Key Terms in Syntax and Syntactic Theory

Also available from Continuum

Key Terms in Linguistics
Howard Jackson

Key Terms in Semiotics
Bronwen Martin and Felizitas Ringham

Forthcoming titles:

Key Terms in Corpus Linguistics
Michaela Mahlberg and Matthew Brook O'Donnell

Key Terms in Pragmatics
Nicholas Allott

Key Terms in Second Language Acquisition
Alessandro G. Benati

Key Terms in Semantics
M. Lynne Murphy

Key Terms in Systemic Functional Linguistics
Christian Matthiessen, Kazuhiro Teruya, and Marvin Lam

Key Terms in Translation Studies
Giuseppe Palumbo

Key Terms in Syntax and Syntactic Theory
Silvia Luraghi and Claudia Parodi

Key Terms in Syntax and Syntactic Theory

Silvia Luraghi and Claudia Parodi

continuum

Continuum International Publishing Group
The Tower Building   80 Maiden Lane, Suite 704
11 York Road   New York
London SE1 7NX   NY 10038

British Library Cataloguing-in-Publication Data
A catalogue record for this book is available from the British Library.

ISBN: 978-08264-9655-3 (Hardback)
       978-08264-9656-0 (Paperback)

Library of Congress Cataloguing-in-Publication Data
The Publisher has applied for CIP data

Typeset by Newgen Imaging Systems Pvt Ltd, Chennai, India
Printed and bound in Great Britain by Cromwell Press, Trowbridge, Wiltshire, UK

Contents

Preface*

Among fields of linguistic research, syntax is presently the one in which competing theories make it harder to grasp the unitary character of linguistic phenomena. Such a wide range of theoretical frameworks triggers a great amount of terminology, which makes it difficult for readers to approach the relevant bibliography in the field of syntax. Problematic aspects of syntactic terminology are two-fold: in the first place, the mere number of terms is very extended; secondly, the same terms are often used with quite different meanings depending on the theory. Furthermore, linguists who subscribe to different theoretical frameworks often have no interest in communicating with one another. These facts can make the field of syntax look esoteric for interested readers. For these reasons, we have decided to include in this book a separate chapter on Key Theories, in which we present a brief overview of the theories that readers are likely to come across in the linguistic literature. Another problematic aspect connected with the understandability of syntactic terminology is the lack of time depth which characterizes much of the field today. Often it is hard for readers to find reference to terms used in the last few decades. Consequently, in the chapter on Key Terms, we give an exhaustive survey of the key terminology which is currently being used in syntax, and also include the basic terminology used in recent works, even when it is no longer current due to fast-developing new theories and versions of theories. Our choice of key terms is coherent with the choice of key theories in the preceding chapter. Finally, in the chapter on Key Thinkers, we have included some linguists who did pioneering research on syntax in the past, as well as some other linguists who are representative of major strands in syntax today. Given its limited scope, this chapter remains necessarily a partial view on current researchers.

Because we think that exposure to linguistic data is of fundamental importance for the understanding of how languages work, we have used a wide variety of examples in the explanation of the concepts discussed in this book. As far as possible, we have tried to always start with English examples; to these we have added examples from several other languages, which are not habitually used in books such as this. To make them accessible to readers that have no knowledge of such languages, we have always provided word-for-word translation and in most cases grammatical glosses as well. Besides, we have refrained from presenting the field of syntax as limited to synchronic description, and have included various key terms which are current in historical linguistics.

We would like to thank friends and colleagues who have helped us with their comments. In particular, thanks are due to Edith Moravcsik and Carlos Quicoli, who patiently read earlier versions of this book and gave us many insightful comments and remarks. Besides, we would also like to thank Liz Goodin-Mayeda for correcting our English. All faults and mistakes remain our own.

*The following entries have been written by Silvia Luraghi: Actant, Adjunct, Adverbial, Adverbial clause, Afterthought, Agreement, Alignment, Anaphor, Anaphora, Animacy, Antecedent, Applicative, Apposition, Attributive clause, Autolexical Grammar, Auxiliary, Behagel, Case (except Abstract Case), Case Grammar, Cataphora, Causative, Chômeur, Circumstantial, Clause, Cleft sentence, Clitic, Cognitive Grammar, Comment, Complement, Complement clause, Complementizer, Configurational vs. nonconfigurational languages, Conjunct, Construction, Construction Grammar/ Radical Construction Grammar, Controller, Converb, Coordination, Coordination reduction, Copula, Copular clause, Core, Core Argument, Coverb, Croft, Delbrück, Demotion, Dependency Grammar, Dependency relation, Dependent, Dik, Direct object, Dislocation, Dixon, Ellipsis, Embedding, Emergent Grammar, Endocentric vs. exocentric construction, Extension, Fillmore, Focus, Functional Grammar, Functional sentence perspective, Gapping, Generalized Phrase Structure Grammar, Generative Semantics, Givón, Goldberg, Governor, Grammatical relation, Grammaticalization, Greenberg, Grounding, Halliday, Head Driven Phrase Structure Grammar, Head vs. dependent marking, Host, Immediate constituent, Incorporation, Indirect object, McCawley, Lakoff, Langacker, Lehmann, Lexical Functional Grammar, Matrix, Modification, Montague Grammar, Nucleus, Null argument, Oblique, P2, Parataxis, Part of speech, Participant, Periphery, Pivot, Pragmatic function, Predicate, Predication, Promotion, Reanalysis, Relational Grammar, Relative clause, Rheme, Role and Reference Grammar, Semantic macro-role, Semantic role, Serial verb, State of affairs, Stratificational Grammar, Subject, Subordination, Systemic Functional Grammar, Tagmemics, Tesnière, Theme, Topic, Transitivity/intransitivity, V2 languages, Valency or valence, Van Valin, Mathesius, Voice, Wackernagel, Weight, Word Grammar, Word order.

The following entries have been written by Claudia Parodi: A-bar position, A-position, Argument, Articulatory and Perceptual properties, Binding, Binding Theory, Bloomfield, Branching, Case (only Abstract Case), Case Filter, Case Theory, C-command, Chain, Chain Condition, Checking, Chomsky, Classical Transformational Generative Theory, Computational system, Conceptual and Intentional properties, Control Theory, Convergence, Copy, Copy Theory, Core Grammar, Covert movement, Covert syntax, Deletion, DP, D-structure, Empty Category, Empty Category Principle, Exceptional Case-Marking Verbs, Expletives, Extended Projection Principle, Extended Standard Transformational Generative Theory, Feature strength, Full Interpretation, Goal, Governing Domain, Government and Binding and Principles and Parameters Theory, Harris, Inclusiveness Condition, Interpretable Features, Island constraint, Jackendoff, Kayne, Lamb, Lasnik, Last Resort Condition, Lexical redundancy rules, Light Verb, Lightfoot, Locality, Logical Form, Logophor, Merge, Minimalist Program, Move alfa or Move α, Movement, Node, NP-Movement, Numeration, Operator, Optimality Theory, Overt movement, Parameter, Parameter setting, Parsing, Postal, Percolation, Phase, Phonetic Form, Phrase, Phrase structure rules, Pike, PRO or big PRO, pro or little pro, Procrastinate, Projection Principle, Raising, Recursion or recursivity, Revised Extended Standard Transformational Generative Theory, Ross, Scope, Scrambling, Sisterhood, Small Clause, Spell-Out, S-Structure, Standard Transformational Generative Theory, Strong Feature, Subcategorization, Subjacency Condition, Superiority Condition, Theta Criterion, Theta role, Tough Movement, Transformational Generative Grammar, Uniformity Condition, Uninterpretable Features, Universal Grammar, Variable, Visibility Condition, Weak Features, Wh-in situ, Wh-movement, X-bar theory.

The authors have worked together on the Introduction and the following entries: Constituent, Grammatical/ungrammatical, Bresnan, Government, Head, Sentence.

List of Abbreviations

Abbreviations used in grammatical glosses

ABL	ablative
ABS	absolutive
ACC	accusative
ADESS	adessive
AOR	aorist
AP	antipassive
APPL	applicative
ASP	aspect marker
CL	noun class marker
CLASS	classifier
CONN	connective
CONSTR	construct state
COP	copula
DAT	dative
DEM	demonstrative
ERG	ergative
F	feminine
FUT	future
GEN	genitive
GER	gerund
IMPF	imperfect
IMPT	imperative
INDEF	indefinite
INF	infinitive
INSTR	instrumental
INT	interrogative
ITER	iterative
LOC	locative
M	masculine
MID	middle
N	neuter

N/A	nominative/accusative neuter
NEG	negation
NOM	nominative
OBJ	direct object
OBL	oblique
PART	participle
PAST	past tense
PF	perfect
PL	plural
POSS	possessive
PRET	preterite
PRS	present
PRT	partitive
PTC	particle
REFL	reflexive
REL	relative
SG	singular
ST	stative
SBJ	subjunctive
SUBJ	subject
TOP	topic
VOC	vocative

Abbreviations used in phrase markers and trees

Adv	Adverb
AdvP	Adverbial Phrase
Aux	Auxiliary
CP	Complementizer Phrase
Deg	Degree
Det	Determiner
DP	Determiner Phrase
Infl	Inflection
IP	Inflectional Phrase
N	Noun
NP	Noun Phrase
S	Sentence

V	Verb
VP	Verb Phrase

Symbols

Ø	zero
=	clitic boundary
-	morpheme boundary
*	(a) ungrammatical form or construction
	(b) reconstructed form or construction

Introduction

1. Linguistics is a comparatively recent endeavor: scientific study of language had its dawn only two centuries ago. Among core levels of grammar, syntax—the architecture of sentences or the principles governing the way in which words and constructions are combined to form sentences—has been the last one to be clearly isolated and to become a matter of research and theoretical discussion.

In the present Introduction, we try to give a brief and summary account of the development of the field. More details are provided in the chapters on Key Theories and Key Thinkers (which are alphabetically and not chronologically ordered). Since our aim is not to write a history of linguistic thought, but rather to help readers find their way through the intricacies of current syntactic terminology, the historical sketch we provide in this chapter contains only some basic information. Interested readers can find more details in various historical introductions, such as Lepschy (1982), Newmayer (1986), Matthews (1993), and Graffi (2001).

In the second part of the Introduction, we give a brief survey of contemporary theories treated later on in the book, highlighting a number of basic differences between 'formal' and 'functional' approaches to syntax. This section must be intended as an introduction to the chapter on Key Theories. Readers who would like to learn more on the different theoretical approaches that we introduce here may consult reference works such as Moravcsik and Wirth (1980), Droste and Joseph (1991), Edmondson and Burquest (1992), and Butler (2003).

2. During the seventeenth and eighteenth century, syntax was conceived of as a direct reflection of thought and logic. Indeed, reflection on language was pursued by philosophers, rather than linguists, and language was not observed in its practical usage in communication, nor through empirical descriptions based on actual data, but rather as an abstract system that mirrored reason. Thus, a logical grammar such as the *Grammaire général* of

Port-Royal focused on language as a valuable field of observation only inasmuch as it could help understand the logical system with which the human mind worked.

Toward the end of the eighteenth century, scholars with different backgrounds, partly philologists and partly philosophers, centered their attention on the diversity of languages. However, comparative and historical linguistics, and later dialectology, especially focused on phonology, while language typology was mainly concerned with morphology. Language typology as worked out by Wilhelm von Humboldt (1767–1835) had strong implications for syntax, since Humboldt regarded some syntactic phenomena as most revealing of the 'inner structure' (*innere Sprachform*) of languages. Nevertheless, his work did not lead to clearly isolate syntactic constructions, such as constituents and sentences, as objects of investigation.

The numerous descriptive and historical grammars produced during the nineteenth century often contained only chapters on phonology and morphology; syntax was mostly treated as an appendix to morphology, under secondary headings such as 'use of cases'. Only toward the end of the nineteenth century some of the Neogrammarians, such as Berthold Delbrück, turned to syntax and worked extensively in the field.

These early scholars mostly worked with no specific theoretical framework: when they started considering the sentence as the relevant unit of syntactic analysis, the only theories that they could turn to (most often with a skeptical and critical attitude) were philosophical or psychological theories, such as the already mentioned *Grammaire général* or the *Völkerpsychlogie*, or 'social psychology', of Wilhem Wundt (1832–1920). Such theories were often at odds with the actual data, which nineteenth century linguists, who mostly had a strong philological background, were very familiar with. Consequently, most definitions of sentence were based on communication: sentence was defined as a unit of communication, that is, an utterance, and there was little interest in sentence structure. This conception was not only widespread among historical linguists and dialectologists, but it was also assumed by many general linguists, such as Otto Jespersen (1860–1943), as argued in Graffi (2001: 113–135).

Jespersen's works are a milestone in the history of linguistic thought. His idea of 'nexus' constitutes a step in the direction of the modern concepts of dependency and government. Such concepts were fundamental in further developments of syntactic description in the works of the European structuralists in the early twentieth century, even when these scholars were not directly influenced by Jespersen.

3. Among various schools of thought within European structuralism, the Prague School deserves special mention as the crane of modern research on discourse and pragmatics. Indeed, the influence of communicative factors on sentence structure had already been the matter of observation by Henri Weil (1818–1868) in the first half of the nineteenth century, but his pioneering ideas had little impact on his contemporaries. Only in the 1910s his work was re-discovered by Czech linguist Vilém Mathesius, who started a flourishing tradition of studies in functional syntax that focused on the communicative dynamism of words and constituents. Under such a view, data from spoken language was crucial for the understanding of sentence structure. Especially in the 1920s and 1930s these ideas were at odds with mainstream European structuralism, which made a sharp distinction between *langue* and *parole*, roughly 'grammar' and 'speech', and only viewed *langue* as a possible field of scientific investigation. (The dichotomy between *langue* and *parole* was introduced by Swiss linguist Ferdinand de Saussure [1857–1913] in the 1910s.)

During the 1930s another important theory emerged in Europe, the theory of Glossematics, developed by Danish linguist Louis Hjelmslev (1899–1965), which aimed to describe the relations between the phonemic and the grammatical systems in algebraic terms. Hjelmslev's work had a great impact on European structuralism, as shown in his correspondence with André Martinet (1908–1999), one of the leading exponents of French functional structuralism, active in the field of syntax as well (see Arrivé and Ablali 2001). Besides, Glossematics played an important role in the development of Stratificational Grammar by American linguist Sydney Lamb. However, the field of research in which Hjelmslev is mostly referred to today is semiotics.

By this time, American structuralism was moving in some interesting directions that must be introduced at this point. Since the beginning of the twentieth century, it had been maintained that sentences—the essential units of syntax—are not free sequences of words, but that they combine forming a structure, the constituent structure, as Leonard Bloomfield (1933) and his followers such as Zelling Harris (1946) and Rulon Wells (1947), called it. Regarding the immediate constituents (IC) of a sentence, Wells (1947: 83) claims that "our general principle of IC analysis is not only to view a sequence when possible as an expansion of a shorter sequence, but also to break it up into parts, of which some or all are themselves expansions." From that time on, IC analysis became a kind of "trademark of American structuralism," as Graffi (2001: 9) points out. Constituents are assumed to be binary, and they are often diagrammed as such. In fact, establishing procedures which help in delimiting IC constituents was one of the main goals of American structuralist syntactic theory during the first half of the twentieth century.

4. The scientific model of early American structuralism was inductive positivism and behaviorism. Explanations were based on observable events analyzed only by principles of mathematics and logic. Following Bloomfield, most American linguists argued against mentalistic and cognitive explanations of language. Thus, they eliminated meaning from their framework. However, during the second half of the twentieth century, Noam Chomsky harshly argued against structural linguistics procedures and the relevance that structural linguists gave to the *corpus* or data collection. Chomsky suggested, instead, that linguistics should be a deductive science that must advance hypotheses, and evaluate them by testing them against evidence provided by native speakers' intuition concerning sentences in their own language.

Chomsky claimed that since any speaker could produce and understand an infinite number of sentences that he or she had never heard or produced before, the proper study of linguistics must be the speakers' underlying knowledge of their language. Chomsky showed that no behaviorist account based on a stimulus-response model of language acquisition could possibly explain the rapidity and ease with which children acquire language. Starting from the 1980s, Chomsky began to combine the innate principles of UG (Universal Grammar) to parameters, the components of languages whose values are not genetically fixed. At this point, language acquisition and language variation became processes of parameter setting in Chomsky's view.

Autonomy of grammar and the modular conception of language are two characteristics that distinguish Transformational Generative Grammar from functional/cognitive theories. According to Transformational Generative Grammar, grammar is an autonomous system due to the fact that its primitives are independent from other human mental capacities. Moreover, language as a system with its own rules, according to Transformational Generative Grammar, is modular. That is, language interacts with other systems, which are governed, as well, by their particular set of general principles.

Autonomy and modularity interact with each other, as Caplan (1981: 60) said: "grammar is a species and domain specific cognitive structure, which interacts with other structures to yield normal intellectual function."

5. During the second half of the twentieth century, several developments regarding syntactic theory occurred in Europe. The most notable and influential advancement was the publication of Lucien Tesnière's book *Éléments de syntaxe structurale* in 1959. In his book, Tesnière introduced the concept of verbal valency, thus challenging the traditional conception that the basic parts of the sentence are the subject and the predicate, which he viewed as conditioned by the tendency to apply the categories of natural logic to language. Thus, Tesnière was pursuing the idea that a sentence has an underlying level of representation, even though he did not elaborate a theory of deep structure, as Noam Chomsky did in the United States. In Tesnière's theory an important role is played by the notions of dependency and government, which, as we have pointed out, conditioned European syntactic theories at least since Jespersen.

Another major trend in European theoretical linguistics had been set by British linguist John Rupert Firth (1890–1960), who created the concept of 'polysystematism'. Following this approach, linguistic patterns cannot be accounted for in terms of one system alone; rather, different systems must be set up to account for different patterns. Firth further highlighted the context-dependent nature of meaning, thus opening the way for his student's M. A. K. Halliday Systemic Grammar, an influential theory which views social interaction as basic for the study of language. Halliday's is one of various functional approaches to syntax and discourse, which conceives of language primarily as a means of communication.

In the 1960s, Chomsky's ideas started to be imported in European universities, and various linguists, such as Luigi Rizzi and Guglielmo Cinque, followed them, thus giving a substantial contribution to the development of Transformational Generative Grammar. However, there were critics as well. Among early critics of the Chomskyan approach there was Dutch linguist Simon Dik, who developed his own theory of Functional Grammar. This theory rejects the assumption regarding the autonomy of syntax and highlights the function of language in communication; in the description of sentence structure, it makes use of Tesnière notion of valency.

In the 1960s, several linguists became critical of Chomsky's theories in the United States as well. The basic matter of dissent concerned the role of semantics and its relation to syntax. This gave rise to the movement known as Generative Semantics, which assumed a nonautonomous view of syntax and a major role of semantics in the generation of sentences. Generative Semantics never became a fully worked out theory; rather, linguists who participated in this movement developed various alternative approaches to syntax, part of which we describe in the chapter on Key Theories in this book.

Regarding the theories that we are going to present in the next chapter, it must be said that they are not all on the same plane in terms of their impact and relevance in the field of syntax. While some of them are currently being used and developed, such as Transformational Generative Grammar or Systemic Functional Grammar, others have been virtually abandoned, such as Stratificational Grammar. Still others, such as Generative Semantics and Case Grammar, have merged with other functional/cognitive approaches and constitute the basis for such productive theories as Cognitive Grammar and Construction Grammar.

Our survey does not cover all syntactic theories ever put forward since the mid-twentieth century. Such an endeavor goes far beyond the scope of the present book, given the proliferation of theories that have grown in various parts of the world, often ignoring one another, in the course of the last decades. Our selection includes the theories that readers are most likely to come across when using the linguistic literature.

6. Speaking of current approaches to syntax, it is customary to make a distinction between 'formal' and 'functional' approaches. In this final section we would like to briefly clarify the meaning of the two terms, which are also used and discussed in the course of the book.

As we pointed out earlier, what unifies current functional approaches is the conception of language as being primarily an instrument of communication. In formal approaches, instead, language is considered primarily an abstract system of knowledge; emphasis is put on the structures. The assumption that communication is the primary function of language is also common to semantic-oriented cognitive approaches, such as Cognitive Grammar.

It must be stressed that what is currently referred to with the term 'formal' is most often Transformational Generative Grammar. The most important difference between this theoretical framework and functional/cognitive approaches lies in the assumption regarding the autonomy of syntax. Most of the functional approaches, which are communication based, and cognitive approaches, which are semantic based, do not view syntax as an autonomous system; consequently, they also hold quite different views on language acquisition than what is common in Transformational Generative Grammar. There are, however, some functionalists that subscribe to the autonomy assumption, as shown in Croft (1995).

Functional approaches are numerous, and their practitioners do not necessarily communicate with one another. The reason for this separation partly lies in different choices regarding specific fields of research. For example, Systemic Functional Grammar focuses most relevantly than other theories on social interaction; linguists working in this framework are mostly concerned with analysis of discourse, rather than with syntactic description.

Another difference between various functional approaches lies in the fact of focusing either on the sentence as basic unit of syntactic analysis, or on discourse. Dik's Functional Grammar differs from other functionalist frameworks in this respect, in that it has been originally worked out as a theory regarding the structure of sentences.

Some functional approaches make use of a certain degree of formalism: in particular, this is the case of Role and Reference Grammar, and, to a lesser extent, of S. C. Dik's Functional Grammar. Apparently, the use of formalism is not a factor that favors the spread of specific functional theories: in fact, the most fast growing functionalist approach today is the so-called West Coast Functionalism, which is not a unitary theory, but rather a collection of partly similar approaches. Linguists that are grouped under this label have a strong typological orientation (although it must be said that the typological orientation is characteristic of functionalist approaches in general), and, besides their stance for functionalism, also accept the basic assumptions of Cognitive Linguistics regarding the basicness and the pervasiveness of meaning. Such an assumption is not per se common to all functional approaches. In S. C. Dik's Functional Grammar, for example, grammatical forms are not conceived of as being meaningful, a position that is in accordance with classical European structuralism, out of which Dik's Functional Grammar originated.

Cognitive Grammar is a direct outcome of Generative Semantics, which, as we have pointed out above, originated within the Transformational Generative Grammar framework, and was indeed a reaction to the autonomy hypothesis. Its assumptions regarding the nature of language are opposite to those of Transformational Generative Grammar: Cognitive Grammar views language as part of human cognitive capacities, and not as an independent module. In this approach, grammar is not conceived of as an abstract set of principles, and it must not be investigated using a hypothetic deductive method, but rather inductively, starting from the actual linguistic data. Besides, the mind, and all mental processes including language, are viewed as embodied, that is, they are conceived of as arising from the brain's and body's physiology. Thus, Cognitive Linguistics overrides the dualistic vision of mind and body, which has been deeply rooted in Western thought ever since antiquity.

Another important strand of research, which is compatible with both functionalism and cognitivism, is the so-called 'Functional-Typological approach', a term used for example in Croft (2003). In fact, typologists such as R. M. W. Dixon, Bernard Comrie, Frans Plank, and many others work within a cognitive/functional framework, even though they cannot be called West Coast functionalists, given the geographical implications of this term.

The inductive approach and emphasis on language usage have provided common ground to Cognitive Grammar, West Coast Functionalism, and the Typological-Functional approach. Thus, the combination of Cognitive Grammar with functionalism currently provides a coherent and exhaustive theoretical framework, which is arguably the most complete alternative to Transformational Generative Grammar to date.

Key Theories

Autolexical Grammar

Autolexical Grammar (AG, earlier Autolexical Syntax) is a theory developed in the late 1980s– early 1990s by Jerrold M. Sadock (see Sadock 1991). It is a nontransformational, monostratal, and multimodular approach to grammar.

AG only assumes one single level of structure, rather than a Deep Structure and a Surface Structure as is commonly assumed in Transformational Generative Grammar. Hence, there is no need for transformations. In AG, separate components (modules) like phonology, morphology, syntax, and semantics have different rules and are understood on different levels of representation. These autonomous representations, produced by the modular grammars, are coordinated by the lexicon and a set of interface principles. By postulating separate components of grammar, AG eliminates the need for movement and deletion rules: for example, cliticization (i.e. the set of rules that determine the position of clitics) is explained as resulting from discrepancies between the phonological and the syntactic component.

Case Grammar

Case Grammar is one of numerous reactions to Transformational Generative Grammar which came to light in the late 1960s and are known under the cover label of Generative Semantics. In 1968, American linguist Charles Fillmore published his seminal paper The Case for Case, in which he elaborated the theory of 'deep cases'. Deep cases, which broadly correspond to semantic roles in current terminology, were conceived as making up part of the deep structure of sentences and were held responsible for determining the syntactic function of constituents. More specifically, Fillmore claimed that the choice of surface subject is based on a hierarchy of deep cases (Agent < Instrumental

< Objective). Deep cases are determined by the frame of individual verbs (corresponding to the semantic valency of predicates).

Deep cases introduced in Fillmore (1968) are Agentive, Instrumental, Dative, Factitive, Locative, and Objective; more cases were added in later writings. In Fillmore's view, the meaning of constituents is crucial in determining the deep case. For example, in sentences:

(1) *Mary opened the door with the key*
(2) *the key opened the door*
(3) *Mary used the key to open the door*

the NP *the key* is assigned the deep case Instrumental in the Deep Structure, although it surfaces as adjunct in (1), as subject in (2), and as direct object in (3). Similarly, toponyms are usually said to have the deep case Locative, such as *Chicago* in (4):

(4) *Chicago is windy*

The frame (or semantic valency) of weather predicates, such as *rain*, *be windy*, etc., is +[_LOC]: they require a NP with the deep case Locative. The deep structure of (4) is:

(5) *it is windy in Chicago*

The surface structure in (4) derives from (5) through a transformation that cancels the preposition.

Fillmore's theory later developed into Frame Semantics, and is one of the theories that inspired Cognitive Grammar.

The influence of Case Grammar was not limited to other semantic-based approaches, but extended to Transformational Generative Grammar, and was incorporated into the Government and Binding model as the Thematic Structure Theory (deep cases correspond to theta roles in this approach).

Classical Transformational Generative Theory

In *Syntactic Structures* (1957), Chomsky proposed a scientific model of grammar that went beyond the taxonomical classification of sentences, that is, the

Immediate Constituents Analysis, common in American structural linguistics. According to this first transformational model, grammar should be the theory of a language able to generate all and only all the grammatical sentences of that language by means of two types of rules: **phrase structure rules** and **transformational rules.** Phrase structure rules or PS rules are rewriting rules of the form X → Y that build phrase markers. A phrase marker enables us to tell where the parts of the string come from. Sentences which are derived from PS terminal strings by the application of phonological rules and obligatory transformations only are called kernel sentences. To these kernel sentence structures singulary transformations are applied, such as affix hopping and passive, and the resultant derived kernel sentences are combined using generalized transformations.

There are two types of transformational rules: obligatory and optional, and each rule must be marked as one or the other. The first part of a rule is its structural description (or SD) specifying the class of strings to which the rule applies. The second part of the rule specifies the structural change (or SC) by means of variable signs with subscript numbers referring to the segments specified in the structural description. For example, the following is the passive optional transformation rule (12) given by Chomsky in *Syntactic Structures*:

Passive, optional
SD: NP – Aux – V – NP
SC: $X_1 - X_2 - X_3 - X_4 \rightarrow X_4 - X_2 + be + en - X_3 - by + X_1$

The rule may be paraphrased as (1) an NP followed by (2) an auxiliary followed by (3) a verb (of a certain class) followed by (4) a second NP may be passivized by switching NPs (X_1 and X_4), by attaching *be + en* to the verb and by placing *by* before the last noun phrase. Thus, the last string of the phrase marker:

(1) *John* + Present + *love* + *Mary*, i.e., *John loves Mary*

may be transformed into the passive string:

(2) *Mary* + Present + *be* + *en* + *love* + *by* + *John*, i.e., *Mary is loved by John.*

Within this framework, there are some optional transformations that operate on two strings at once, conjoining them or embedding one into another. Such rules are called **generalized** or **two string transformations**. These rules, in addition, provide recursion, which is essential in language. The generalized transformation for sentential subjects or nominalizing transformation for examples such as:

(3) *to prove the theorem is difficult*

given by Chomsky in *Syntactic Structures* as generalized transformation number (24), is the following:

SD of S_1: NP – VP

of S_2: X – NP – Y (X or Y may be null)

SC: $(X_1 - X_2; X_3 - X_4 - X_5) \rightarrow X_3 - to + X_2 - X_5$

This generalized transformation deletes the subject NP of S_1, prefixes it by the lexical item *to* and inserts the result into a NP (subject) position in another clause. Then, given the kernel sentences S_1 and S_2, this generalized transformation produces the sentence S_3 as shown below:

S_1: John—prove the theorem

S_2: 0 it—is difficult

S_3: —to prove the theorem—is difficult

(Note that the numbers (12) and (24) maintain the numeration given by Chomsky in *Syntactic Structures*)

According to Chomsky (1986: 5), this research program from the mid-1950s "led to the development of cognitive sciences in the contemporary sense sharing the belief . . . that certain aspects of the mind/brain can be usefully construed on the model of computational systems of rules that form and modify representations, and that are put to use in interpretation and action." The proposed format for rules in this framework was adapted from traditional descriptive grammars and historical grammars and recast in terms of ideas developed in the theory of computation, such as recursion and the theory of algorithms. Figure 1 shows the order of operations in a derivation of a single sentence within the classical model.

PS rules

↓

P-Marker with terminal string

↓ *Singularly transformations (or other transformations)*

PRE-Sentence

↓ *Morphophonemics*

Sentence

Figure 1 Classical model

Cognitive Grammar

Cognitive Grammar is not a syntactic theory, but rather a semantically based theory of language that developed out of Generative Semantics and of Fillmore's research on Case Grammar (later Frame Semantics). An early version of Cognitive Grammar is Space Grammar (Langacker 1982). Cognitive Grammar rejects the idea that syntax is a separate component of language. Besides, Cognitive Grammar assumes a nonmodular structure of the human mind: consequently, it views language as integrated into the general cognitive capacities of the human mind, and similarly structured.

In Cognitive Grammar, languages consist of symbolic units (conventional pairings of form and meaning). Crucially, all units of language are equally meaningful, including grammatical forms, such as bound morphemes.

Another characteristic feature of Cognitive Grammar, as opposed not only to formal approaches, such as Transformational Grammar, but to many other structural approaches as well, is that it assumes a prototype view of category structure. Under this assumption, category members are not all on the same plane: rather, they may be more or less central, depending on the number of features they share with the most central member of the category. In addition, category borders are not clear cut but are rather structured as a continuum between different categories.

Cognitive Grammar is sometimes considered as a type of Construction Grammar.

Construction Grammar/Radical Construction Grammar

Construction Grammar (CxG) is a theory connected with Cognitive Grammar and developed in the late 1980s and 1990s, but has its root in Fillmore's pioneering work on Case Grammar and Frame Semantics. Its basic assumption is that all constructions have meaning. The meaning of constructions is partly determined by their structure: this is a crucial assumption, because it implies that constructions that differ in structure also have different meanings. A further consequence of the assumption that the structure of a construction contributes to its meaning is that the meaning of constructions is noncompositional, that is, it does not consist of the sum of the meanings of its parts. CxG is a monostratal approach, which does not assume different levels of structure; syntax and the lexicon are not viewed as strictly distinct components: rather, CxG assumes a **syntax-lexicon continuum**. Furthermore, the assumption of the basicness of semantics leads CxG to reject the idea that pragmatics and semantics can be viewed as separate.

An early study based on the assumptions of CxG appeared as an appendix in Lakoff (1987) and concerned the *there* construction. Another, partly different outline of CxG Fillmore, Kay, and O'Connor (1988). CxG has been developed in particular by Adele Goldberg, and received a full account in Goldberg (1995).

Goldberg (1995) explains what it means that constructions have meanings by analyzing the so-called dative shift. Sentences (1) and (2):

(1) *Paul gave Mary a present*
(2) *Paul gave a present to Mary*

are often said to convey the same meaning. In the CxG approach this cannot be true: Goldberg captures this difference in terms of topicality. While in (1) the recipient (*Mary*) is topical and the object (*the book*) is focal, the contrary holds for (2): the recipient is focal and the object is topical. This explains why in certain cases only the dative shift construction may occur, as in (3a), while (3b) is ungrammatical:

(3) a. *Paul gave Mary a push*
    b. **Paul gave a push to Mary*

According to Goldberg (1995), the reason for the ungrammaticality of (3′) lies in the fact that it is always the object that is focused with such verbs, rather than the recipient.

Networks of families of constructions, taxonomically arranged, constitute the grammar of a language. Constructions share the basic properties typical of categories in Cognitive Grammar (e.g. prototypicality). In general, construction grammars purport a usage-based model approach, which views language structure as emerging from language use, a position which is in accordance with the assumption that a theory of grammar must not posit phonologically unrealized underlying representations. In usage-based models of language, language structure in grounded in the actual instances of language (usage-events).

A variant of CxG is Radical Construction Grammar, developed in Croft (2001), who states that the goal of this approach "is to represent universals of human language in a way that is plausible as a model of the knowledge of an individual speaker of a particular language." Because Radical Construction Grammar is especially designed for typological purposes, it adopts the semantic maps model, a tool used by typologists for comparing different exponents of a certain category (e.g. passive) across different languages. In the semantic maps model the distributional patterns of language particular categories are mapped onto a conceptual space which is conceived of as being universal. Croft stresses the common assumption of CxG according to which the meaning of a construction is not the sum of the meaning of its parts by pointing out that the parts receive their meanings from the meaning of the whole construction. This is in accordance with basic assumptions of *Gestalt* theory, a theory of mind developed in Germany during the early twentieth century that assumes that the mind operates according to holistic principles.

Suggested link: http://www.constructiongrammar.org/

Dependency Grammar

The name 'dependency grammar' is a translation from French *grammaire de la dependance*. This theory was developed in Tesnière's posthumous book *Elément de syntaxe structurale* (1959) and had several instantiations thereafter. The name 'dependency grammar' was not created by Tesnière, who always used 'structural' to define his theory, as shown in the title of his book.

However, the word 'structural' has a special meaning in Tesnière's work, because it refers to the sentence structure underlying its linear order. This assumption makes the idea of structure in Tesnière crucially different from that of American structuralists, in particular Bloomfield.

Structural syntax according to Tesnière focuses on dependency relations within sentences, and investigates the hierarchical structure of sentences. Tesnière describes three types of relation: *connexion*, *translation*, and *jonction*. Connection corresponds to subordination in traditional grammatical description; connection relations, also called dependency relations, hold between a *regissant* ('governor') and a *dependant*, and it is said that the governor *régit* ('governs') the dependent. (Note that *régir* is usually translated 'govern', but Tesnière's notion of *rection* is crucially different from the current notion of 'government'.)

Contrary to former descriptions, Tesnière conceives of the subject as being one of the dependents of the verb, much in the same way as the direct object or other complements. Before Tesnière, the subject had always been assumed to have a special relation with the verb (or predicate), different from the relation between the verb and other complements. The change in perspective can be captured by the two schemes in Figure 2, which represent sentence (1):

(1) *Alfred hits Bernard*

While syntactically the superordinate element governs the subordinate one, semantically the subordinate element determines or completes the superordinate. In particular, an attributive adjective is governed by its head noun and determines the head noun, while a noun that depends on a verb completes it (it is the verb's complement). The whole formed by a governor

Figure 2 Two models of sentence structure (adapted from Schwischay ms.)

and all its subordinate elements constitutes a 'structural node' (*noeud structural*), and the function of the governor is called *fonction nodale*.

Tesnière distinguished three subordinate functions: *actant, épithète,* and *cicumstant*. Actants are arguments that saturate the valency of the verb: the first actant is the subject, the second is the direct object, and the third the indirect object. Epithets are modifiers of nouns, and circumstants are non-obligatory constituents, such as adverbs and other adjuncts. Additionally, Tesnière classifies parts of speech in *mots pleins*, literally 'full words', and *mots vides*, 'empty words'. The former correspond to open classes (verbs, nouns, adjectives, and adverbs), while the latter include articles, prepositions, pronouns, conjunctions, and other parts of speech which have mostly grammatical function. Among the *mots pleins*, verbs are always governors; for the other three classes, Tesnière seeks to establish a biunivocal correspondence with functions: nouns function as actants, adjectives as epithets, and adverbs as circumstants.

Prepositional phrases often function as circumstant: this happens on account of the second type of relation, *translation*, by which a *mots vide* or a bound morpheme transfers a lexical item from one class to another. In the case of prepositional phrases, a preposition transfers a noun to the class of adverbs.

The last type of relation, junction, corresponds to coordination in traditional terminology.

As shown above, the highest ranking part of a sentence is held to be the verb, which determines the number and function of its dependents based on its valency, a concept taken from chemistry, indicating the combining power of an element (for this reason, Dependency Grammar is sometimes called Valency Grammar) . Thus, a monovalent verb, such as *run*, has a combining power of 1, a bivalent verb such as *push* has a combining power of 2, etc. Valency relations are obligatory: in other words, if an item has a valency, the valency must be saturated.

Not all dependency relations are determined by valency; in particular, relations in which the dependent determines the governor (attributive relations) are nonobligatory.

After Tesnière's seminal work, the notion of valency has been progressively incorporated into an increasing number of theories, either by direct derivation from Tesnière, or by being rediscovered (as in Lexical Functional Grammar). Models based on dependency are numerous and often use different terminologies. For example, Bartsch and Vennemann (1972) provide a comprehensive model which accounts for interactions between syntax and semantics based on dependency relations; they use the term 'operand' for head and 'operator' for dependent.

Emergent Grammar

Emergent Grammar is a usage-based approach to the study of language, which views language structures as emerging from the use of language in communication. The name of Emergent Grammar was introduced in a 1987 paper by Paul Hopper, who borrowed the term 'emergent' from anthropology. According to Hopper, grammar "is not the source of understanding and communication, but a by-product of it. Grammar is, in other words, epiphenomenal" (1998: 156). This assumption clearly rests on psycholinguistic views opposite to those which are commonly argued for in Transformational Generative Grammar, in that there is no assumption of innate UG which provides speakers with a set of parameters: rather, language users construct grammar in the process of communication.

Emergent Grammar brings together Cognitive Linguistics and Construction Grammar with functional approaches known under the label of West Coast Functionalism, best represented by works by Givón and his associates, and follows the tradition of functional typology, initiated by Joseph Greenberg in the 1960s. Being usage based, it takes as its field of observation spoken rather than written language, and discourse rather than single sentences.

As pointed out in Tomasello (2002: 3–4), as soon as one turns to spontaneous spoken speech the basicness of sentences consisting of a subject, a verb, and a direct object such as *John bought a motorcycle*, which are usually assumed as prototypical utterances, becomes questionable. Such sentences almost never occur in actual discourse, but are rather generated in the metalinguistic contexts of grammatical description. Frequency in actual usage is a key concept in Emergent Grammar. Frequency can be of two types: **token frequency** (i.e. the frequency of individual items), and **type frequency** (i.e. the frequency of patterns). Both token and type frequency have consequences on the **entrenchment** of items and constructions, and contribute to the ongoing construction of grammar in the events of communication.

Emergent Grammar does not draw a sharp distinction between syntax and the lexicon, and between syntax and morphology. In fact, Emergent

Grammar draws heavily on research on grammaticalization and on the emergence of morphology from frequent collocations. An effect of frequency on syntax, according to Bybee (2007: 313–335), is constituency: following this approach, constituency is viewed as emerging from sequenciality in discourse, rather than as deriving from the underlying hierarchical structure of constructions.

Extended Standard Transformational Generative Theory

One of the rival developments following Chomsky's theory exposed in *Aspects* (1965) (i.e. the Standard Theory) was Generative Semantics, a theory in which semantic representations were identified with syntactic deep structures. This model implied a powerful conditioning of syntax by semantics. Chomsky, however, strongly disagreed with the Generative Semantics principles and developed an alternative model, the interpretive or Lexicalist Grammatical Model, within the framework he called Extended Standard Theory (EST). In this new version of the Standard Theory, deep structures became closer to surface structures since it was not possible to transform an adjective or a verb into a noun or vice-versa, as a consequence of the lexicalist hypothesis (Chomsky 1970). A noun, for example, should enter the lexicon as such and not as a result of a derived transformation from a related verb or adjective. Within this framework, the semantic component does not generate deep structures, since they are generated by the syntactic component. Interpretive semantic rules form part of a separate semantic component that takes syntactic structures as its input. Moreover, rules of semantic interpretation apply to surface syntactic structures as well as to deep structures, as shown in Figure 3. For example, within the EST, pronominalization is not

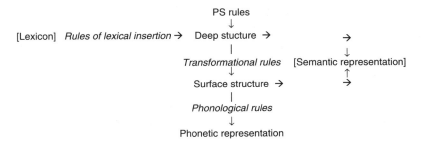

Figure 3 EST Model

handled by transformations because pronouns are lexical elements present at deep structure. This implies the existence of interpretive rules to assign coreferentiality between pronouns and their correspondent NPs at surface structure. Figure 3 depicts the main features of the EST (modeled upon Newmeyer 1986: 140).

Functional Grammar

S. C. Dik's Functional Grammar (FG) is one of the various approaches that have developed out of Dependency Grammar. It is functional in that language is conceived of as a tool for verbal interaction, and it is assumed that grammar must be understood and explained as far as possible within the framework of language usage. The first complete account of FG is Dik (1978); later elaborations of the theory are incorporated into Dik (1997), which was published posthumously.

FG seeks to conform to three criteria of adequacy:

a) pragmatic adequacy: linguistic theory must assume linguistic descriptions which can be interpreted in the wider framework of a pragmatic theory of verbal communication;
b) psychological adequacy: FG strives to develop a theory in agreement with the findings of current psycholinguistic research on language acquisition, language processing, and language production;
c) typological adequacy: the theory of FG must apply to all languages, regardless of their typological features.

The structure of FG is given in Figure 4 on p. 21.

In FG the sentence is the basic domain of syntax; it is conceived of as having a layered structure, which includes a core and a periphery, and sentence constituents are viewed as functioning on three distinct relational levels: semantic, syntactic, and pragmatic. Accordingly, each constituent is assigned a semantic, a syntactic, and a pragmatic function within each given sentence.

In order to attain high practical applicability, FG refrains from using abstract concepts typical of formal approaches such as Transformational Generative Grammar. In particular, it avoids making use of structure-changing

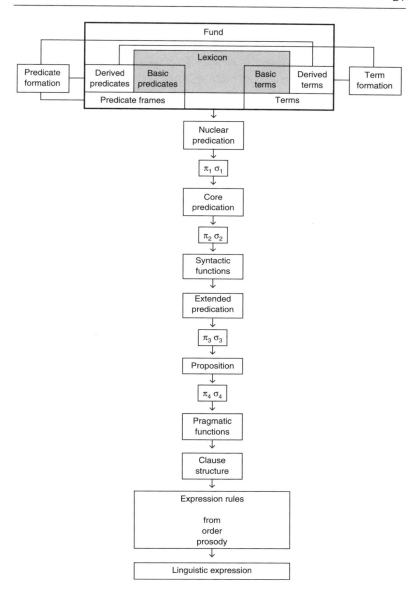

Figure 4 The structure of Functional Grammar (from Dik 1997: 60)

operations (transformations); if an element is not overtly realized, it is not postulated that an empty element exists at some level in the underlying structure; there are no filter devices, and abstract lexical decomposition is not applied.

FG describes linguistic constructions in terms of abstract underlying predications, consisting of predicates and terms; inasmuch as predicates and terms cannot be formed through productive rules, they constitute the lexicon of a specific language. Each predicate has a predicate frame, which specifies its semantic and syntactic properties. The formal structure of underlying predications is highly uniform across languages; differences appear especially at the level of concrete predicates, and of the rules that specify the terminal form of underlying predications (expression rules).

After the appearance of Dik's (1978) account of the theory, Functional Grammar gained many supporters, especially in the Netherlands, Belgium, and Spain. A recent development in Functional Grammar is Functional Discourse Grammar, which takes acts in discourse rather than sentences as the basic units of analysis (see Hengeveld and Mackenzie 2005).

Suggested link: http://www.functionalgrammar.com/

Functional Sentence Perspective

Functional Sentence Perspective (FSP) is not a theory of syntax in the strict sense, but rather a theory of discourse. It was developed, starting in the 1910s by various scholars connected with the Prague School, among them Vilém Mathesius, and later Jan Firbas, and František Daneš. In FSP, sentences are analyzed based on their information structure, that is, in terms of the theme-rheme articulation (Mathesius is credited with having introduced these terms in 1911). According to the Prague School, language is a system of elements used in communication; accordingly, emphasis is placed on the communicative function of linguistic items. FSP is functional in the sense that it does not take forms as starting point, but rather functions: according to Mathesius, 'traditional' approaches considered forms as basic, and tried to determine their functions; in his approach, functions are considered basic, and forms are taken into account only inasmuch as they implement specific functions.

FSP is especially relevant to the study of word order, since it assumes that specific positions in the sentence are associated with different degrees of communicative dynamism of constituents. Constituent structure, anaphoric processes, and null anaphora are other fields that can profitably be investigated in light of FSP.

Generalized Phrase Structure Grammar

Generalized Phrase Structure Grammar (GPSG) originated in the first half of the 1980s. It was developed by Gerald Gazdar and Geoffrey K. Pullum as an alternative to Transformational Generative Grammar (see Gazdar, Pullum and Sag 1985).

GPSG is monostratal: it only assumes one level of syntactic description; consequently, it does not assume transformations. In GPSG, languages are described in terms of context-free phrase structure rules, in much the same way as in Lexical Functional Grammar. Each rule is connected by a biunivocal relation with a semantic rule which defines the meaning of the resulting constituent. The meaning of a construction is conceived of as a function of the meanings of its constituents. To describe semantic rules, GPSG makes use of a logical-intensional system, as defined in Montague Grammar. In this respect, GPSG can be conceived of as a version of Montague Grammar that operates with a syntax based on phrase structure.

Evidence that grammars are context sensitive at least to some extent led to the formulation of Head Driven Phrase Structure Grammar.

Generative Semantics

Generative Semantics (GS) was developed in the 1960s as a reaction to Transformational Generative Grammar. Key exponents of Generative Semantics were mostly former students and collaborators of Noam Chomsky and they received their education at MIT. Prominent linguists who contributed to the development of GS are John R. Ross, Paul Postal, James McCawley, and George Lakoff. An important role was also played by some linguists who did not receive their education at MIT, and did not start as Chomskyans, most notably Charles Fillmore. The clash between Chomsky and generative semanticists was so harsh that it was referred to as 'the linguistic wars' (see Harris 1993).

The word 'generative' in GS is opposed to 'interpretive'. In transformational syntax, semantics was considered interpretive, in the sense that well-formed sentences generated by syntactic rules were assigned an interpretation based on a separate semantic component: crucially deep structures were not generated by the semantic component, but by the syntactic component alone. Consequently, syntax was viewed as autonomous with respect to semantics. In GS, semantic interpretation is generated directly at the deep structure level, which implies a strong conditioning of syntax by semantics. In practice, the semantic structure corresponded to the deep structure.

Early GS assumed a level of deep structure that accounted for semantic interpretation of sentences. Under this approach, deep structures became increasingly complicated, until the multistratal conception of language was generally abandoned in favor of monostratal approaches. By this time, scholars who initially contributed to the birth of GS had developed different theories, separated and sometimes as different from each other as from Transformational Generative Grammar.

Government and Binding and Principles and Parameters Theory

The goal of Government and Binding (GB) and Principles and Parameters (P&P) Theory is to move toward a modular model of syntax and toward a program of comparative syntax and Universal Grammar (UG). The key works of the GB Theory are Chomsky's *Lectures of Government and Binding* (1981), which is an elaboration of the 'On binding' (1980) model, *Some concepts and consequences of the theory of government and binding* (1982). In this model, syntax is formulated as a modular theory divided in several sub-theories or modules which have their own independent principles. The modules are sub-theories such as:

a. Bounding theory: principles that set limits on the domain of movement rules
b. Government theory: principles that define the relation between the head of a phrase and the categories depending on it
c. Theta theory: principles that assign theta roles
d. Case theory: principles that assign abstract Case
e. Control theory: principles that determine the reference of PRO
f. X-bar theory: principles that constrain the base component of grammar
g. Trace theory: principles that set the properties of traces
h. Binding Theory: principles regulating the interpretation of anaphors, pronouns and referential expressions.

Within this framework, linguistic variation results from each language setting different **parameters** or values for one or more principles of these sub-theories. Thus, when children acquire their native languages, in addition to being innately endowed with a system of principles common to the human species or UG, they have to set the parameters of the language or languages they are exposed to. From a typological perspective, it is important to determine which clusters of properties separate one set of languages from other sets of languages. For example, Italian and Spanish conform to the pro-drop or null subject parameter differing from English and French in that:

a. They allow null subjects (EC) of conjugated verbs: **EC** *comemos manzanas* "**we** eat apples"
b. They allow subject inversion: *come manzanas* **Juan** "eats apples **John**"
c. They allow subject extraction out of a subordinate wh (interrogative) clause: *la mujer* **que**$_j$ *no se cuándo* **t**$_j$ *haya telefoneado* "the woman who$_j$ I do not know when **t**$_j$ (she) has called"
d. They allow *that*- trace violations: *¿Quién crees que vendrá?* "who do you think **that** will come?"
e. They allow empty resumptive pronouns (EC): *el muchacho que*$_j$ *no se quien haya dicho que EC*$_j$ *ha llegado* "the boy who$_j$ I don't know who said (**he**$_j$) has arrived"

Within this framework, phrase structure rules and all the base component rules of previous models are eliminated and the X-bar phrase model is adopted in building sentences. Moreover, GB theory advances the understanding of empty NP elements whose distribution is accounted for by Binding Theory and Government Theory. Thus, NPs can be anaphors, pronominals, or referential expressions; traces must be properly governed, according to the Empty Category Principle (ECP). During this period there was much discussion about the levels—D-Structure, S-Structure, or Logical Form (LF)—in which the principles of Binding Theory and the ECP should be applied. There were several definitions of government, which despite their small differences had major consequences for the ECP and for Binding Theory. The definition of government was given in terms of the basic notion of **c-command**. As a continuation of the lexicalist hypothesis, Chomsky (1981) introduced the Projection Principle and the Theta Criterion as structure preserving constraints, conditions that had to be met by entire derivations. The **Projection Principle** states that subcategorization properties of lexical items must be maintained at D-Structure, S-Structure, and LF. This principle is structure preserving, since it ensures that the phrase structure configuration of a sentence remains constant throughout the derivation. The **Extended Projection Principle**, which requires that all sentences have a subject, was an important addition to the Projection Principle because it explains the need of small *pro* in languages that may not have an overtly realized subject. The Theta Criterion demands that each argument bears one and only one thematic role and that each theta role be assigned to one and only one argument. Case Theory is also responsible for the distribution of NPs in sentences. In fact, in this model each NP must be assigned abstract Case, to conform to the Case Filter. Different categories assign Case: Agreement assigns Nominative Case, a verb assigns Accusative Case, and a preposition assigns Accusative or Oblique Case. With the exception of Genitive, Case is assigned under government. An important function of Case is to force movement. For example, in passive, the NP object moves to subject position to get nominative Case.

Since the publication of the paper 'On binding' (1980), specific movement transformations were replaced by one movement rule, **move** α, where α is a syntactic category. This extremely simple rule allows "moving anything anywhere in the sentence." To preclude chaos, the sub-theories or modules with their own independent principles control overgeneration and restrict the operation move α. This system allows to eliminate independent rules such as Passive, Raising, Relativization or Question Formation that were part of earlier generative theories. There are still two main types of movement: NP movement (to an A position, or Argument position, where the NP gets Case) and Wh-movement (to an A-bar position, or non-Argument position, which lacks Case, but allows the wh-operator to bind a variable). Within this framework a sentence has four levels of representation that are reached through move α: D-structure (Deep Structure), S-structure (Surface Structure), LF (Logical Form), and PF (Phonetic Form). The LF representation of a sentence is an intermediate level between S-structure and full semantic representation. This level represents the interpretation of scope-taking elements, such as wh-phrases and quantifiers. PF is the level of representation that encodes the surface properties of a sentence, usually corresponding to its pronunciation.PF is derived from S-structure and is considered the interface with the articulatory-perceptual system. Both PF and LF are subject to the principle of Full Interpretation. That is, every element of PF and LF must receive an appropriate interpretation and

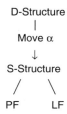

Figure 5 T-Model

fulfill well-formedness conditions on syntactic structure. The four levels are represented in the T-model depicted in Figure 5.

Head Driven Phrase Structure Grammar

Head Driven Phrase Structure Grammar (HPSG) was developed in the late 1980s by Pollard and Sag. It is a successor of Generalized Phrase Structure Grammar and an alternative to Transformational Generative Grammar (see Pollard and Sag 1994). Unlike GPSG, HPSG incorporates some of the features of Government and Binding Theory.

HPSG is "a non-derivational, constraint-based, surface oriented grammatical architecture" (Kim 2000: 7). In other words, it does not assume transformations and conceives of different representations as subparts of a single larger structure, related by constraints. Thus, some constructions usually derived through transformational rules in Transformational Generative Grammar are generated by lexical rules in HPSG. An example is the passive lexical rule, which generates a passive verb from a transitive verb, as shown in Figure 6.

Under this perspective, a passive sentence does not derive from an active one through a transformation; rather the active/passive alternation is handled in the lexicon. In this respect, HPSG is similar to Lexical Functional Grammar.

Figure 6 The passive lexical rule in HPSG (from Kim 2000: 16)

HPSG further rejects the idea that there are phonologically unrealized elements such as big PRO, the subject of controlled nonfinite verbs in GB Theory. This is because in HPSG lexical specifications, such as subcategorization requirements, are explicitly represented. It is the lexical specification of the control verb that explains why controlled infinitives allow different controllers, as in:

(1) a. *I persuade him to leave*
    b. *I try to leave*

Basic linguistic items are signs. Signs are divided into two subtypes, words and phrases; they are described as bundles of features, which determine phonological (PHON), syntactic and semantic (SYNSEM) constraints. Feature structures of signs are represented as attribute value matrices (AVMs).

As an example of what a lexical entry looks like in HPSG consider the verb *put* in Figure 7.

In the top left corner a label specifies this sign as a word (rather than a phrase). PHON refers to the phonological representation of the word. The SYNSEM constraints specify category properties (this word is a verb with a specific valency), and content properties, which correspond to the semantic roles of the NPs that saturate the valency of this verb or its combining potential.

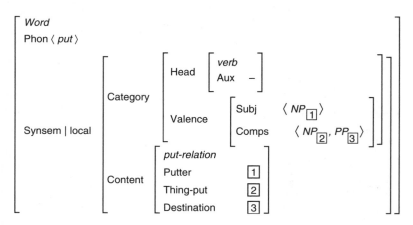

Figure 7 A lexical entry in HPSG (from Levine and Meurers 2006: 238)

HPSG incorporates a version of the X-bar theory under the name of Immediate Dominance Principle (ID).

Suggested link: http://www.ling.ohio-state.edu/research/hpsg/

Lexical Functional Grammar

Lexical Functional Grammar (LFG) was developed in the late 1970s by Joan Bresnan, who had received training in Transformational Generative Grammar at the Massachusetts Institute of Technology (see Bresnan 2001). It is one of the various theories that have risen out of criticism for mainstream generative theory.

LFG is lexical in that it assumes a richly structured lexicon, in which lexical relations capture linguistic generalizations, while there is no need for transformations or operations on phrase structure trees (i.e. LFG is monostratal). The crucial difference between LFG and Transformational Generative Grammar (Standard Theory) lies in the nature of subcategorization. While in Transformational Generative Grammar subcategorized items are specified in terms of syntactic categories, in LFG subcategorization specifies grammatical functions (grammatical relations in most other terminologies). Thus, a verb such as *see* is specified as follows:

(1) *see* V Pred = 'SEE <SUBJ, OBJ>'

LFG is functional in the sense that certain grammatical functions, such as subject and object, are considered primitives and accordingly are not further defined in terms of phrase structure configuration or semantic roles (in very much the same way as in Relational Grammar), even though a current thread of research in LFG investigates the pairing of grammatical function and semantic (or thematic) roles.

Note that the word 'functional' in LFG is used with a meaning which is different from the meaning it has in S. C. Dik's Functional Grammar, and in general when one speaks of 'functional approaches': as shown above, it refers to grammatical functions as primitives of the theory and not to a special vantage point that takes the function of language in verbal communication as central. (In practice, the term 'functional' in LFG corresponds to the term 'relation' in Relational Grammar.)

In LFG there are two fundamental levels of syntactic representation: constituent structure (c-structure) and functional structure (f-structure):

- C-structures have the form of context-free phrase structure trees; they follow the X-bar theory and assume that all constructions, except sentences are internally headed and thus endocentric; they represent word order and phrasal constituenthood: consequently, they may vary across languages, depending on specific word order and on its function (in English, the position of the subject NP defines its function, in Russian it does not).
- F-structures represent abstract grammatical functions such as subject and object and features such as tense, case, person, gender, and number.

In contrast with the Chomskyan tradition from which it developed, LFG assumes that many phenomena can be more naturally analyzed in terms of grammatical functions as represented in the lexicon or in f-structure, rather than on the level of phrase structure. An example is the alternation between active and passive, which is handled in the lexicon, rather than being treated as a transformation (see Bresnan 1982). Grammatical functions are not derived from phrase structure configurations, but are represented at the parallel level of functional structure.

In a sentence such as:

(2) *Mary ate the steak*

Mary is the subject and *the steak* is the object. This information is represented by an attribute-value structure, the f-structure, in which the value of the SUBJ feature is the f-structure for the subject, and the value of the OBJ feature is the f-structure for the object, as shown in Figure 8.

Grammatical functions are a closed set of universally available primitives, which include the following (from Dalrymple 2006: 85):

$$
\begin{bmatrix}
\text{PRED} & \text{'EAT}\ \langle\ \text{SUBJ, OBJ}\ \rangle\text{'} \\
\text{SUBJ} & [\text{PRED 'MARY'}] \\
\text{OBJ} & \begin{bmatrix} \text{SPEC} & \text{THE} \\ \text{PRED} & \text{'STEAK'} \end{bmatrix}
\end{bmatrix}
$$

Figure 8 An example of f-structure in LFG

- SUBJ: subject;
- OBJ: object;
- COMP: sentential or closed (nonpredicative) infinitival complement;
- XCOMP: an open (predicative) complement, often infinitival, whose SUBJ function is externally controlled;
- OBJ_θ: a family of secondary OBJ functions associated with a particular, language-specific set of thematic roles; in English, only OBJ_{THEME} is allowed, while other languages allow more than one thematically restricted secondary object;
- OBL_θ: a family of thematically restricted oblique functions such as OBL_{GOAL} or OBL_{AGENT}, often corresponding to adpositional phrases at c-structure.

Languages differ as to which of these functions are relevant, but in many languages, including English, all of them are used. (Note that the function PRED applies to all lexical items that convey semantic, as opposed to grammatical information.)

LFG uses three distinct layers of structure for representing the relations or functions of arguments: θ-structure (thematic structure), a-structure (argument structure), and f-structure (functional structure), which expresses grammatical relations. Argument structure corresponds to what is commonly called 'verbal valency' ('predicate frame' in S. C. Dik's Functional Grammar).

Suggested link: http://www.essex.ac.uk/linguistics/LFG/

Minimalist Program

Chomsky's *Minimalist Program* (1995) proposes a tentative research program that further develops conceptions of economy to find out universal principles and parameters. This model uses mainly notions required by 'virtual conceptual necessity'. Thus, while Government and Binding Theory required several levels of representations (D-structure, S-structure, PF, and LF), the Minimalist Program regards sentences as pairings of sounds (π or PF) and meanings (λ or LF). The pair (π and λ) is subject to Full Interpretation. That is, the Minimalist Program requires that all the features of the pair be legible at these interfaces. In Minimalist terminology, a sentence is the interface of articulatory and perceptual (A–P) properties and their conceptual and intentional (C–I) characteristics. For this reason D-structure and S-structure are excluded in the Minimalist Program, but PF and LF carry on in it. In this Program, the language faculty is the optimal realization of interface conditions. In fact, particular phenomena are not overdetermined by linguistic principles. Moreover, Chomsky (1995) stresses the relevance of concepts related to economy, such as **least effort, shortest move** and **last resort movement** to address movement. Minimalist approaches to phrase structure have resulted in attempts to eliminate the X-bar scheme. Due to the principle of economy of derivation, movement only occurs to match **interpretable features** with **uninterpretable features**. In the Minimalist Program traces are replaced by copies that have the same features as the moved elements.

The derivation procedure in the Minimalist Program is currently construed as a step-by-step bottom-up process. This is different from the X-bar schema in the Government and Binding Theory, where the selection and subcategorization properties of the lexical items were projected into D-structures in an all-at-once and top-down process. Moreover, in the Government and Binding Theory, functional elements such as Agreement, Tense, and their inflectional morphemes, were independently base-generated. The lexical elements (stem of a verb or a NP), were raised to the functional nodes to adjoin to their inflections. In the Minimalist Program, the notion of affixation has been abandoned since the lexical items are introduced with the **numeration** fully inflected, accompanied with their Case, agreement, and Φ features (person, gender, and number). These formal features are licensed by checking against those associated with the functional nodes, that is, by raising to the specifier positions of the functional heads. In this Program the notion of government is replaced by the notion of Spec(ifier)-head agreement, which is local in character. In particular, Case-assignment is substituted by Case-feature-checking. Uninterpretable features (such as those for Case), if unchecked, will cause a derivation to crash. In the version outlined by Chomsky (2000, 2001, 2004), the derivation proceeds by phase. That is, syntactic structures are built in a bottom-up, one-phase-at-a-time fashion. Phases, which according to Chomsky include the propositional categories CP and (transitive) *v*P, can be seen as defining local computational domains, as the cycle did in previous models. Phases are constructed by successive application of the two basic structure-building operations **Merge** and **Move**. Overt movement, which presupposes abstract agreement, is induced only by heads that carry the Extended Projection Principle feature. Agreement—and hence, movement—is triggered by the need to eliminate uninterpretable features of both the attracting head (the **Probe**) and the attractee (the **Goal**).

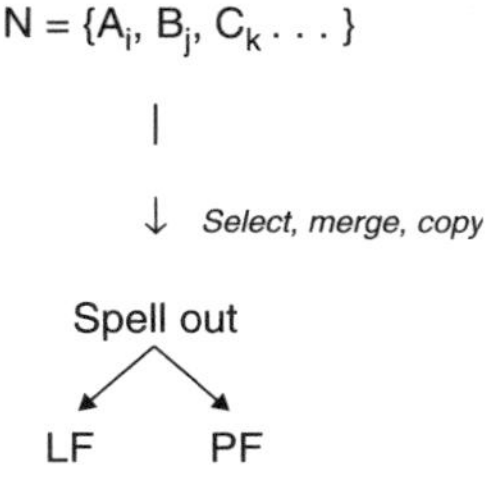

$$N = \{A_i, B_j, C_k \dots \}$$

$$|$$

$\downarrow$ *Select, merge, copy*

Spell out

LF   PF

Figure 9 Minimalist Program Model

The Minimalist Program has produced important revisions of earlier proposals. For example, by eliminating D-structure, the recursive feature of the grammar has to become the province of generalized transformations. Whatever its ultimate success, however, Minimalism continues the pursuit of the broad goals of descriptive and explanatory adequacy enunciated in Chomsky's earliest work. The Minimalist model, with no D-structure nor S-structure, contains Numeration, a movement rule that selects, merges elements and leaves copies; PF and LF still are part of the system, as shown in Figure 9 (modeled upon Boeckx 2006).

Suggested link: http://minimalism.linguistics.arizona.edu/AMSA/ archives.html

Montague Grammar

Montague Grammar owes its name to American logician Richard Montague, whose main intention was to work out a logical model of universal grammar, capable of accounting for natural as well as formal languages.

Montague's most influential writings date to the early 1970s, and focus especiallyon on formal semantics. At the time of their publication, Montague's semantic theory appeared as a possible 'third way' between interpretive and generative semantics and was incorporated in some theories alternative to Transformational Generative Grammar, such as Generalized Phrase Structure Grammar. One of the basic tenets of Montague Grammar is the Principle of Compositionality, according to which the meaning of a whole is a function of the meanings of its parts and the rules of their combination.

Because in dealing with natural languages one runs the risk of being overwhelmed with data, Montague worked out the method of 'fragments'. Accordingly, Montague's papers contain descriptions of limited subsets (fragments) of the grammar of a natural language. This method is still followed in computational semantics, perhaps the field to which Montague Grammar has given its most relevant contribution (see Partee and Hendricks 1997).

Grammatical models such as Montague Grammar are called **categorial grammars**. Categorial grammars take a logic based approach to language, and adopt the terminology and methods of classical logic for language description.

Optimality Theory

Optimality Theory (OT) arose in the 1990s as a branch of Transformational Generative Grammar that uses constraints to explain variability in language, mainly in phonology. Thus, it differs substantially from previous models that use rules and constraints, since it eliminates derivations, simplifying the SPE (Sound Patterns of English) model and other generative models. This theory is also applicable to other subfields, such as syntax and language acquisition. In OT the constraints (CON) are considered part of innate Universal Grammar (UG). However, languages can violate universal constraints, since constraints are in conflict with each other. Thus, individual grammars must regulate conflicts between constraints in order to select the optimal output. This is achieved by ranking universal constraints. Ranking varies across languages, originating cross-linguistic variation. Each violation of a higher-ranked universal constraint is more costly than a lower ranked violation. The optimal output candidate incurs in minimal violations of higher-ranking constraints, but it may infringe several lower-ranking violations. There are two basic types of constraints: **Faithfulness constraints** and **Markedness constraints**. Faithfulness constraints require that the surface or output, match the input. That is, these constraints require identity between input and output. Markedness constraints impose requirements on the structural well-formedness of the output. The universal nature of CON predicts types of languages (typology), since grammars vary in their different rankings of CON. Thus, the set of possible human languages is determined by the constraints. However not all possible rankings of all existing constraints are attested, which may in part be due to accidental gaps in language typology or to different rankings producing the same optimal outputs.

In syntax, the *input* in OT is defined in terms of the argument structure of lexical heads. For example, consider the sentence in (1):

(1) *what did John eat?*

At the level of input, the lexical head *eat* takes two arguments, which are assigned to two lexical heads (*John* and *what*). At the level of generation (GEN), all possible candidates, such as the examples in (2), are produced within the universal structural requirements of a theory. In this case, it is X-bar theory.

(2) a. *John ate what?*
    b. *what John ate?*
    c. *what ate John?*
    d. *what did John eat?*

All these candidates correspond to grammatical sentences in different languages, for example, among others, Chinese (a), Czech and Polish (b), Dutch, Spanish, and Italian (c), English (d). Then the candidates are submitted for evaluation (EVAL). Each of the examples in (2) violates one or more constraints, but each one is maximally optimal with respect to some ranking in the specific language in question. The English sentence (d) can be evaluated in OT using the universal well-formedness constraints included in (3), proposed by Grimshaw (1997):

(3) *No lexical head movement (No-Lex-Mvt)*
        A lexical head cannot move
    Operator in specifier: (Op-spec)
        Syntactic operators must be of specifier position
    Obligatory heads (Ob-hd)
        A projection has a head
    Economy of movement (Stay)
        Trace is not allowed
    Full Interpretation (Full-Int)
        Lexical conceptual structure is parsed

In the process of evaluation (EVAL), all candidates are compared against the ranked universal constraint list. In this way it is possible to see which candidate violates fewest higher-ranking constraints. The constraints in (3) are self-explanatory, except *Full Int,* which bans semantically empty auxiliary verbs

{*say* (x,y), x=*Mary*, y=*what*, tense=past}	No-Lex-Mvt	Op-Spec	Ob-Hd	Full-Int	Stay
→ What **did** Mary **e** say t				*	* *
What **e** Mary said t			* !		*
What **e** Mary **did** say t			* !	*	*
What **e** Mary **e** said t			* !		*
What said Mary **e** t	* !				* *

Figure 10 The constraint tableau

as is *do-support* in English. Since this violation is minimal, semantically empty verbs are used only when necessary. The evaluation of the candidates is displayed on the *constraint tableau,* such as Figure 10, where each violation is indicated with an asterisk, a fatal violation is marked with an asterisk and an exclamation mark, and the optimal representation is preceded by an arrow.

In Figure 10 it is clear that the optimal or most harmonic representation of the English sentence *What did Mary say?* violates few of the lowest-ranked constraints: *Full interpretation* and *Stay.* In other languages the ranking is different. Thus, other violations and various outputs are obtained.

Suggested link: http://roa.rutgers.edu/index.php3

Relational Grammar

Relational Grammar (RG) is a multistratal theory developed in the 1970s by Paul Postal and David Perlmutter. In RG the grammatical relations Subject, Direct Object, Indirect Object, and Oblique are considered linguistic primitives, not to be further defined. RG was conceived as a universally valid model: the assumption of grammatical relations as primitives is a consequence of the fact that representations based on phrase structure rules, used in Transformational Generative Grammar, fail to account for some universal phenomena, such as the passive, in a way that is valid for all languages. (Note that these assumptions are similar to some of the basic assumptions of Lexical Functional Grammar.)

In RG, a sentence is conceived of as a net constituted by the basic relations Subject (1-relation), Direct Object (2-relation), and Indirect Object (3-relation); the sentence has different syntactic levels, represented as arcs on the network of relations specified by the predicate. Each constituent bears one of the basic

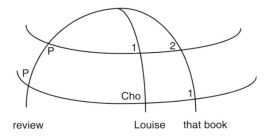

Figure 11 The representation of a passive sentence in RG

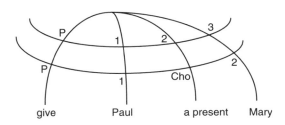

Figure 12 The representation of dative shift in RG

relations at every level. A passive sentence involves detransitivization of the predicate, which no longer requires a subject and an object (i.e. 1 and 2), but only a subject, along with promotion of the object to subject, that is, promotion from 2 to 1, and demotion of the subject. The demoted subject no longer occupies one of the basic relations, and is said to become a chômeur ('jobless'), as in the representation in Figure 11.

(1) *That book was reviewed by Louise*

Dative shift constructions also imply promotion (from 3 to 2) and consequent demotion to chômeur, as shown in Figure 12.

(2) *Paul gave Mary a present*

The structure of final levels is constrained by the Final 1 Law, which states that the 1 relation (subject relation) must be covered at all syntactic levels.

This implies the assumption of nonovertly realized dummies for sentences that do not contain an overt subject, such as:

(3) *è tardi*
is late
"It's late." (Italian, Romance, Indo-European)

Since RG originated as an answer to problems raised by the application of Transformational Generative Grammar to the description of languages other than English, in which constituency played a different role, and it aimed at being universally applicable, it has been tested on numerous typologically different languages, and relational grammars of a high number of languages, including lesser described ones, have appeared especially in the early 1980s. A refined version of RG is Arc Pair Grammar (Johnson and Postal 1980).

Revised Extended Standard Transformational Generative Theory

The paradigmatic paper by Chomsky 'Conditions on transformations' (1973) altered the generative conception of grammar and the perception of language at the time. In this paper Chomsky explores the effects of the desirable blind applications of transformations. This program led him to discover important constraints on transformations such as the **Specified Subject Condition**, the **Principle of Subjacency,** and the **Tensed Sentence Condition**, all of which preclude certain transformations to apply or limit their movement to one cyclic domain. For example, the Tensed Sentence Condition prevents moving a syntactic element in a tensed sentence as in (1a) to a position outside this sentence as in (1b):

(1) a. *the students **each** expected that the other would pass the class*
b. **the students **expected** that **each** other would pass the class*

Moreover, Chomsky and his associates discovered that every time an NP or a wh-element moves, it leaves a trace (**t**) which is coindexed with the moved NP or wh-element as in (2):

(2) **who**$_i$ *did she say John hit **t**$_i$?*

This discovery gave rise to **trace theory**, which assigns different properties to different traces. Thus, while NP traces act as anaphors bound by the moved NP phrases, wh-traces, such as **t** in (2), act as variables bound by the moved wh-phrase (which acts as a logical quantifier). Most importantly, NP movement transformations were replaced by one movement rule, **move NP**. In addition, in 1977 Chomsky in his 'On wh-movement' paper derived by a single rule of **Wh-movement** the effects of relative clauses, questions, and several constructions—some of which did not have an overt wh-word—such as comparative sentences and topicalized sentences among others. Deletion rules were used to remove nonoccurring wh-phrases in these constructions and filters were used to avoid the generation of ungrammatical sentences. In the Government and Binding model, NP movement and Wh-movement would become part of a more general syntactic movement, **move α**.

Since surface structures contained traces of movement, there was no need for semantic rules to apply at deep structure, as in the previous model. Thus, Chomsky proposed a set of semantic rules (SR-1) that mapped surface structure onto Logical Form (LF) and another set of semantic rules (SR-2) that took LF as input to determine other semantic relations, such as inference and conditions of appropriate use. The main features of the REST model are depicted in Figure 13 (modeled upon Newmeyer 1986:163).

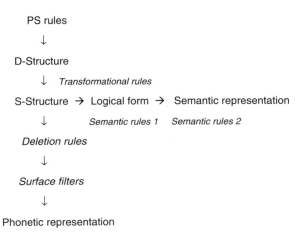

Figure 13 Revised Extended Standard (REST) Model

Role and Reference Grammar

Role and Reference Grammar (RRG) is a functional model of grammar which was developed primarily by Robert Van Valin Jr., in collaboration with other linguists, notably William Foley, in the 1980s. Similar to S. C. Dik's Functional Grammar, RRG holds that language is primarily a tool for verbal communication. Accordingly, sentences are described in the first place in terms of their semantic and communicative functions. Because it was developed by typologists, RRG has as one of its primary motivations to avoid an English biased perspective on grammatical structure, as is typical of many other theories.

RRG is a monostratal theory. The syntactic representation of a sentence corresponds to its actual structure, including actual word order and morphology; it is connected to the semantic representation through discourse pragmatic principles. Figure 14 illustrates the structure of the theory:

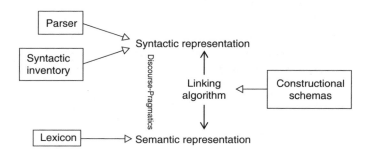

Figure 14 The structure of RRG (from Van Valin 2006: 641)

As in Dik's Functional Grammar, in RRG the clause is assumed to have a layered structure, which includes the nucleus (the predicate), the core (the predicate and the arguments), and the clause (the core and the periphery, i.e. other possible constituents). The representation of a sentence in RRG is as follows:

(1) *the man saw the woman in the mountains*

Figure 15 shows the layered structure of a clause in RRG and Figure 16 the layered structure of a phrase in RRG.

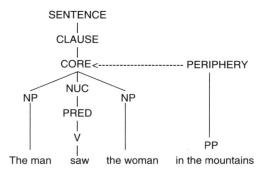

Figure 15 The layered structure of a clause in RRG (adapted from Van Valin and LaPolla 1997: 33)

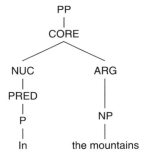

Figure 16 The layered structure of a phrase in RRG

Constituents also have a layered structure. The structure of the PP *in the mountains* is given in Figure 16.

Suggested link: http://linguistics.buffalo.edu/research/rrg.html

Standard Transformational Generative Theory

The problems of the classical model, such as the application of generalized transformations and the information included in phrase structure rules, triggered deep changes in the model of *Aspects of the Theory of Syntax* (1965), a book by Chomsky from which the Standard Transformational Generative model emanates. As other generative grammars, the Standard Model "must be the 'output' of an acquisition model of language" (Chomsky 1965: 75). The order of the application of generalized transformations and the way recursion was implemented in the classical model of *Syntactic Structures* was left unexplained (see Fillmore 1963). This was corrected in the *Aspects* model. Thus, recursion is handled by phrase structure rules that generate a lexically specified phrase marker (or **deep structure** tree) serving as input to the transformational rules. The level of deep structure in the *Aspects* model is defined by the application of phrase structure rules, subcategorization rules, and lexical insertion rules. The resulting phrase marker or tree contains nodes labeled with a category symbol such as S (sentence), NP (noun phrase), N (noun), VP (verb phrase), V (verb) etc. Universal grammatical relations such as **subject, predicate,** and **direct object** are placed in the semantic component, leaving syntax to operate only on phrasal categories (e.g. a NP, PP, or VP). Thus, the subject is formally defined as the NP immediately dominated by S and the direct object is a NP immediately dominated by VP, and so on, as shown in sentence (1), which has the structure given in (2):

(1) *Mary loves the boy*

(2)

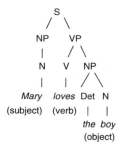

In this model, there are three kinds of subcategorization rules: context-free rules, context-sensitive rules, and selectional rules. The first type of rules has the form in (3):

(3) N → [+N, ±Human, ±Common]

The second type of rules shows the syntactic frames in which lexical categories occur. Thus, a verb preceding a noun phrase would have the feature + [__ NP]. Finally, the third type of rules subcategorizes verbs on the basis of the features of the categories with which they cooccur. Thus, the feature

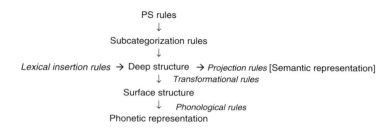

PS rules
↓
Subcategorization rules
↓
Lexical insertion rules → Deep structure → Projection rules [Semantic representation]
↓ Transformational rules
Surface structure
↓ Phonological rules
Phonetic representation

Figure 17 Standard Model

+[+Human __] would be assigned to a verb occurring after a human subject. The transformational rules were applied orderly at the level of deep structure to the output of subcategorization rules and lexical insertion rules. In this model, phrase structure rules applied recursively, and transformational rules applied cyclically from the most embedded sentence to the highest sentence. Global transformations were abandoned, but singulary transformations, such as passive, were kept as in the *Syntactic Structures* model.

Summarizing, the Standard Model is characterized by the introduction of deep structure and by moving recursion to the base, which allows for a more restricted theory of grammar. A restrictive theory is always desirable as it brings us closer to the central goal of explaining how language acquisition is possible. Figure 17 shows the organization of the Standard Model.

Stratificational Grammar

Stratificational Grammar is a theory developed in the 1960s by American linguist Sydney Lamb, in which language is analyzed as having multiple levels, or strata. According to Lamb (1966), basic strata are phonology, grammar, and semology, each of which is further subdivided into two strata. In particular, grammar is subdivided into the morphemic and the lexemic strata. The latter is the level of syntactic analysis, syntax being said to concern combinations of lexemes. Language structures at each level of representation are represented by linguistic graphs, made up of lines and nodes (intersections of lines). There are two types of analysis, again operating at each level: tactic, concerning distribution patterns, and realizational, concerning the combination of units (horizontal), and the structure of paradigmatic relations (vertical). Stratificational Grammar conceives of the linguistic system as a network of relations holding between different strata. It later developed into Neurocognitive

Linguistics, whose main interest is to investigate the relationship between language and the brain.

Suggested link: http://www.ruf.rice.edu/~lngbrain/

Systemic Functional Grammar

Systemic Functional Grammar (SFG) is a functional approach to language developed by British linguist Michael Alexander Kirkwood Halliday, based on work by his teacher, John Rupert Firth, who was active in the 1920s–1950s. The word 'functional' in SFG refers to the communicative function of language, with special emphasis on the social aspect of linguistic interaction. According to Matthiessen and Halliday (forthcoming), grammar is "a resource for creating meaning by means of wording."

In SFG, syntax is not assigned a special status; rather, it is a part of lexico-grammar (a combination of syntax, lexicon, and morphology), which accounts for linguistic structure. According to Halliday, there is no clear-cut separation between grammar (including syntax) and semantics. In SFG, the latter also incorporates what is usually considered pragmatics in most other approaches.

Following the central relevance of social interaction for linguistic analysis, SFG focuses on discourse structure, rather than on sentence structure: basic units of linguistic analysis are not sentences, but texts.

The word 'systemic' in SFG refers to the existence of various simultaneous systems, the three basic ones being transitivity, mood, and theme. Connected with these grammatical systems are three metafunctions:

- ideational, which analyzes language as message, something that expresses ideas: this metafunction has as its main grammatical system the system of transitivity, which serves the purpose of structuring our experience as structural configurations (processes);
- interpersonal, which analyzes language as interaction, something that allows people to interact with one another: its main grammatical system is mood, which can be understood as the grammaticalization of social interaction;
- textual, which analyzes language as text: it "serves to enable the presentation of ideational and interpersonal meaning as information that can be shared" (Matthiessen and Halliday forthcoming) by creating "its own parallel universe in the form of discourse" (Halliday 2006: 445). In practice,

it provides an information structure (theme vs. rheme) to a certain unit of discourse, for example, a sentence.

Each system consists of sets of choices, as shown in Figure 18:

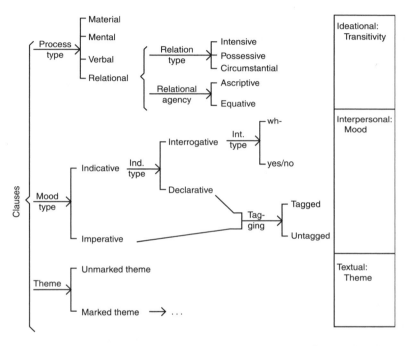

Figure 18 Metafunctions as manifested in the system network of the English clause (from Matthiessen and Haliday forthcoming)

Suggested link: http://www.isfla.org/Systemics/index.html

Tagmemics

Tagmemics was developed by American linguist and anthropologist Kenneth Lee Pike in the 1950s and 1960s. Tagmemics conceives of language as a part of human behavior, and consequently rejects strict mentalism. Basic axioms of linguistic theory are claimed to hold for human behavior in general, and not for language behavior alone.

Tagmemics assumes four basic postulates on human behavior (see Jones 1980). In the first place, purposive behavior, such as language, can be analyzed in discrete units recognizable by the distinctive features that contrast units with one another. In the second place, tagmemics highlights the role of context: since units do not occur in isolation, they should be studied within the appropriate context (accordingly, sentences should be studied in discourse rather than in isolation). Thirdly, units form part of hierarchies. Hierarchies relevant for language are the phonological, grammatical, and referential hierarchies. Of these three, it is the grammatical hierarchy that accounts for structure, including syntax (which is viewed as not being separate from morphology). Finally, tagmemics also puts emphasis on the observer, stating that, depending on the observer's perspective, linguistic description can be static, dynamic, or relational.

Grammatical units are called tagmemes, and consist of two elements, a slot (the relation of the unit to other units on the same constituency level), and a class (the type of unit). Tagmemes build syntagmemes or constructions. So for example, a sentence such as (1):

(1) *the girl sings*

is in the first place a tagmeme (it is an independent unit); being a construction, it can be analyzed as a syntagmeme constituted by two tagmemes, *the girl* (slot: subject, class: noun phrase), and *sings* (slot: predicate, class: verb). These two tagmemes are themselves syntagmemes, and can be further analyzed. In particular, since, as noted above, syntax and morphology are not two separate levels of analysis in tagmemics, the form *sings* is considered a construction containing two tagmemes, one of which is the inflectional ending *-s*.

The lexicon has a relevant place in tagmemics, acting as an interface between the three hierarchies (phonology, grammar, and reference). Syntactic analysis does not assume transformations (i.e. the theory is monostratal). Rules of tagmemics are formulas that consist of sets of successive choices, and generate all and only specific units of the language implied by specific formulas (Jones 1980: 90).

Suggested link: http://personal.bgsu.edu/~edwards/tags.html

Transformational Generative Grammar

Transformational Generative Grammar attempts to construct a formalized theory of language within a framework that assumes the existence of rules or devices that modify or transform one linguistic structure into another structure in order to explain an array of phenomena pertaining to human language, mainly syntax. There have been several versions or models of Transformational Generative Grammar since its inception in 1955, when Noam Chomsky wrote his dissertation *The Logical Structure of Linguistic Theory*. The first published version of this theory appeared in 1957 with Chomsky's *Syntactic Structures*. Most of them correspond to changes introduced by Chomsky himself in several key works:

- Classical Transformational Generative Theory (1950–1957)
- Standard Transformational Generative Theory (1965)
- Extended Standard Transformational Generative Theory (1970)
- Revised Extended Standard Transformational Generative Theory (1973–1977)
- Government and Binding/Principle and Parameters Theory (1980–1993)
- Minimalist Program (1995)

Despite the fact that there were previous modern attempts to develop transformational grammars, such as Harris (1951, 1957), Noam Chomsky's publication of *Syntactic Structures* (1957) was the breaking groundwork that changed the field of contemporary linguistics.

Word Grammar

Word Grammar is a theory developed by Richard Hudson in the 1980s (see Hudson 1984). It partly grew out of Systemic Functional Grammar. It is monostratal, and does not assume transformations.

Word Grammar purports to be a cognitive approach to language. Similar to Cognitive Grammar, Word Grammar conceives of language as part of human cognition, rather than as an independent module. Grammar is conceived of as a set of units connected by a network. Words are connected to meaning, phonological representation, and morphological properties (the idea of a network operating on various levels derives from Stratificational Grammar).

The most important relation in Word Grammar is the concomitance relation, a subtype of which is dependency. Dependency is claimed by Hudson to replace constituency (1980a, b). The concomitance relation is a relation of cooccurrence explicitly granted by grammar. In (1):

(1) *Elizabeth likes plain yogurt*

the grammar must specify that *Elizabeth* and *likes* can occur together, but no rule refers to the cooccurrence of *Elizabeth* and *yogurt*. In much the same way, grammar specifies the cooccurrence of *plain* and *yogurt*, but not of *plain* and *Elizabeth*. Relations have a specific direction: they proceed from the nucleus or head to the dependent. Hence, sentence (1) can be represented as in Figure 19.

Note that this type of representation with tree diagrams does not always make clear the actual word order. This problem can be avoided with another type of representation:

(2)
        Elizabeth likes   plain   yogurt

Crucial to this view of sentence structure is the notion of head. In particular, it is of central importance to be able to identify the head of a construction. This issue has been a frequent topic of discussion for scholars working in this framework.

An earlier version of Word Grammar was called Daughter-Dependency Grammar.

Suggested link: http://www.phon.ucl.ac.uk/home/dick/wg.htm

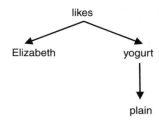

Figure 19 A tree-diagram representation of a sentence in word grammar

Key Terms

A-position

A-position stands for argument position. It is a position in the phrase marker (tree) occupied by an argument (subject or object). Theta-roles are assigned in A-positions. Consider (1):

(1) [$_{IP}$ [$_{VP}$ Silvia [$_V$ loves linguistics]]]

In sentence (1), *Silvia* and *linguistics* are in A-positions.
See *D-structure* and *Theta-role*.

A-bar position

A-bar position stands for a non-Argument position. A-bar positions are positions occupied by operators such as *what* in (1):

(1) **what** *did you buy?*

Typically the Spec of CP (Complementizer Phrase) is an A-bar position.
See *Operator*.

Absolutive see *Case*.
Accessibility hierarchy see *Relative clause*.

Actant

An item which saturates the valency of a predicate, an argument. On the sentence level, actants are expressions that indicate obligatory participants, and are opposed to circumstants, which are not obligatory. This terminology goes back to Tesnière (1959); in general, actant corresponds to argument and circumstant to adjunct.

Actants can be syntactic but not semantic, in case they are nonreferential and saturate only a syntactic valency of a predicate. For example, in (1):

(1) *il pluit*
    it rains
    "It is raining." (French, Romance, Indo-European)

the dummy subject *il* is nonreferential; it is a syntactic actant, but not a semantic one. In (2):

(2) *il est tombé sur le trottoire*
    he is fallen on the pavement
    "He fell on the pavement." (French, Romance, Indo-European)

the subject *il* is a referential expression, and it is both a syntactic and a semantic actant.

See also *Adjunct*, *Argument*, and *Valency*.

Active see *Voice*.
Active language see *Alignment*.
Actor see *Semantic macro-role* and *Semantic role*.
Actualization see *Extension*.

Adjunct

An adverbial constituent, not required by the verbal valency, such as *at nine o'clock* in (1):

(1) *the children had breakfast **at nine o'clock***

Adjuncts of this type provide information regarding the setting of an event, or its circumstances; for this reason, they are also sometimes called circumstantials. In the layered structure of the sentence according to functional approaches, adjuncts are peripheral constituents.

While 'adjunct' may be used as a cover term for nonarguments, adjuncts are sometimes divided into adjuncts proper, as in (1), disjuncts and conjuncts.

Disjuncts are adverbials and adverbs that modify a whole sentence, as in (2):

(2) ***according to my mother**, all my boyfriends were silly*

Conjuncts convey information which is not relevant for the propositional content of a sentence, but they help us to understand its relation with the rest of the discourse:

(3) *I started cooking late.* **In addition**, *I wasted a lot of time looking for a pan.*

In Systemic Functional Grammar, the above three types of adjuncts are called 'experiential adjuncts' (adjuncts 'proper'), 'interpersonal adjuncts' (disjuncts), and 'textual adjuncts' (conjuncts).

See also *Adverbial, Argument, Circumstantial*, and *Valency*.

Adposition see *Part of speech*.
Adverb see *Part of speech*.

Adverbial

(a) Any constituent that is not an argument. Because they do not belong to the core or nucleus of the predication, adverbials are said to stand in its periphery. In S. C. Dik's Functional Grammar adverbials are called **satellites**.

(b) A constituent which has the same distribution as an adverb. According to this definition, some prepositional phrases that function syntactically as arguments are called adverbials, such as in *on the table* in example (1):

(1) *I put the book* **on the table** */ I put the book* **there**

(c) An adverbial subordinate clause.

See also *Adverbial clause, Adjunct, Argument,* and *Valency*.

Adverbial clause

An adverbial clause is a subordinate clause that does not function as an argument and is not a modifier of a head noun, but adds information regarding the circumstances of the predication in the main clause. For this reason, adverbial clauses are also called circumstantial clauses. In (1), the clause *when his dad left* is an adverbial clause:

(1) *the child cried* **when his dad left**

The adverbial clause in (1) indicates a temporal circumstance and is called a temporal clause. Other types of adverbial clauses are given below:

(2) *the child cried **because his dad left*** (causal)
(3) ***if it rains**, I'll go to the movies* (conditional)
(4) *Mary went to the store **to buy milk*** (final, or purpose clause)
(5) *the children had so much ice cream **that they couldn't finish their meal*** (consecutive)

In English, subordinate clauses can be finite, if they contain a finite verb form, as (1), (2), (3), and (5), or nonfinite, if they contain a nonfinite verb form, as (4) and (6):

(6) ***going home,** I met your cousin*

See also *Clause, Converb, Sentence,* and *Subordination.*

Afterthought

An afterthought constituent is a right dislocated constituent, placed outside the sentence boundary, which adds some piece of additional information to an otherwise syntactically complete sentence, as the NP *your little brother* in (1):

(1) *I haven't met him yet, **your little brother***

Afterthought constituents are especially relevant in OV languages, where the external character of their position is shown by the fact that they occur after the finite verb.

Afterthought constituents are sometimes called **tails**, as for example in S. C. Dik's Functional Grammar.

See also *Dislocation.*

Agreement

A phenomenon by which a controller triggers the expression of certain features on a target:

(1) **Paul is** reading **his** book

(2) *w-attomer*   *ha-'išša*
and-say:IMPF.3SG.F the-woman
"the woman said" (Biblical Hebrew, Semitic, Afro-Asiatic)

In (1) *his* is masculine and singular, because its controller, the NP *Paul*, is masculine and singular; in addition, the verb form *is* is third person singular because the subject, again *Paul*, requires a third person singular. In (2) the finite verb *tomer* agrees not only in person and number (third person singular) but also in gender with the subject, which is feminine (the third person masculine would be *yomer*).

As shown by the examples, agreement can be quite pervasive; its degree of obligatoriness may vary even within the same language. **Gender agreement** is stronger inside the noun phrase:

(3) *ein schönes Mädchen*
a:N pretty:N girl:N
"a pretty girl" (German, Germanic, Indo-European)

(4) *ich habe ein Mädchen gesehen, das/die*   *sehr schön aussieht*
I have a:N girl:N seen who:N/who:F very pretty looks
"I saw a girl who looks very pretty." (German, Germanic,
Indo-European)

In (3) the adjective *schönes* 'pretty' agrees with the head noun *Mädchen* 'girl' (both are neuter); in (4) the relative pronoun can either be *das* (neuter), which agrees with its controller, again the noun *Mädchen*, in gender (neuter) and number, or *die* (feminine), which only agrees in number but displays a different gender. The reason for this lack of grammatical agreement lies in the conflict between the grammatical gender of *Mädchen* and its referential properties: the grammatical gender of the word *Mädchen* is neuter, but its possible referents are females, and the feminine gender is usually associated with female human beings in German. The phenomenon by which a noun such as *Mädchen* can trigger feminine agreement in certain targets is known as **semantic agreement**. Semantic agreement is not limited to gender. It can appear with number, as in:

(5) *vi*   *gente*   *que comía/comían*   *peras*
see:PRET.1SG people:SG that eat:IMPF.3SG/3PL pear:PL
"I saw people eating pears." (Spanish, Romance, Indo-European)

In (5) the NP *gente* 'people' is singular, but, being a collective noun, it refers to a plurality of entities. For this reason, it can occur with a verb in the singular (grammatical agreement) or in the plural (semantic agreement).

A peculiar type of agreement is double case, also known as **suffix copying**, as for example in (6):

(6) *wagal-* **ni- ngu** *gudaga-***ngu** *mujam*   *bajal*
    wife-GEN-ERG   dog-ERG   mother:ABS bites
    "(My) wife's dog is biting (my) mother." (from Dixon 1980: 300)
    (Yidin, Pama-Nyungan, Australian)

In (6) the case suffix *-ngu* of the ergative indicates the function of the head noun *gudaga* 'dog', but it also appears on the modifier *wagal* 'wife', which is marked as modifier by the genitive suffix *-ni*. Double case is known from several languages of Australia, Old Georgian, and some ancient languages of the Caucasus.

The function of agreement is to indicate that certain items belong together: for example, agreement inside the NP indicates what items belong to it. Typical targets of agreement are attributive adjectives, articles, relative and anaphoric pronouns. Subject verb agreement is common in the Indo-European languages, but the subject is by no means the only item that can trigger agreement on the verb. In Italian, compound verb forms of transitive verbs also agree with the direct object when this is a clitic pronoun:

(7) *io   non **le**   ho   ancora **viste***
    1SG NEG 3PL.F have:1SG yet   seen:PL.F
    "I haven't seen them yet." (Italian, Romance, Indo-European)

In (7) the verb form *ho viste*, which contains an auxiliary and a past participle, agrees with the clitic direct object *le* in gender (feminine) and number (plural). When the object is not a clitic, but an accented constituent, the verb form is always inflected in the masculine singular, independent of gender and number of the direct object (*ho visto*).

In many non-Indo-European languages, agreement of the verb with arguments other than the subject is more widespread as shown in example (8):

(8) *guk   zu   liburu   hau eman d-i-zu-gu*
    we:ERG you:DAT book:ABS this give   3SG-have-2SG-1PL
    "We have given you this book." (Basque, isolate)

In (8), the verb form *dizugu* bears agreement markers with the subject, the direct object, and the indirect object: it contains a third person singular absolutive, *d-*, the root of the verb, *i*, a polite second person dative, *-zu,* and a first person plural ergative, *-gu.*

See also *Subject.*

Alignment

The term 'alignment' refers to the way in which the "syntactic-semantic prim-itives" intransitive subject, transitive subject, and transitive object are marked (Dixon 1994: 6). Types of alignment are **nominative-accusative** (also called accusative), **ergative**, and **active** or active-stative. In nominative-accusative languages, such as English, the subject of transitive verbs and the subject of intransitive verbs are encoded through the same case (called nominative), and contrast with the direct object of transitive verbs, which is encoded through a different case (called accusative):

(1) *he went home*
(2) *he saw her*

In ergative languages, instead, the subject of intransitive verbs is encoded in the same way as the patient of transitive verbs (through the absolutive case), while the agent of transitive verbs is encoded through a special case (called ergative). This is illustrated by Basque in (3) and (4):

(3) *umea   kalean   erori da*
    child.the:ABS street.in fall   3SG:be
    "The child fell in the street." (Basque, isolate)
(4) *emakumeak   gizona   ikusi   du*
    woman.the:ERG man.the:ABS 3SG:see 3SG:have
    "The woman saw the man." (Basque, isolate)

In (3) the subject of an intransitive verb is *umea* 'child', in the absolutive case; in (4) the subject of a transitive verb is *emakumeak* 'women' in the erga-tive, while the direct object is *gizona* 'man', in the absolutive.

Many languages exhibit what is called **split-ergativity**, that is, they pres-ent ergative alignment limited to a given verbal tense or aspect, as in Georgian and Hindi-Urdu, or to nouns that rank low on the animacy scale.

A third type of alignment is active, or active-stative alignment. Active languages are languages in which the subject of some intransitive verbs is coded as the agent of transitive verbs, while the subject of some others is coded as the patient of transitive verbs, depending on the degree of volitionality and/or control. The phenomenon underlying active alignment has been referred to as **split-intransitivity** (Van Valin 1990) or **split-S** (Dixon 1994). Thus, "in Waurá, an Arwak language spoken . . . in Brazil . . . a transitive clause shows basic constituent order A[ctive subject] VO; the verb has a pronominal prefix cross-referencing the A[ctive subject] NP" (Dixon 1994: 77), as in (5):

(5) *yanumaka ɨnuka   p-itsupalu*
    jaguar   3SG:kill   2SG.POSS-daughter
    "The jaguar killed your daughter." (Waurá, Arwakan,
    Equatorial-Tucanoan)

Waurá has two classes of intransitive verbs. In one, the subject behaves as an active subject, that is, it precedes the verb and the verb bears a pronominal suffix that refers to the subject, as shown in (6):

(6) *wekɨhɨ katumala -pai*
    owner 3SG:work -ST
    "The owner worked." (Waurá, Arwakan, Equatorial-Tucanoan)

In the other class of intransitive verbs, the subject follows the verb and there is no prefix cross-referencing it on the verb (it behaves as the object of transitive verbs). An example is given in (7):

(7) *usitya   ikísii*
    catch.fire thatch
    "The thatch caught fire." (Waurá, Arwakan, Equatorial-Tucanoan)

See also *Animacy, Control, Transitivity,* and *Voice.*

Anaphora

A construction in which an item called **anaphor**, often a pronoun, refers back to some entity already introduced in discourse, which may or may not be present in the sentence:

(1) *I have met **your brother**_i before, but I wouldn't be able to recognize **him**_i*

In (1), *him* is an anaphoric pronoun: it refers back to *your brother*, which is called its antecedent (or controller), and triggers certain features on the pronoun (in the case of English third person pronouns relevant features are number and gender). It is the antecedent that helps interpret the reference of the anaphoric element.

Depending on the context, Ø can function as an anaphor, for example in coordinated clauses:

(2) *Mary said goodbye and Ø left*

or in control constructions:

(3) *Paul wants Ø to go home*

In (2) and (3) Ø refers to *Mary* and *Paul* respectively.

In the Government and Binding framework of Transformational Generative Grammar, an anaphor must be bound by an antecedent within its binding domain, usually the sentence. For example, in sentence (4) *herself* is bound by *Mary*, its antecedent:

(4) *Mary loves herself*

Traces of NP movement are anaphors within this framework.

Anaphoric pronouns can be used cataphorically, that is, referring to some entity which is introduced later in discourse. The term 'anaphora' is sometimes used to encompass both processes.

Anaphora comes from Greek *anaphorá*, 'carrying back', and means 'repetition'. In some approaches, the word 'anaphora' is used as a quasi-synonym of 'pronoun'.

See also *Cataphora or big PRO*.

Anaphor

An item with anaphoric function.
See *Anaphora* and *Logophor*.

Animacy

A semantic feature of nouns that often has morphosytactic reflexes.

Animate nouns are not simply nouns that have animate referents: from the point of view of morphosyntax, nouns that refer to animals behave more frequently as inanimate nouns, rather than as animate ones. Animacy is connected with volitionality, rationality, and individuation: the more individuated an entity and the more capable of acting rationally on its own accord, the higher it will rank on the animacy scale. Thus a collective noun such as *crowd*, which has a low degree of individuation, ranks lower than a plural count noun such as *persons* or *men*. According to Corbett (2000: 55), the animacy scale is as follows:

(1) speaker > addressee > 3rd person > kin > human> animate > inanimate
      (1st person (2nd person
      pronouns)   pronouns)

In many languages there are further distinctions: we have already mentioned collective nouns which rank low on the scale in spite of having animate (or even human) referents; among inanimate nouns, those that refer to natural forces (i.e. dynamic entities), such as *earthquake, wind, storm,* often rank higher than other inanimates.

See also *Part of speech* and *Semantic role*.

Antecedent

A constituent that precedes another constituent, typically a pronoun, triggers some of its morphosyntactic features and/or determines its reference. An antecedent is a type of controller in certain theories, and the word that is controlled is called a target.

The antecedent of the relative pronoun in (1) is *man*:

(1) **the man whose** *son I met yesterday is my teacher*

In (2) the antecedent *einen Sohn* triggers gender and number agreement on the relative pronoun:

(2) *Klaus hat einen   Sohn, den   ich   noch nicht kennegelernt habe*
Klaus has a:ACC.M son REL.ACC.M I   yet   not   met   have
"Klaus has a son that I haven't met yet." (German, Germanic,
Indo-European)

The word antecedent literally means 'that comes before', but antecedents
do not necessarily precede controlled elements in all languages.
See also *Anaphora* and *Controller*.

Antipassive see *Voice*.

Applicative

Applicative is a **valency-changing** operation similar to **causative**, by which
an adverbial constituent comes to be included into the verbal valency, thus
being treated as an argument. Examples of applicatives are the following:

(1) a. *m-geni **igula** u-gimbi*
     CL-guest buys CL-beer
     "The guest is buying beer."
   b. *m-geni **igulila** va-ndu   u-gimbi*
     CL-guest buys:APPL CL-person CL-beer
     "The guest is buying beer for people." (from Ngonyani and
     Githinji 2006: 4) (Ngoni, Bantu, Niger-Congo)
(2) a. *Ted   **schmierte** Butter auf   die Tischdecke*
     "Ted smeared   butter onto the tablecloth."
   b. *Ted   **beschmierte** die Tischdecke mit Butter*
     "Ted smeared   the tablecloth with butter." (German,
     Germanic, Indo-European)

Ngoni, as well as other Bantu languages, has an applicative suffix -*il*-:
in (1b) the beneficiary *vandu* 'people' is included in the verbal valency. In
German, the prefix *be*- functions as an applicative, as shown in (2b), where
the locative expression *auf die Tischdecke* 'on the tablecloth' of (2a) becomes
an argument of the prefixed verb.

Applicative is similar to causative, another valency increasing operation, and to
voice, except for the fact that it is generally derivational, while voice is inflectional.
See also *Causative, Valency*, and *Voice*.

Apposition

A construction in which two constituents are juxtapposed, without being in a syntactically hierarchical relation with each other, and in which one of the two constituents specifies the other:

(1) *my friend Paul*

In (1) *Paul* is said to be in apposition to *my friend*. The NP in (1) is an example of **restrictive** apposition, because *Paul* narrows down the scope of *my friend* and conveys information that is essential to identify the referent. On the other hand, in (2):

(2) *Paul, a friend of mine*

the apposition is **nonrestrictive**, because it does not restrict the scope of *Paul*, but simply adds some nonessential piece of information.

See also *Relative clause*.

Argument

Arguments are items that saturate the valency of a predicate. Every predicate is specified by the number of arguments it requires. Verbs, nouns, adjectives, and prepositions have an **argument structure** or **predicate frame** which is lexically coded.

Verbs. The argument structure of a verb, also called its valency, determines the elements of the sentence that are obligatory. For example, in sentence (1) there are two arguments, *John* and *Mary*:

(1) *John saw Mary*

Both constituents are obligatory.

The lexical representation of verbs can be improved by specifying the number of arguments they have. Both in Dependency Grammar and in Transformational Generative Grammar, this notation eliminates the terminology transitive, intransitive, ditransitive. Dependency Grammar introduces the terms monovalent, bivalent, and trivalent. In Transformational Generative Grammar, subcategorization frames are often substituted by lexical representations of verbs. This is shown in (2):

(2) see,   verb,   1   [DP/NP], 2 [DP/NP]
    smile,   verb,   1   [DP/NP]
    dance,   verb,   1   [DP/PN]
    give,   verb,   1   [DP/NP], 2 [DP/NP], 3 [PP]

In some cases, one argument can be omitted, changing the meaning of the sentence, as in (3a) and (3b):

(3) a. *John bought Mary a book*
    b. *John bought a book*

In (3b) it is understood that John bought a book for himself, but *himself* may not be expressed. In this case, it is considered optional. Optional elements are placed in parenthesies, as shown in (4):

(4) buy, verb, 1 [DP/NP], (2 [DP/NP]), 3[DP/NP]

Nouns. Nouns that derive from verbs, or are related to verbs, may have the same argument structure. However, the presence of the arguments is usually optional (the relationship between a noun and its dependents is a **modification relation**, i.e. it is not obligatory). In other words, the semantic valency of derived nouns may correspond to the valency of the verb which serves as the base of derivation, but not the syntactic valency. Examples are *destruction* and *destroy* in number (5):

(5) a. *John destroyed the car*
    b. *The destruction of the car by John was impressive*
    c. *John's destruction of the car was impressive*
    d. *The destruction of the car was impressive*
    e. *The destruction was impressive*
    f. **John destroyed*

In this case, the notation of the noun *destruction* is as shown in (6):

(6) destruction, noun, 1 ([PP/DP/NP]), (2 [PP])

Adjectives. The arguments of adjectives are often optional, as in (7a):

(7) a. *John is envious*
    b. *John is envious of his sister*

In this case, too, the PP is not obligatory, as compared to the obligatory complement of the verb *envy*:

(8) a. *John envies his sister*
    b. **John envies*

Then, the notation of the argument structure of the adjective *envious* is as in (9):

(9) envious, adjective, 1 [DP/NP], (2 [PP])

Prepositions. Prepositions have an argument structure as well. In (10) *between* has three obligatory arguments: *the house, First Avenue,* and *Madison*:

(10) *the house between First Avenue and Madison*

See also *Predicate* and *Valency*.

Argument structure see *Valency.*

Articulatory and Perceptual properties (A–P system)

Within the Minimalist Program, the Articulatory and Perceptual (or A–P) properties compose a formal system of language that interfaces with the PF (Phonetic Form) level of representation. The A–P properties of language are independent of the modality of the output system, since they capture both spoken and sign languages. However, most of the time this level is phonetic. Within the Minimalist Program framework, all levels of representation in former Transformational Generative Grammar, other than PF and LF (Logical Form), are dispensed with.

See also *Conceptual and Intentional properties.*

Attribute see *Modifier.*

Attributive clause

A clause that functions as a modifier (attribute) for a nominal head. Relative clauses are attributive clauses; other types of attributive clauses involve the occurrence of nonfinite verb forms as in (1) and (2):

(1) *I saw an old man **walking towards me***

(2) *okul- da bulun-an kisi-ler arkadaš-lar-ım degil-dir*
    school-LOC be-PART person-PL friend-PL -POSS1SG not be
    "The people who are in the school are not my friends." (Turkish, Turkic, Altaic)

In (1) the verb of the attributive clause is *walking*. In English, one could also have a relative clause with a pronoun and a finite verb form:

(3) *I saw an old man **who was walking towards me***

In Turkish, attributive clauses can only be made with nonfinite verb forms, as the participle *bulunan* in (2).

See also *Relative clause* and *Subordination*.

Auxiliary

An item, typically a verb, that carries grammatical information and forms part of a compound verb form with another verb, called the main verb, which carries lexical information. English is very rich in auxiliaries: ***have** gone*, ***would** buy*, ***will** see*, ***does** not know*, ***am** eating* are all compound verb forms in which a finite auxiliary that carries inflectional markers cooccurs with a nonfinite main verb. Note that the main verb is such only from the point of view of lexical information; from the structural point of view, it is the auxiliary that has the main function in the phrase, being the head of the compound verb form.

Many auxiliaries, when occurring alone, have a specific lexical meaning and function as lexical verbs. Indeed auxiliaries are the product of grammaticalization and have developed their grammatical function from lexical verbs in the course of history, even if their original meaning can no longer be detected. Compare:

(1) *I **have** a book*

(2) *I **have** been to Rome many times*

In (1) *have* is a verb with its lexical meaning ('possess'); in (2) the same form is an auxiliary that indicates that the event referred to by the main verb has taken place at some unspecified time in the past.

Different verbs can develop into auxiliaries, as shown by numerous unrelated languages. However, from the point of view of their meaning, potential auxiliaries constitute a relatively small set. In general, one would not expect a verb like *sleep* or *drink* to develop into an auxiliary; on the other hand, such a development is much more predictable with verbs such as *have, be, do, stand, become,* modal verbs and motion verbs. These are verbs with a generic enough meaning (they refer to 'basic events' in the terms of Heine 1993: 27–45) that tend to be associated with other verbs in phrasal constructions, out of which they can develop into auxiliaries by a process of semantic bleaching.

Typically, auxiliaries constitute a closed subclass of verbs in a given language, characterized by special syntactic constraints (e.g. they occur in fixed positions), and build a complex verb form with a nominal form of another verb, as in the English examples above. Functionally similar to auxiliaries may be serial verbs, which, in contrast, present quite different morphosyntactic features.

See also *Grammaticalization, Reanalysis,* and *Serial verb.*

Behagel's Law See *Word order*.

Binding

Syntactic relation by which one constituent binds another sentential constituent if certain conditions such as c-command and coindexation are met. More formally binding can be defined as in (1):

(1) α (alfa) binds β (beta) iff α c-commands and is coindexed with β

Consider the example in (2):

(2) *John$_i$ loves himself$_i$*

In sentence (2) *John$_i$* binds *himself$_i$* because *John$_i$* c-commands and is coindexed (i.e. it is coreferential) with *himself$_i$*.

There are two types of binding: A-binding and A-bar binding. A-binding is a relation in which the antecedent is in an A-position (Argument position), as in (1). A-bar binding is a relation in which the antecedent is in an A-bar position (non-Argument position). Non-Argument position is the position occupied by operators such as *what* or *who* in wh-questions, such as *who* in (3):

(3) **who** *does John love t?*

In (3) **who** binds the trace *t* which represents a variable in the position that occupied **who** before the question was formed: John loves **who**.

See also *C-command, A-position*, and *A-bar position*.

Binding Theory

Within the Government and Binding framework, binding theory is the module of grammar that regulates the interpretation of DP/NPs. From this point of view, DP/NPs can be reflexives (*himself/herself*), pronouns (*him/her*), and referential expressions (*John, the boy*). The reference qualities of each one of these categories can be defined by using the features [+/– *pronominal*] and [+/– *anaphor*]. Thus, DP/NPs can be defined as in (1):

(1) a. *Reflexives* (and *reciprocals*)
        [+anaphor –pronominal]
    b. *Pronouns*
        [–anaphor +pronominal]
    c. *R-expressions*
        [–anaphor –pronominal]

In addition, in this framework, the interpretation of these categories is measured in terms of locality, considering the position of the antecedent. Anaphors need a local antecedent; pronouns may have an antecedent, but this antecedent must be outside a certain local domain. Referential expressions must not have an antecedent; they must be free. These referential properties are encapsulated in three principles: principle A, principle B, and principle C as shown in (2), (4), and (6):

(2) *Principle A*: An anaphor (reflexive or reciprocal) must be bound in its governing domain, as shown in (3a) and (3b):
(3) a. *Ann$_i$ loves herself$_i$*
    b. **Ann$_i$ thinks John loves herself$_i$*

In (3a) the sentence is grammatical because the anaphor *herself* is bound in its governing domain. In (3b), the sentence in ungrammatical because the anaphor *herself* is not bound in its governing domain, but outside it. It violates principle A.

(4) *Principle B*: A pronoun must be free (not bound) in its governing domain, as shown in (5a) and (5b):
(5) a. *Ann$_i$ thinks John loves her$_j$*
    b. **Ann$_i$ loves her$_i$*

In (5a) the sentence is grammatical because the pronoun *her* is not bound inside its governing domain; it refers to an antecedent outside (*Ann*) its governing domain. In (5b), the sentence is ungrammatical because the pronoun *her* is bound in its governing domain, violating principle B.

(6) *Principle C:* A referential expression (R-expression) must be free everywhere, as shown in (7a) and (7b):

(7) a. **she$_i$ thinks John loves Ann$_i$*

    b. ***she$_i$** *thinks that Peter said that Mary claimed that John loves Ann$_i$*

In (7a) the sentence is ungrammatical because the R-expression *Ann* corefers with the pronoun *she*. In this case the sentence is ungrammatical, even if binding takes place outside the governing domain of the R-expression. In (7b), the sentence is ungrammatical even if three clause boundaries intervene between the pronoun and the R-expression *Ann*. The R-expression is distantly bound. Thus it violates principle C.

Within the Minimalist Program, with the elimination of DS (D-Structure) and SS (S-Structure) Binding Theory can only apply at LF (Logical Form). This eliminates problems of overgeneration of structures created by theories that allowed DS and SS. The problem of overgeneration is shown in examples such as (8):

(8) *Ann$_i$ wondered which portrait of herself$_{ij}$ Mary$_j$ liked*

Example (8) is ambiguous because *herself* can have *Mary* or *Ann* as antecedent. The ambiguity could be solved by checking the coreference *Ann-herself* at S-Structure or at LF, and the second ambiguity *Mary-herself* can be checked either at DS or in the course of the derivation. However, this is not an economical or a restrictive way to solve the ambiguity. In Minimalist grounds the meanings of this sentence must be interpreted at LF only. Thus, the other two levels of representation were eradicated.

See also *Binding* and *Governing domain*.

Branching

The concept of branching refers to the phenomenon by which complex constituents are built. Branching may operate rightward, if constituents are mostly expanded by adding dependents on their right side, or leftward, if constituents are expanded by adding dependents on their left side. SOV languages are mostly left branching, while VSO and SVO languages are usually right branching. English is right branching in some respects: for example, the verb, which is the head of the VP, precedes its complements, while in others it is left branching (the attributive adjective precedes the head noun). Syntactic structures with phrases that contain more than two immediate constituents are ruled out.

After Kayne (1994) only left branching is allowed in Transformational Generative Grammar; different word orders are obtained through recursive movement.

See also *Word order* and *X-bar theory*.

Case

An inflectional category of nouns that helps identify a NP's grammatical relation and/or semantic role; often also called 'morphological case' to distinguish it from abstract Case, a concept used in some formal approaches (see below), and from deep cases, assumed in Fillmore's Case Grammar, which correspond to semantic roles.

The process by which nouns and related lexical categories take case is called **case marking**. In languages with case marking, case usually manifests itself on nouns, adjectives, and pronouns, but it can be more limited. In English, for example, case marking is limited to certain pronouns that distinguish between nominative (*he, who*), oblique (*him, whom*), and genitive (*his, whose*). Many Indo-European and non-Indo-European languages have case marking, as for example Russian:

nominative	*kniga* 'book'
accusative	*knigu*
genitive	*knigy*
dative	*knige*
instrumental	*knigoj*
prepositional	*knige*
(Russian, Slavic, Indo-European)	

In languages such as Russian, core grammatical relations are distinguished by case marking: the **nominative** is the subject case, the **accusative** the case of the direct object, and the **dative** the case of the indirect object. The **genitive** case most often indicates nominal dependency, that is, it marks a noun as a modifier of another noun, as in:

(1) *timor   hostium*
     fear:NOM enemy:GEN.PL
     "fear of the enemy" (Latin, Italic, Indo-European).

Other cases may have more of a semantic function and often indicate semantic roles, such as the **instrumental**, that usually indicates instrument and agent of passive verbs.

The Russian case called **prepositional** can only occur within prepositional phrases; it corresponds to the **locative** case of some other Slavic languages that indicates location. The locative is called a **local or spatial case**; other frequently found local cases are the **ablative**, which indicates source or origin, the **allative**, which indicates direction, and the **perlative**, which indicates path through which. Some non-Indo-European languages have very complex systems of local cases, such as for example Hungarian:

inessive	a *ház-ban*	"in the house"
superessive	a *ház-on*	"on the house"
adessive	a *ház- nál*	"near the house"
elative	a *ház-ból*	"from inside the house"
delative	a *ház-ról*	"from the top of the house"
ablative	a *ház- tól*	"from near the house"
illative	a *ház-ba*	"into the house"
sublative	a *ház-ra*	"to the top of the house"
allative	a *ház-hoz*	"to the house"

(Hungarian, Finno-Ugric, Uralic)

Ergative languages have two special cases: the **ergative** which indicates the agent of transitive verbs, and the **absolutive** which indicates the subject of intransitive verbs and the patient of transitive verbs. Typically the absolutive case has no marker. (Note that the absolutive is often called nominative in grammatical descriptions of specific ergative languages.)

Many languages have a special form of nouns, mostly personal names, used to address someone and called the **vocative**, cf. Latin *Paulus* 'Paul' (nom.)/*Paule* (voc.), *filius* 'son' (nom.)/*fili* (voc.). Some languages have a special case for the predicate nominal of predicative verbs indicating temporary states, such as the **essive** case in Finnish: *lapsi* "child"/*lapsena* "as a child," "when one was a child." In the Finno-Ugric languages, a **comitative** case occurs, which indicates accompaniment, and many Australian languages have an **aversive** case, which is used for the complement of verbs of fearing.

It is questionable whether the **partitive**, found in some Finno-Ugric languages and in Basque, is a real case. It is used when the referent of a NP is only partially involved in an event, but it does not indicate a specific semantic role, and it is not connected with a specific grammatical relation. For example, in Finnish one may find partitive objects and/or partitive subjects as in example (1):

(1) **sotilait-a**   tuli   illa-lla

soldier-PRT.PL come:IMPF.3SG evening-ADESS

"Some soldiers came in the evening." (Finnish, Finno-Ugric, Uralic)
(from Sulkala and Karjalainen 1992: 211).

Grammatical and semantic cases. A distinction is sometimes made between grammatical and semantic or concrete cases, that is, cases that mostly or exclusively mark core arguments and express grammatical relations, and cases that mostly or exclusively mark peripheral constituents (adverbials) and express semantic roles. In other words, grammatical cases are those that are taken by governed constituents, and are determined by the verb, while concrete cases are independent of the verb, and express a meaning by themselves or, more frequently, in association with the lexical features of the NP they mark. This distinction is also captured by saying that **case assignment** is **contextual** with grammatical cases and **inherent** with concrete ones. Other pairs of names found in the literature for grammatical and semantic cases are **relational** and **adverbial**, **core** and **peripheral**, **abstract** and **concrete**. Note that this distinction, which was first introduced in Kuryłowicz (1949), has never worked out well, because of the tendency for most cases to have both grammatical and semantic functions, albeit to a different extent.

A further distinction, partly similar to the one described above, is made between **direct** and **oblique cases**: direct cases are the nominative and the accusative, oblique cases are all the others. In languages that only have a distinction between a subject case and a nonsubject case, the term oblique may be used as synonym of nonsubject.

Abstract Case. In Transformational Generative Grammar, abstract Case is part of Universal Grammar. All languages, including those that do not have morphological case marking, such as English or Irish, are held to have abstract Case. There are two types of abstract Case: Structural Case (Nominative and Accusative) and inherent Case (e.g. English or Spanish Genitive, *house of John, casa de Juan*).

1. *Structural Case.* Nominative Case is assigned to a DP/NP subject by I in IP (inflectional phrase), Accusative Case is assigned to an object DP/NP by V in VP (verb phrase) or by P in PP (prepositional phrase). The Case assigner must govern the Case assignee. Structural Case is blind to thematic relations.

2. *Inherent Case.* Inherent Case can only be assigned to a given DP/NP by a category that governs and also assigns a theta-role to that DP. For example,

nouns and adjectives assign inherent genitive Case to a DP/NP. In English *of* is a morphosyntactic marker of this Case.

Abstract Case is part of Case Theory in the framework of Government and Binding Theory.

See also *Case Filter, Case Theory*, and *Semantic role*.

Case Filter

Within the Government and Binding framework of Transformational Generative Grammar, *Case Filter* requires that every overt DP/NP be assigned abstract Case. This requirement acts as a filter because it excludes any nominal construction which is not assigned abstract Case. Since the Case Filter does not explain why Case is obligatory, it has been linked to other properties of grammar such as the Visibility Condition.

See also *Case, Case Theory*, and *Visibility Condition*.

Case Theory

Within the Government and Binding framework, Case Theory is a module of grammar that accounts for some of the properties of overt DP/NPs and integrates the notion of Case into Transformational Generative Grammar. It includes, among other things, the key concepts of a abstract Case (Structural and Inherent), the Case Filter, and the Visibility Condition.

See also *Case, Case Filter*, and *Visibility Condition*.

Cataphora

A pronoun that refers forward to a constituent introduced later on in discourse, as in:

(1) *What determined the speech that startled **him** in the course of **their** encounter scarcely matters, being probably but some words spoken by **himself** quite without intention—spoken as **they** lingered and slowly moved together after **their** renewal of acquaintance. **He** had been conveyed by friends an hour or two before to the house at which **she** was staying; the party of visitors at the other house, of whom **he** was*

*one, and thanks to whom it was **his** theory, as always, that **he** was lost in the crowd, had been invited over to luncheon.* (Henry James, *The Beast in the Jungle*)

The above example contains the first few sentences of a short story. Various forms of third person pronouns, masculine and feminine singular and plural, introduce the two characters of the story, whose names will appear only later. They are used cataphorically, to refer to participants that are yet unknown to the reader, and are overtly introduced later on in the course of the text.

Cataphora comes from Greek *kataphorá*, which means 'carrying forward'. In principle, it is the mirror image of anaphora, albeit much less frequent; in some descriptions the term 'anaphora' is used to cover both.

See also *Anaphora*.

Causative

A **causative construction** is one in which a participant causes another participant to do something. In (1):

(1) *Mary made John leave*

there are two participants, Mary and John, and it is said that Mary causes John to perform the action of leaving. The semantic role of the NP *John* is called **causee**, or secondary agent.

Several languages have morphological causatives, or **causative verbs**. In example (2), the verb form *sallanun* 'I promoted' is a causative of *sallai-* 'to grow (intransitive)', formed with adjunction of the causative suffix *-nu-*:

(2) **sallanun**=   *war=an   kuit   ammuk*
    promote:1SG.PRET PTC   3SG.ACC because   1SG.NOM
    "because I promoted him" (from Otten 1981 iv 11–15) (Hittite, Anatolian, Indo-European)

Causativization is a **valency changing** operation, which increases the valency of a verb: causatives of intransitive verbs are transitive, as in the case of (2) *sallai-* 'grow (intransitive)'/*sallanu-* 'make greater, promote (transitive)', while causatives of transitive verbs are often **ditransitive** (they take a double object) or **trivalent** (they take a direct object and an indirect object).

Some languages, such as English, do not have morphological causatives; they rather have analytic causatives. In English, a sentence like the one in (1) is analyzed as containing two clauses, *Mary made*, which is the main clause, and *John leave*, the complement clause. In some other languages, such as Italian and French, analytic causatives can be analyzed as constituting a single verb complex, with an auxiliary and a main verb. Compare:

(3) a. *gli ospiti* **sono entrati**
      the guests are come.in
      "The guests   came in."

   b. *Paolo* **ha fatto entrare** *gli ospiti/Paolo* **li**   *ha   fatti   entrare*
      Paul   has made come.in the guests/Paul **them** has made come.in
      "Paul let the guests come in./Paul let them come in."

(4) a. *il   direttore* **ha scritto** *la   lettera*
      the chairman has written the letter
      "The chairman wrote the letter."

   b. **ho fatto scrivere**   *la lettera al direttore*
      I   have write   the letter to the chairman
      "I had the chairman write the letter." (Italian, Romance,
      Indo-European)

In Italian, the verb *fare* 'make' which is used in causative constructions, cannot be separated from the second verb. It has the syntactic behavior of other auxiliaries, and the causee, which is the subject of the noncausative sentences (3a) and (4a), can be analyzed as a direct object in the causative sentences (3b) and (4b) (although it must be said that French causatives with *faire* 'make' display some features of two-clause constructions; see Comrie 1976: 296–303). In (3b) the causative construction is transitive: the causee is marked as a direct object. In (4b) the causee is marked as an indirect object with the preposition *a* 'to'. The causative construction is trivalent.

Being a valency changing operation, causative is similar to voice; the reason why it is usually not viewed as a voice is that, even in languages with morphological causatives, it is usually derivational, while voice is usually inflectional.

See also *Applicative, Valency,* and *Voice.*

Chain

In the Government and Binding framework, chains are created as a result of movement. The moved element is the **head** of the chain and each trace is a **link** of the chain. The last link is the **tail** or **foot** of the chain. When the head of a chain is in an A-position, it is an A-chain. When the head of a chain is in an A-bar position, it is an A-bar chain. Chains have a theta-role and Case, and must comply with the Chain Condition.

See also *Chain Condition*.

Chain Condition

The Chain Condition states that a well-formed chain must contain a theta-marked position and a Case-marked position. In A-chains the head is Case-marked and the tail is theta-marked. In A-bar chains, the tail of the chain, which is a variable, is bound by an operator (the wh-word) and it may be theta-marked or A-bound to a theta-marked element.

See also *Traces, NP-movement*, and *Wh-movement*.

Checking

In the Minimalist Program, **checking** replaces the term **assignment** of the Government and Binding Theory. For example, Case assignment is replaced by Case checking. This change allows delaying Case checking until Logical Formal (LF) with no empirical cost and with the advantage to dispense with S-Structure. Then the **Case Filter,** a former condition at S-structure, becomes a LF condition in the Minimalist Program. In this framework, the Case Filter would state that Cases must be appropriately checked at LF. In addition, feature checking in the Minimalist Program is triggered by the need to eliminate **uninterpretable features** from the computation. Once uninter-pretable features are checked, they can be deleted. The features that share two elements that enter in a relationship must be erased as well, other-wise the derivation crashes. Features are checked by matching the features of the checked elements under sisterhood or by spec-head agreement. Consider (1):

(1) *who did you talk to?*

In (1) the wh-feature is checked in the (Spec, CP) against the feature [+wh] in C. If checking does not take place, the derivation is ill formed because the [+wh] feature is not checked (i.e. eliminated), as shown in (2):

(2) *[+wh] you talked to who?

See also *Feature strength* and *Uninterpretable features*.

Chômeur

In Relational Grammar, a syntactic construction that bears no primitive grammatical relation, such as subject or direct object, as a result of demotion. For example, in (1):

(1) *this book has been read **by everyone***

the NP *by everyone* is a chômeur, because it has been demoted from its original subject relation, and it does not bear any primitive grammatical relation.

The word 'chômeur' comes from French and means 'jobless', 'unemployed'.

See also *Demotion* and *Promotion*.

Circumstantial

A peripheral constituent, not required by the verbal valency, which specifies the circumstances for a predication, such as *yesterday* in (1):

(1) ***yesterday*** *I came home late from work*

See also *Adjunct* and *Adverbial*.

Clause

A simple sentence, either independent (main clause) or dependent (subordinate clause). Subordinate clauses may function as modifiers of a constituent of the main clause (attributive clauses), as complements of the predicate of the main clause (complement clauses), or as adverbials.

In the overall organization of information in discourse, main clauses are more central: they usually encode foregrounded information, whereas subordinate clauses encode backgrounded information. Main and subordinate clauses are also distinct in illucutionary force. Main clauses can be assertions, and accordingly can be negated, as in (1) and (2):

(1) *I left*
(2) *I didn't leave*

Sentence (1) is true iff sentence (2) is false.

On the other hand, subordinate clauses are presupposed and do not have assertive force of their own. Consider:

(3) *since I left, John came in*

The parallel sentence (4) with a negation in the subordinate clause does not imply that (3) is false:

(4) *since I didn't leave, John came in*

Rather, (3) is false if one negates the predicate of the main clause, as in (5):

(5) *since I left, John didn't come in*
   (see Lambrecht 1994).

In Cognitive Grammar, a subordinate clause is a clause whose profile is overridden by the main clause: this is another way to say that subordinate clauses are not asserted, and that they convey additional information, while main clauses convey essential information.

See also *Grounding*, *Sentence*, and *Subordination*.

Cleft sentence

A sentence formed by a main clause and a relative clause, in which the main clause is a copular clause, its subject is Ø or an expletive form (*it* in English), and the predicate noun is a NP which heads the relative clause:

(1) *it is Claudia who wrote this book*

The meaning of the complex sentence in (1) is the same as the meaning of the simple sentence in (2), but its information structure is different:

(2) *Claudia wrote this book*

In (2), the NP *Claudia* can be assumed to function as topic, while in (1) it is focused. Thus, cleft sentences are a means for indicating focus. Null subject languages do not require an expletive subject in the main clause:

(3) è   *Claudia che ha*   *scritto*   *questo libro*
    be:PRS.3SG Claudia that have:PRS.3SG write:PART this   book
    "It is Claudia who wrote this book." (Italian, Romance, Indo-European)

A special type of cleft sentence is **pseudo-cleft**, in which the head of the relative clause is an interrogative pronoun, as in (4):

(4) *what Claudia wrote is this book*

In pseudo-cleft sentences, the relative clause precedes the main clause. If the order is reversed, we have an **inverted pseudo-cleft**:

(5) *this book is what Claudia wrote*

See also *Focus*.

Clitic

A lexical item that does not bear an accent, and constitutes a phonological unit with some other adjacent item, as the form of the auxiliary *'ll* in:

(1) *I'll never go there*

In general, clitics can be said to be morphological but not phonological words. Depending on theoretical assumptions, clitics may be considered **phrasal affixes**. The word to which clitics attach phonologically is called their **host**. According to their position, clitics can be classified in several ways.

In the first place, a distinction can be made between **proclitics** and **enclitics**. Proclitics precede their host, while enclitics follow it. The Italian clitic pronoun *mi* 'me' is proclitic in (2a) and enclitic in (2b):

(2) a. **mi** *stava*   *guardando*
     me stay:3SG.IMPF look:GER
     "S/he was looking at me."
   b. *guarda**mi**!*
     look:2SG.IMPT+me
     "Look at me!" (Italian, Romance, Indo-European)

The position of *mi* is determined by its phonological status; the corresponding accented form would occur in another position:

(3) *stava*   *guardando*   **me**
   stay:3SG.IMPF look:GER   me
   "S/he was looking at me." (Italian, Romance, Indo-European)

In examples (2a) and (2b), **proclisis** vs. **enclisis** is determined by the verbal mood: in the Modern Romance languages, pronominal clitics can be either proclitic or enclitic, depending on the mood of the verb to which they attach. At earlier stages in the history of the Romance languages, clitics had a higher freedom, and could be placed both before or after the same type of verb forms. In Medieval Romance, clitics could occur to the right or to the left of the verb when the verb was in sentence-internal position, but they could only follow the verb (i.e. be enclitic) when the verb was sentence initial. This constraint is known as the **Tobler-Mussafia Law** (see Wanner 1987).

Italian clitic pronouns are arguments of the verb and belong into the VP; they attach to the verb and form a constituent with it. This is not the case in all languages: in some, clitics do not necessarily attach to the constituent to which they belong syntactically, or to any specific type of constituent; rather, they always occur in a specific position in the sentence, regardless of the constituents that occur in the adjacent positions. This is the case for **P2 clitics**, also called **Wackernagel clitics** from the name of the scholar who first described them. Consider the following example from Hittite:

(4) *piran=**ma**= at=*   **mu**   mDXXX.DU-*as* DUMU ᵐ*zida maniyahhiskit*
   before CONN 3SG.N/A 1SG.OBL A:nom   child   Z. administrate:
   3SG.PRET.ITER
   "Before me Armadatta, the son of Zida, had administrated it." (from Otten 1981: i 28) (Hittite, Anatolian, Indo-European)

In example (4), the word in initial position is an adverb, *piran* 'before', here functioning as an adposition. It hosts three enclitics: the adversative conjunction =*ma* and two pronouns, =*at* 'it', the direct object of the verb in final position and a part of the VP, and =*mu* 'me', which can be considered a complement of *piran* (but it is hosted by *piran* only on account of its position).

A distinction is sometimes made between phonological and structural host (Klavans 1985). The **phonological host** of a clitic is the word or constituent that constitutes a phonological unit with it, while the **structural host** is the constituent that builds a syntactic unit with the clitic: in the case of (5), the phonological host of =*at* is *piran*, while its structural host is the verb *mani-yahhiskit*, the head of the VP. In the case of Italian clitic pronouns, the structural and the phonological host necessarily coincide; in the case of Hittite clitic pronouns they need not coincide and often do not. Note that in example (4) the connective =*ma* and the pronominal particle =*at* have the same phonological host (the adverb *piran*) but their structural host is different: while the clitic pronoun is hosted by the verb, the connective is hosted by the sentence. The sentence is not only its structural host, but it is the phonological host as well: the connective is placed at the sentence border (second position is the leftmost position accessible to an enclitic, which must be preceded by an accented word, see Luraghi 1990).

Both Italian and Hittite clitics have special placement rules, but this is not the case for all clitics. English nonemphatic pronouns are unaccented and are hosted by the verb. Consider the examples in (5):

(5) *I saw* **him**

In (5), if no special emphasis is placed on the pronoun *him*, this word does not receive an independent accent, and builds a phonological unit with the verb *saw*. In this case, *him* can also be considered a clitic; contrary to Italian and Hittite clitics, it shares the distribution of accented pronouns, and does not undergo any special placement rule.

Italian clitic pronouns, and Romance clitics in general, as well as Wackernagel clitics, do not share their distribution with the correspondent accented forms and undergo special placement rules as shown in the above examples. For this reason, such clitics are called **special clitics**, a term first introduced in Zwicky (1977).

Because clitics lack phonological independence and have fixed positions, it can sometimes be hard to distinguish them from affixes. English *'s* (genitive), for example, can be considered a clitic or a phrasal affix.

See also *P2*.

C-command

C-command stands for constituent command. c-command is a binary relationship between nodes of a tree or phrase marker that reflects structural properties of languages. Beyond dominance and precedence relations, c-command is crucial to explain relations among constituents in linguistic structures. The definition of c-command is given in (1):

(1) A node A c-commands B if and only if
   (i) A does not dominate B and B does not dominate A, and
   (ii) The first branching node dominating A also dominates B

C-command is used as a diagnostic to determine the internal workings of certain syntactic structures, such as government and reflexive binding. In reflexive binding, a reflexive must be coreferential with a c-commanding expression as in sentence (2):

(2) *he$_j$ loves himself$_j$*

In sentence (2) the reflexive *himself* is c-commanded by the coreferential subject pronoun *he* in VP as shown in (3):

(3)
$$
\begin{array}{c}
\text{VP} \quad \leftarrow \textit{first branching node}\\
\diagup \;\; \diagdown\\
\text{(A) he}_j \quad \text{V'}\\
\diagup \diagdown\\
\text{loves} \;\; \text{himself}_j \;\; \text{(B)}
\end{array}
$$

In (3) the pronoun *he* (A) does not dominate *himself* and *himself* (B) does not dominate *he*. VP, the first branching node, dominates *he* and dominates *himself*. Thus the sentence is grammatical. However, (4) is ungrammatical:

(4) **himself$_j$ loves he$_j$*

In (4), even though *he* and *himself* corefer, the ungrammaticality of the sentence is due to the fact that the reflexive *himself* is *not* c-commanded by its coreferential expression *he* because the first branching node that dominates *he* does not dominate *himself,* as shown in (5):

(5)
$$
\begin{array}{c}
\text{VP} \\
/ \ \backslash \\
\text{(B) himself}_j \quad \text{V' } \leftarrow \textit{first branching node} \\
/ \ \backslash \\
\text{loves} \quad \text{he}_j \text{ (A)}
\end{array}
$$

After the first attempts by Klima (in his 1964 paper on negation) and by Langacker (in his 1969 paper on pronominals), Reinhart (1983) defined and discussed c-command in depth. Since then it has been steadily used in Transformational Generative Grammar.

See also *Binding* and *Government*.

Comment

Comment is what is being said about a topic in an utterance. Comment, which corresponds to rheme in the Functional Sentence Perspective of the Prague School and to focus in S. C. Dik's Functional Grammar, typically conveys new information, as opposed to topic, which is old, or shared information. For example, in sentence (1):

(1) *ice cream, I like*

I like is the comment and *ice-cream* is the topic.

See also *Focus* and *Topic*.

Complement

a) Complement clause.
b) An item governed by another item (e.g. the complement of a preposition).
c) The grammatical relation borne by an argument of a predicate, other than subject, direct object, or indirect object. For example, the NP *patientia nostra* in (1) can be said to be a complement, since it is required by the verbal valency, but is not a direct object, because it is not inflected

in the accusative and cannot be passivized in the way accusative direct objects can:

(1) *quo   usque tandem Catilina   abutere   patientia   nostra?*
REL.ABL until   then   Catiline:VOC abuse:FUT.2SG patience:ABL our:ABL
"How long yet, Catiline, do you mean to abuse our patience?"
Cicero, *Against Catiline* 1.1 (Latin, Italic, Indo-European)

See also *Complement clause, Government, Grammatical relation,* and *Valency.*

Complement clause

A subordinate clause that functions as an argument of the predicate of the main clause, as in:

(1) *Mary thinks **(that) John's a fool***
(2) ***that John's a fool** is by no means certain*

The complement clause *that John's a fool* is an **object clause** in (1) and a **subject clause** in (2). Complement clauses may be marked as such by the occurrence of an overt **complementizer**, such as *that*, or by their position with respect to the main clause, as is the case in (1), where the complementizer can be left out. **Indirect questions** are another type of complement clause:

(3) *I'm wondering **whether I should go to the movies***

In this type of clause, the complementizer is typically a wh-word. Complement clauses that do not have an overt complementizer may be marked as such by the occurrence of nonfinite verb forms:

(4) *non mi   pare una buona idea **andare al   cinema questa sera***
not to.me seems a   good idea go   to.the cinema this evening
"I don't think it's a good idea for me to go to the movies tonight."

In (4) ***andare al cinema questa sera*** is a subject clause: it is the subject of the verb form *pare* 'seems'.

In English, some verbs admit **subject-to-object raising** with complement clauses:

(5) *I didn't expect* **him to be such a fool**

In (5) the third person subject of the complement clause is 'raised' to the main clause, where it takes the function of direct object of the main verb. In other analyses, *him* stays in the subordinate clause, and receives case from the main verb via the ECM mechanism. Under the latter analysis, the whole clause functions as direct object of the main verb.

See also *Argument, Clause, ECM verbs, Raising, Sentence*, and *Subordination*.

Complementizer

An item that marks a subordinate clause as a complement, such as *that* in English. In X-bar theory the complementizer is the head of the complementizer phrase or CP.

See *Complement clause, Subordination*, and *X-bar theory*.

Computational system

Within the Minimalist Program, the computational system is a mechanism that arranges lexical items in such a manner as to form a syntactic object (e.g. a sentence). These lexical items must converge or be interpreted at Phonetic Form (PF) and at Logical Form (LF). To build a syntactic structure, the computational system accesses lexical items in the **numeration**. Then, it selects one lexical item at a time (operation **select**), it reduces the index of the lexical item by one, and applies the operations **Merge** and **Move**. During the derivation (in the vP and CP phases), constituents must be checked for convergence or well-formedness. If they converge or are interpretable, the derivation continues to be built, otherwise it crashes. Finally the procedure employs the operation **Spell-Out** and the sentence is uttered and interpreted. For example, the numeration in (1) has the lexical items and indices to build the sentence in (2):

(1) $N = \{the_2, boy_1, ate_1, apples_1\}$
(2) *the boy ate the apples*

See also *Logical Form, Merge, Movement, Numeration, Phase, Phonetic Form,* and *Spell-Out.*

Conceptual and Intentional properties (or C–I system)

Within the Minimalist Program, Conceptual and Intentional (C–I) properties of language form the system of meaning of languages. They interface with the Logical Form (LF) level of representation. Within the Minimalist Program framework, other than Phonetic Form (PF) and LF all levels of representation that were part of the Government and Binding framework, such as D-structures and S-structure, have been eradicated.

See also *Articulatory and Perceptual properties.*

Configurational vs. nonconfigurational languages

Configurational languages are languages in which constituent structure, or **constituency**, plays some relevant role. In English, for example, constituents cannot easily (or not at all) be split up by items that do not belong to them. In nonconfigurational languages, on the other hand, constituency is much less relevant. For this reason, while **government relations** are common in configurational languages, in nonconfigurational languages **modification relations** predominate. Typical features of nonconfigurationality are free word order on the phrase level and widespread use of null arguments. Besides English, configurational languages are for example the Romance languages and the other modern Germanic languages; nonconfigurational ones are Warlpiri (Australian) or Japanese. The ancient Indo-European languages, such as Vedic Sanskrit and Homeric Greek, display many features of nonconfigurationality as well.

See also *Constituent, Government, Modification*, and *P2.*

Conjunct

(a) A type of adjunct.
(b) A member of a coordinated construction.

See *Adjunct* and *Coordination.*

Constituency see *Configurational vs. Nonconfigurational languages* and *Constituent*.

Constituent

A constituent is a word or construction which is part of a wider construction. The word 'constituent' indicates that a certain unit is a part of a whole. Constituents are typically words, phrases (i.e. constituents below the clause level), or clauses that have a certain function (e.g. subject, direct object, etc.), functioning as a single unit within a given structure (e.g. a sentence).

Constituents are syntactic constructions. Constituents below the clause level, also called **phrases**, are of various types, depending on their head: **noun phrase** (NP), as in *red hat*, *Mary*, *my father's car*, *the boy who is running in the street*; **verb phrase** (VP), as in *eat meal*, *have gone*, *think that he should leave*; **adjectival phrase** (AP), as in *very good*, *much greater*; **adverbial phrase** (AdvP), as in *slowly*, *very early*, *over there*; **prepositional phrase** (PP), as in *on the table*, *at six o'clock*. Of these, the first four types are endocentric, while PPs are exocentric; they are considered endocentric within the X-bar theory. (Note that the term 'prepositional phrase' only applies to languages which have prepositions. Since many languages have postpositions, or both pre- and postpositions, and since there is a word, adposition, that refers to both prepositions and postpositions, a better term, which is usable for all languages, is **adpositional phrase**.)

Depending on their internal structure, constituents can be more or less complex: a NP such as *the boy who's running in the street* is more complex than a NP without modifiers, such as *the boy*, or than one consisting of a pronoun, such as *he*. Internal categorial complexity of constituents is also called **constituent's weight**: less complex constituents are said to be **light**, while more complex ones are said to be **heavy**.

That a certain group of words is actually a constituent can be shown through **constituency tests**, like the **substitution test**. In the sentence:

(1) *I don't know **the boy who's running in the street***

the NP *the boy who's running in the street* is indeed a syntactic unit, because, among other things, it can be replaced by a pronoun:

(2) *I don't know **him***

A second test of constituency is based on the fact that, in languages such as English, constituents most often cannot be split up by another word/constituent. One can say:

(3) *I saw a man with **a red hat** yesterday*

but not:

(4) **I saw a man with **a red** yesterday **hat***

This is by no means a universal property of constituents. In several free word order languages, constituents may be split up by the occurrence of words that belong to other constituents. For example, in Latin we find:

(5) *arma   virumque   cano,   Troiae   qui   primus   ab*
weapon:N/A man:ACC+and sing:PRS.1SG Troy:GEN REL.NOM first:NOM from
oris   Italiam . . . Laviniaque   venit   litora
shore:ABL.PL Italy:ACC   Lavianian:N/A.PL+and come:PRET.3SG coast:N/A.PL
"I sing the arms and the man who came first from the shores of Troy to Italy and to the Lavinian coast." Virgil *Aeneid* 1–3 (Latin, Italic, Indo-European)

In example (5) two constituents, *ab oris Troiae* 'from the shores of Troy', and *Lavinia litora* '(to) the Lavinian coast', are split up by other words, in a way which would be completely impossible in English. Example (5) is from a highly artificial register; nevertheless, it demonstrates that under appropriate circumstances constituents could be discontinuous in Latin. Languages that allow for discontinuous constituents are called nonconfigurational languages, while languages like English are configurational.

The larger constituents into which a construction can be split are called **immediate constituents**. Such constituents may often be divided into further constituents. In sentence (6):

(6) *the girl with the lollipop used to play in the garden next to my home*

the NP *the girl with the lollipop* and the VP *used to play in the garden next to my home* are immediate constituents; they can further be analyzed into smaller constituents: for example, the NP can be divided into another NP, *the girl*, and a PP, *with the lollipop*.

See also *Configurational vs. nonconfigurational languages, Construction, Head, Parts of speech, Phrase, Weight,* and *X-bar theory.*

Construction (or syntactic construction)

An ordered set of units, arranged in a way to build a larger unit, such as a sentence or a phrase. Constructions may be endocentric or exocentric.

Endocentric constructions are those whose head belongs to the same form-class as one of its parts (see Bloomfield 1933: 195), and can stand for the whole construction. For example, *poor John* is a NP, it belongs to the same form-class as *John*, which is called the head of the NP and is itself a NP; similarly in the VP *eat meal*, the head *eat* is also a VP, and so on. On the other hand, in the PP *on the table*, an **exocentric construction,** the preposition *on* is not itself a PP, and cannot stand alone for the whole phrase. Certain prepositions can function as independent adverbs. It is possible to say:

(1) *I am* **in my office**
(2) *I am* **in**

However, there is a categorial difference between *in my office* (PP) and *in* (AdvP): even if *in* can stand alone, it is not the case that it can be labeled as a PP if it does not have a complement.

Note that within X-bar theory, all constituents are considered to be endocentric, including prepositional phrases and sentences.

Syntactic constructions can be contrasted with grammatical constructions, which may involve bound morphemes and are relevant to morphology.

In Construction Grammar, no difference is made between syntactic and grammatical constructions. A construction is defined as "[a] symbolic structure involving the syntagmatic combination of morphemes and/or larger expressions." (Langacker 1987: 489). As pointed out in Croft and Cruse (2004: 257), constructions are similar to the lexicon in other syntactic theories, and are at least partially arbitrary.

See also *Constituent* and *X-bar theory.*

Contact clause see *Relative clause.*

Control Theory

Within the Government and Binding framework of Chomsky (1981), Control Theory is one of the subsystems of UG (Universal Grammar). It is devoted to determining the potential for reference of the abstract element PRO. The term *control* is used to refer to a relation of referential dependency between an unexpressed subject (the controlled element), usually the subject of an infinitival or gerund verb, and an expressed or unexpressed constituent (the controller), which determines the meaning of PRO. Thus, the referential properties of the controlled element are determined by those of the controller (see Landau 2001). This is shown in sentence (1):

(1) *Mary$_i$ went to the store PRO$_i$ to buy a book*

In sentence (1) *Mary*, being the controller, determines the properties of PRO, which is interpreted as 'Mary'.

See also *PRO*.

Controller

(a) An item that controls another item and triggers the expression of certain morphological features on a target or determines the reference of an anaphor. In (1) the NP *Mary* controls the anaphoric pronoun *her*:

(1) ***Mary$_i$** left and everybody misses **her**$_i$*

A controller is an antecedent: the two different terms capture different features of the phenomenon of control.

(b) A participant that exerts control on a state of affairs, that is, that has the capability of bringing about a state of affairs, typically an agent or a natural force. In this sense, control must not be confused with intentionality: natural forces can be conceived of as controlling events, even if they do not act voluntarily.

See also *Anaphora, Antecedent, Control theory, PRO, Semantic role*, and *State of affairs*.

Converb

An adverbial form of the verb, such as the English gerund:

(1) a. **coming** *home, I stopped to buy some milk*

Converbs often do not indicate a specific semantic relationship with the main clause, and can take the place of various types of adverbial clauses, their meaning being specified by the context. In this case, they are called **contextual converbs**. The English gerund is a contextual converb: it can have the function of a temporal clause, as in (1a), which corresponds to:

(1) b. **while I was coming home**, *I stopped to buy some milk*

or of a causal clause, as in (2):

(2) a. *I broke my leg* **falling from the stairs**
    b. *I broke my leg* **because I fell from the stairs**

See also *Adverbial subordinate clause* and *Subordination*.

Convergence (Converge)

In the Government and Binding Program a convergent derivation is a well-formed or grammatical derivation. In the Minimalist Program a convergent derivation satisfies the conditions at the Phonetic Form (PF) and Logical Form (LF) interfaces. A derivation crashes if it is not convergent.

During each step of a derivation or phase, the constituents must be checked for convergence. If they converge or are interpretable, the derivation continues to be built. If they do not converge, they are uninterpretable, and the derivation crashes.

See also *Computational system*.

Coordinand see *Coordination*.

Coordination

Coordinated constructions are series of two or more items connected with some kind of conjunction (**syndetic coordination**) or simply juxtaposed (**asyndetic coordination**) that must be understood as constituting a single unit with a unitary syntactic status, rather than in a hierarchical relation with each other:

(1) *John **and** Mary went to the party*

In (1) two coordinated NPs, *John* and *Mary*, constitute a single unit from the point of view of sentence structure; the NP *John and Mary* is the subject of the verb *went* and the two NPs are syndetically coordinated by means of the coordinating conjunction *and*.

The conjunction *and* demonstrates **conjunctive coordination**; other types of coordination are **disjunctive** (*or*) and **adversative** (*but*):

(2) *John will go to the party **or** to the movies*
(3) *John went to the party, **but** Mary remained home*

Members of coordinated constructions are called **coordinands** or **conjuncts**. The order of conjuncts is often said to be reversible, as shown in (4):

(4) *Mary and John = John and Mary*

However, this is not always the case: in coordinated clauses, anaphors and Ø (ellipses) can only stand in the second conjunct, as shown under **coordination reduction**.

The type of coordination found in English expressions such as (1) is also called **symmetric coordination**. Some languages may have **asymmetric coordination** as well:

(5) *ja **s** **Mišoj*** *pošli* *v* *kino*
I with Misha:INSTR go:PAST.PL in cinema
"I and Misha went to the movies." (Russian, Slavic, Indo-European)

In (5) the second conjunct *s Mišoj*, literally 'with Misha', is morphologically coded as a comitative adverbial; still, it builds a single unit with the first conjunct, as shown by the fact that the verb is inflected in the plural.

In S. C. Dik's Functional Grammar and in Transformational Generative Grammar, (symmetric) coordination is used as a test for the semantic (or thematic) role of constituents, since it is assumed that only constituents with the same semantic role can be coordinated.

See also *Coordination reduction*.

Coordination reduction

In coordinated clauses, some items that are coreferential need not be repeated. This is called coordination reduction, and applies most often to the subject:

(1) **Susan**$_i$ *kissed the children and* **Ø**$_i$ *left*

Many languages of various language families also allow coordination reduction with direct objects, as is the case in Turkish:

(2) *raftan*   **kitab**$_i$ *alkyor ve*   **Ø**$_i$ *okuyorum*
    shelf:ABL book:ACC take   and   read:1SG.PRS
    "I take **the book** from the shelf and read **it**." (Turkish, Turkic, Altaic)

Coordination reduction in such occurences is also called **equi NP deletion**. Coordination reduction must not be confused with gapping. While gapping can occur both leftward and rightward, mostly based on the word order type of a given language, coordination reduction can only operate rightward, and it is not connected with other word order features, but rather with general properties of anaphoric processes. In other words, it is not possible to say:

(3) a. ****Ø**$_i$ *kissed the children and* **Susan**$_i$ *left*

in much the same way as one cannot say:

(3) b. ****she**$_i$ *kissed the children and* **Susan**$_i$ *left*

which is ungrammatical with the interpretation *she = Susan*.
    See also *Anaphora, Binding, Coordination*, and *Gapping*.

Copula

A device, often an existential verb, used to express verbal categories with nominal predicates, such as the verb *be* in English:

(1) *the girls* **were** *beautiful*

In (1) the predicate is the adjective *beautiful*, which lacks verbal categories; the latter are supplied by the verb form *were*, which does not carry any lexical meaning, but indicates tense and agreement. The phenomenon by which nominal predicates acquire verbal categories by being accompanied by a copular item is sometimes called **copula support**.

Many languages have zero copula, especially in the present tense. In some languages, such as Latin, the copula is optional; in others it never occurs, as in Russian and Hungarian:

(2) *devuškij - krassivyj*
    girl:NOM.PL   beautiful:NOM.PL
    "The girls are beautiful." (Russian, Slavic, Indo-European)

(3) *a lány szép*
    the girl beautiful
    "The girl is beautiful." (Hungarian, Finno-Ugric, Uralic)

Some languages have more than one copula, such as Spanish, in which both *ser* and *estar* share the function of English *be*. The former is the existential verb, and usually indicates a permanent state:

(4) *Dolores **es** guapa*
    "Dolores is beautiful." (Spanish, Romance, Indo-European)

Estar, instead, when not used as copula, means 'be' in the sense of 'be somewhere', 'stand', as in (5):

(5) *el vaso **está** en la mesa*
    "The glass is on the table." (Spanish, Romance, Indo-European)

When used as a copula, *estar* indicates a temporary state as in (6) or a change of state as (7):

(6) *Dolores está guapa hoy*
    "Dolores is beautiful today."

(7) *el vaso está roto*
    "The glass is broken." (Spanish, Romance, Indo-European)

Thai also has two copulas, the copula /pen/ used as classifying (*Paul is a teacher*), and the copula /khɯɯ/ used as equational (*Paul is my brother's teacher*), as in:

(8) *cOOn1* **pen1** *khruu1*
    John   COP   teacher
    "John is a teacher."
(9) *khOn1 thii3 chan4 rak4* **khUU1** *cOOn1*
    person REL   1SG   love COP   John
    "The person that I love is John." (from Takahashi and Shinzato 2003: 133) (Thai, Tai, Tai-Kadai)

The copula need not be a verb: anaphoric and demonstrative pronouns are another frequent source of copulas. For example, the Chinese copula *shì* was originally a demonstrative.

See also *Predicate*.

Copular clause

A clause that contains a copula.
    See also *Copula*.

Copy

Within the Minimalist Program, copy is equivalent to the trace of a moved element in a sentence in the Government and Binding Theory. The operations Move and Merge produce movement in a sentence. A copy is whatever the moved element is. After movement, the copy or copies of the moved element must disappear for the structure (phrase marker or tree) to be linearized or to have its linear word order. While a syntactic structure is a two-dimensional structure (it has breath and depth), its output, which is a sentence, is a one-dimensional item with a linearized   word order. This requires copies to disappear from the tree before the sentence reaches PF (Phonetic Form) or it is pronounced. In (1) the lower relative pronoun must be erased for the sentence to be interpreted linearly:

(1) *what did John eat* ~~what~~?

In Government and Binding Theory there are NP-traces and Wh-traces. NP-traces are anaphors and must comply with Principle A of Binding Theory. Wh-traces are R-expressions and must comply with Principle C of Binding Theory. Since traces are empty elements, they must comply with the Empty Category Principle (ECP).

See also *Binding Theory, Copy Theory, Merge and Movement*.

Copy Theory

Within the Minimalist Program Copy Theory of movement pertains to the movement property of languages. In this theory, movement, the result of copy/move plus Merge, leaves copies that must be erased in the phrase marker. The Copy Theory of movement absorbs Trace Theory of the Government and Binding framework. Copy Theory improves Trace theory because it does not introduce new theoretical elements, the traces, which are not present in the numeration (they are not lexical items). Copy Theory complies with the Inclusiveness Condition.

Core

The inner part of a sentence, as opposed to the periphery. The core consists in the predicate and its arguments, as shown in:

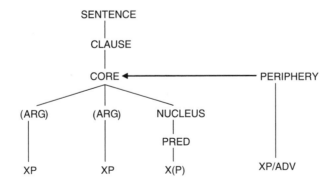

(from Van Valin and LaPolla 1997: 31).

Thus, in example (1):

(1) *I had a snack in the afternoon*

the NPs *I* and *a snack* are two arguments, and the verb *had* is the predicate; the verb is also the nucleus of the predication and builds its core together with the two arguments. The PP *in the afternoon* stands in the periphery.

The predication that builds the core of a sentence or clause is sometimes called **nuclear predication**, and the word *nucleus* is considered synonym of *core* in certain terminologies.

See also *Nucleus, Sentence*, and *Valency*.

Core Argument

An argument that belongs to the core of the sentence, that is, to the nuclear predication.

See also *Argument* and *Nucleus*.

Core Grammar

In Transformational Generative Grammar, Core Grammar refers to the general principles of grammar which derive from universal principles of UG (Universal Grammar). Core Grammar is opposed to the periphery, which is the idiosyncratic part of grammar of a particular language.

See also *Interpretable features* and *Uninterpretable features*.

Cosubordination see *Serial verb*.

Coverb

A type of Chinese serial verb that functionally corresponds to English prepositions:

(1) wǒ **gěi** Wáng jì xìn
    I   give Wang send letter
    "I send a letter to Wang." (Chinese, Sinitic, Sino-Tibetan)

In example (1) the verb **gěi** 'give' functions as a preposition 'to'.
See also *Serial verb*.

Covert movement

In the Government and Binding framework, **covert movement** is a type of movement that takes place from S-structure to Logical Form (LF). Covert movement is a semantic movement. The output of covert movement does not have a phonetic reflex. Examples of covert movement include wh 'in situ', expletive replacement, and anaphor raising. The sentence in (1) is an example of wh 'in situ' in Chinese:

(1) *Paul mǎi le*   **shénme?**
    Paul buy ASP what
    'What did Paul buy?' (Chinese, Sinitic, Sino-Tibetan)

In (1) the wh-element **shénme** 'what' is assumed to move covertly at LF to the beginning of the sentence.

In the Minimalist Program, **covert movement** is used to check **weak features** due to **Procrastinate.** For example, verb movement in English must proceed covertly (at LF) to check the **weak** V-feature of Infl. This explains why English has no overt verb movement in the syntax in examples such as (2a). French, instead, has **overt verb movement** in the syntax because French has a strong V-feature in Infl. This is shown in (2b):

(2) a. *John often **eats** apples*
    b. *Jean **mange** souvent des pommes* (French, Romance, Indo-European)

In (2a) the verb follows the adverb *often* because it did not move. In (2b) the verb moved, and it precedes the adverb *souvent*. In this proposal, due to Pollock (1989), the Adverbial Phrase has a fixed position in the tree in all languages.

See also *Movement* and *Overt Movement*.

Covert syntax

Covert syntax is the part of syntax ordered after Spell-Out. It has no effects in the sound structure of language.

See also *Covert movement* and *Spell-Out*.

Dative See *Case*.
Dative shift See *Indirect object*.

D-structure (Deep structure)

In Transformational Generative Grammar until Minimalism, D-structure (formerly Deep structure) encodes the basic thematic relations in the sentence as determined by the argument structure of the predicate. It is the input of the transformational component. Thus, a sentence such as (1) has the D-structures in (2), following X-bar theory:

(1) *John ate the apples*
(2)

```
                        CP
                       / \
                    Spec  C'
                         / \
                        C  IP
                          / \
                       Spec  I'
                            / \
                           I  VP
                     [+Tense] / \
                        past DP  V'
                            Δ  / \
                        John  V  DP
                           ↑  ate  Δ
                           θ   →   the apples
```

In (2) the verb assigns the theta-role (theme) to the internal argument or object and the theta-role (agent) to the external argument or subject. In addition to the D-structure representation, which reflects lexical properties, a sentence is associated with a second level of representation, which is called S-structure or surface structure. Movement operations (transformations) map D-structures onto S-structures.

Within the Minimalist Program, the linguistic levels of representation are restricted to only the ones that are required by conceptual necessity. These are the A–P (Articulatory Perceptual)-Interface and the C–I (Conceptual Intensional Interface). Thus, D-structure and S-structure are levels that have been eradicated in this framework.

See also *Articulatory and Perceptual Properties, Movement*, and *S-structure*.

Deletion

Deletion consists in the erasing of an element in a construction. In early Transformational Generative Grammar only elements that can be recovered may be deleted due to the Principle of Recoverability of Deletion, which states that only recoverable items may be deleted.

See also *Coordination reduction*.

Demotion

In Relational Grammar, the phenomenon by which a constituent that bears a certain relation at a deeper layer of structure is demoted to another relation at a lower level (e.g. from subject to direct object), following the hierarchy subject > direct object > indirect object.

See also *Chômeur* and *Promotion*.

Dependency relation

A syntactic relation by which an item, called the dependent, depends on another item, called the head. Dependency relations are of two basic types: government and modification. In government relations the dependent is obligatory, such as *noon* in (1):

(1) *my brother came home at noon/*my brother came home at*

In modification relations, instead, the dependent is nonobligatory, as *slowly* in (2):

(2) *she drove home slowly/she drove home*

See also *Dependent, Government, Head,* and *Modification*.

Dependent

An item that depends on another item, either through a relation of government, or through a relation of modification. The item on which the dependent depends is called the head. Dependency relations can be marked on the dependent, on the head, or on both.

See also *Dependency relation, Government, Head vs. Dependent marking,* and *Modification*.

Determiner see *Part of speech*.

Direct object

A constituent (often simply called 'object') that saturates the valency of transitive verbs, such as *pasta* in:

(1) *Paul eats pasta*

In nominative-accusative languages, the direct object is typically marked by the accusative case, and can become the subject if a sentence is turned into the passive:

(2) a. *everybody saw me*
    b. *I was seen by everybody*

Some pro-drop languages that allow for null subjects also allow for null direct objects, albeit less frequently. This happens most often in coordinated clauses that contain conjunctive coordinators (coordination reduction), but it is by no means limited to them, as shown in:

(3) *hoi   mèn beltíous   poioûntes   autoùs$_i$ pántes*
    DEM.NOM.PL PTC better:ACC.PL make:PRS.PART.NOM.PL 3PL.ACC all:NOM.PL
    ánthrōpoi   eînai, heîs   dé   tis   ho   diaphtheírōn Ø$_i$?
    man:NOM.PL be:PRS.INF one:NOM PTC INDEF.NOM DEM.NOM injure:PRS.PART.NOM
    "(that) those who make **them** better are all mankind, while he who injures **them** (is) some one person?" Plato, *Apology* 25b (Classical Greek, Indo-European).

Several languages display **differential object marking**, a phenomenon by which the direct object is encoded by means of different cases other than the accusative, most often depending on definiteness and/or animacy. In

Turkish, indefinite objects are marked by Ø, while definite ones are marked by
the ending -i (or -ı):

(4) a. *bir defter   aldı*
       a   copybook buy:PAST.3sg
       "He bought a copybook."
    b. *defter-i   aldı*
       copybook-ACC buy:PAST.3sg
       "He bought the copybook." (Turkish, Turkic, Altaic)
(5) a. *ekmek yedi*
       bread eat:PAST.3sg
       "He ate (some) bread."
    b. *kadın-ın   ekmeg-ini   yedi*
       woman-GEN   bread-POSS3SG.ACC eat:PAST.3sg
       "He ate the woman's bread." (Turkish, Turkic, Altaic)

In various Romance languages, among which Spanish and Romanian, animate (mostly human) direct objects are marked by a preposition (*a* in Spanish,
pe in Romanian), while inanimate ones are not:

(6) a. *estoy buscando a mi amigo*
       "I am looking for my friend."
    b. *estoy buscando mi coche*
       "I am looking for my car." (Spanish, Romance, Indo-European).

(Animate objects can occasionally occur without preposition if they are
nonreferential or indefinite.)
    See also *Coordination reduction, Grammatical relation, Transitivity*, and
Valency.

Disjunct see *Adjunct*.
Ditransitive see *Transitivity* and *Valency*.
Double case see *Agreement*.

DP (Determiner Phrase)

In 1987 Abney provided arguments for the idea that the determiner head
projects a Determiner Phrase (DP), like other functional elements, such as

the complementizer, which projects a complementizer phrase or CP. This proposal, labeled DP-Hypothesis, reassesses various aspects of noun phrases within the Government and Binding framework. The structure Abney proposed follows X-bar theory. Thus, the phrase *the house* has the basic—expected—representation given in (1):

(1)
```
              DP
             / \
              D'
             / \
            D   NP
            |   Δ
           the house
```

The DP structure establishes a structural parallel between noun phrases and sentences. The head D can be [+Definite] or [–Definite].

DP may have more structure than just (1). For instance, DP structure allows formalizing the fact that gerunds may be nominal categories containing a VP, satisfying the endocentric requirement of X-bar theory. Thus, in a sentence such as:

(2) **John's writing poems** *impressed his students*

the DP *John's writing poems* is the complement of D in the following structure (3):

(3)
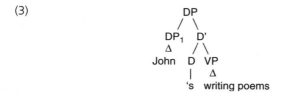
```
                DP
               /  \
            DP₁    D'
             Δ    / \
           John  D   VP
                 |   Δ
                's  writing poems
```

Moreover, there is internal movement in DPs, as in sentences. For example in (3), the triangle in DP₁ abbreviates the movement of *John* in this DP. In fact, in DP₁ *John* has moved from the head of NP to the head of DP₁, as is shown in (4):

(4)

```
              DP₁
             /  \
              D'
             / \
            D   NP
            |   Δ
         John i  ti
              ←
```

This movement is frequent with proper nouns, but infrequent with common nouns in English and other languages. Proper nouns may be inherently definite singular, thus they do not have a definite article and they may move in DP. Common nouns are not inherently specified for definiteness. Thus, they may require a phonetic article, as in (1). However, there is variation with regard to this among languages, since there are examples such as (5) in Spanish and other languages:

(5) *el Juan*
   the John
   "John" (Spanish, Romance, Indo-European);

DPs may have a more complex functional structure with quantification and agreement elements, such as Number Phrase and Quantifier Phrase, as in Spanish *cinco libros,* 'five books'.

Summarizing, the DP hypothesis makes two important claims:

   a. The structure of DPs fully conforms to the X-bar theory.
   b. The structural relation between D and NP is a head/complement relation.

See also *Constituent, Head*, and *X-bar theory*.

Dislocation

The placement of a constituent in a position which is not its habitual one, usually at one of the sentence boundaries. In (1) the constituent *ice cream* is left dislocated, while in (2) the constituent *that big ice cream* is right dislocated:

(1) **ice cream**, *I like*
(2) *I don't know how you could eat **it** up,* **that big ice cream**

Dislocation may be indicated by special features, like a pause, as in (1), or a coreferential pronoun, as in (2), in which the pronoun *it* is coreferential with the right dislocated constituent.

Dislocation is used for pragmatic purposes, such as topicalization.
See also *Afterthought, Topic, Topicalization*, and *Word order*.

Ellipsis

Ellipsis consists in the leaving out of a constituent which should be syntactically realized in a sentence. Ellipsis can concern the subject or another constituent. A special case of ellipsis is constituted by **VP ellipsis**, as in (1):

(1) *he always **tells lies**, and his sister **does** too*

In (1) two coordinated clauses have the same predicate, *tells lies*. The VP *tells lies* is overtly expressed in the first clause, but it is not repeated in the second: the auxiliary *does* occurs instead.

See also *Coordination reduction, Gapping*, and *Null argument*.

Embedding

The process by which an item is inserted (embedded) in another item. In (1):

(1) *the girl with the lollypop*

the PP *with the lollypop* is part of an NP, and it is said to be embedded in the NP. Subordinate clauses are embedded in the main clause. Embedding may involve the addition of material at the left or at the right of a constituent, or in its center. The latter process, known as **center embedding**, has been paid special attention to because, in languages that have it, it exhibits a low degree of recursivity. This is not a consequence of grammatical or structural constraints, but rather of the limitation of human short-term memory. Thus, a sentence with several levels of center embedding, such as (2), is said to be grammatical, but unacceptable:

(2) *the boy that the teacher that the girl that the lady that the taxi driver picked up from home accompanied to school had never met before scolded came in late*

In (2) we find a governing clause, *the boy came in late*, with a number of relative clauses, subordinated to each other. Each relative clause is embedded into the one that contains its head: *that the teacher scolded* is subordinated to the main clause, and has the NP *the boy* as its head; *that the girl had never met before* has the NP *the teacher* as its head; *that the lady accompanied to school* has the NP *the girl* as its head, and finally the clause *that the taxi driver picked up from home* is headed by the NP *the lady*.

See also *Grammatical/Ungrammatical*.

Empty Category

Within Government and Binding theory, there are four empty or nonovertly realized categories such as little *pro,* big PRO, NP trace and wh-trace. In sentence (1) there is a nonpronounced, empty subject or little *pro:*

(1) **pro** *nieva*
        snow:3sɢ
    "It is snowing." (Spanish, Romance, Indo-European)

In (2), there is an nonovertly realized empty subject of the infinitival verb, big PRO:

(2) *Silvia₁prefers* **PRO**₁ *to invite Claudia*

In (3) there is a NP-trace, which is the result of *John* moving to the subject position through NP-movement:

(3) **John**₁ *is loved* **t**₁ *by Mary*

In (4) there is a wh-trace, which is the result of the wh-word *what* being moved to the Spec of CP (Specifier of the Complementizer Phrase) through wh-movement:

(4) **what** *did John eat* **t**₁*?*

The existence of NP-trace and wh-trace is related to movement. In (3) the trace is left by NP-movement, while in (4) the trace is left by wh-movement. Empty categories have the same features and behavior as their phonetic counterparts as shown in chart (i).

NP-traces are subject to principle A of Binding Theory, little *pro* is subject to principle B of Binding Theory, wh-traces are variables, subject to principle C of

Non-overt	Overt	Type
NP-trace	anaphors	[+anaphor −pronominal]
pro	pronouns	[−anaphor +pronominal]
Wh-trace	R-expressions	[−anaphor −pronominal]
PRO	-------	[+anaphor +pronominal]

Chart i Typology of empty categories

Binding Theory. PRO is not subject to any principle of Binding Theory because it is [+anaphor +pronominal].

See also *Binding Theory, Empty Category Principle*, and *Variable*.

Empty Category Principle (ECP)

In the Government and Binding framework, the Empty Category Principle or ECP applies to traces, which are always either theta-governed (NP-traces) or antecedent governed (wh-traces). Formally, the Empty Category Principle or ECP states that:

(1) *Empty Category Principle: ECP*
Traces must be properly governed:
A properly governs B iff A theta-governs B or A-antecedent governs B
A properly governs B iff A governs B and A theta-marks B
A-antecedent governs B iff A governs B and A is coindexed with B
(Hageman 1991: 404)

See also *Government*.

Enclitic see *Clitic*.

Endocentric *vs.* exocentric construction

According to Bloomfield (1933: 195), an endocentric construction is one in which "the resultant phrase belongs to the same form-class as one of the constituents, which we call head." Thus, the head of an endocentric construction can substitute the whole construction. In the endocentric construction *poor John,* the head *John* can substitute the whole construction. The NP *poor John* is also called a "subordinative endocentric construction" (*ib*). Endocentric constructions can be coordinative, when "the resultant phrase belongs to the same form-class as two or more of the constituents" (*ib*). An example is *boys and girls.* Endocentric constructions are said to be internally headed.

Exocentric constructions, such as for example prepositional phrases, are not internally headed. In exocentric constructions, "the resultant phrase [belongs] to a form-class other than that of any constituent" (Bloomfield 1933: 194). Sentences are exocentric constructions. In:

(1) *John ran*

we find a NP *John* and a VP *ran*; the resulting construction is neither a NP nor a VP, but rather a sentence, and has different functions and a different distribution.

See also *Constituent, Construction, Phrase,* and *X-bar theory.*

Equi NP deletion see *Coordination Reduction.*
Ergative language see *Alignment.*

Exceptional Case Marking Verbs (ECM Verbs)

Within the Government and Binding framework, Exceptional Case Marking Verbs (ECM Verbs) are those verbs that assign accusative Case to the subject of an infinitival subordinate clause, as in sentence (1):

(1) *John believes* **her** *to be a genius*

In sentence (1), the verb *believe* takes the infinitival clause *her to be a genius* as its internal argument. Since neither *to* nor the infinitive can assign Case to a phonetic DP, such as *her*, the verb *believe* is the only Case assigner available. In order to assign Case, the subordinate clause does not project a subordinate CP phrase in this particular type of sentence, as is shown in (2):

(2)

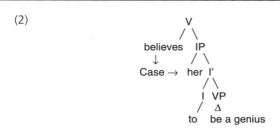

The exceptionality of these constructions is related to the fact that the main verb assigns Case only if the lower sentence does not project a complementizer phrase (CP). However, when a CP is projected, it becomes a barrier for Case assignment from the outside, as in (3a):

(3) a. *he_i doesn't know [$_{CP}$ whether [$_{IP}$ him_i to go on vacation tomorrow]]

Thus, PRO is the only possible subject for a sentence with a CP, as in (3b):

(3) b. he_i doesn't know [$_{CP}$ whether [$_{IP}$ PRO_i to go on vacation tomorrow]]

See also *Raising*.

Expletives

Expletives are items (typically pronouns or adverbs) that do not refer and have no semantic role, such as *it*, and *there* in English in examples (1a) and 1(c). In Transformational Generative Grammar, little *pro$_{expl}$* in null subject languages is also considered an expletive, and it is said that expletives are not assigned a theta-role.

Expletives do not refer to anything, as shown in:

(1) a. ***it** rains*
    b. ***pro$_{expl}$** llueve*
        "It is   raining." (Spanish, Romance, Indo-European)
    c. ***there** is a man in the garden*

See also *Null argument* and *Valency*.

Extended Projection Principle (EPP)

Within Transformational Generative Grammar, Government and Binding and the Minimalist Program, the **Extended Projection Principle** (EPP) asserts that all clauses or sentences must contain a subject. This principle reflects a general property of sentences and it yields the structural requirement that inserts expletives such as *it* and *there* in subject position in examples such as (1a) and (1b):

(1) a. **it** *rains*
     b. **there** *is a man in the garden*

This principle is extended to the **nonovert** or **null subjects** little *pro* and big *PRO*, as in (2a) and (2b):

(2) a. **pro**$_{expl}$ *nieva*
            snow:3SG
         "It is snowing." (Spanish, Romance, Indo-European)
     b. *Mary expects* **John**$_i$ **PRO**$_i$ *to leave*

Within the Minimalist Program, the EPP is reinterpreted morphologically as a strong D or N feature of IP (Inflectional Phrase). Thus, I, the head of IP, has a strong D feature or a strong N feature. Then another constituent, usually the subject which has a D or N feature, must move to the Spec of IP to check the strong feature of I (the head of IP) before the computation splits to Spell-out and Phonetic Form (PF).

See also *Feature strength*.

Extension

Extension is one of the basic mechanisms of syntactic change. Extension "results in the surface manifestation of a pattern" but "does not involve immediate or intrinsic modification of underlying structure" (Harris and Campbell 1995: 51).

An example of extension is the change of some German postpositions to prepositions, such as *wegen* and *statt*, as argued in Givón (1971: 401–402). In particular, in the case of *wegen* one can observe two changes connected with extension. Consider example (1):

(1) a. *des schlechten Wetters   wegen   sind wir nicht hier geblieben*
   the:GEN bad   weather:GEN because are   we not   here remained
   b. *wegen   des   schlechten Wetters   sind wir nicht hier geblieben*
   because the:GEN bad   weather:GEN are   we   not   here remained
   c. *wegen   dem   schlechten Wetter   sind wir nicht hier geblieben*
   because the:DAT bad   weather are   we not   here remained
   "Because the weather was bad, we didn't remain here." (German,
   Germanic, Indo-European)

In (1a) *wegen* is used as a postposition and takes the genitive case.
Historically, this is its most ancient construction; it is still used today, but less
frequently than patterns (1b) and (1c), and it belongs to a high stylistic register. Pattern (1b) is considered the standard today, and it is the one described
in reference grammars. It started occurring at a later time than pattern (1a).
The reason for adopting it lies in the fact that German adpositions are for the
most part prepositions: an uncommon pattern (noun-postposition) is abandoned in favor of a common one, which is extended. Example (1c) is presently
more common in the spoken language, even if it is still considered substan-
dard and accordingly is generally not included in reference grammars.
It contains a prepositional phrase with *wegen* and the dative case, instead
of the genitive found in (1a) and (1b). It attests to a more recent change,
which is also an extension: in German, the number of prepositions that
take the genitive is comparatively small, in comparison to the number of prepositions that take the accusative or, even more frequently, the dative. Thus,
the change from (1b) to (1c) also involves abandoning an infrequent pattern
in favor of a frequent one. This type of extension can also be seen as
an instance of **actualization,** that is, the "gradual mapping out of the
consequences of the reanalysis" (Timberlake 1977; see further Harris and
Campbell 1995: 80–81 on the relation between extension and actualization), because it involves extension of the normal prepositional pattern to a
postposition which was created as such out of reanalysis of a pattern involving a NP constituted by a genitive modifier followed by a head noun (Givón
1971: 402).

Since it consists of the extension of an already existing and frequent
pattern, which replaces an infrequent one, extension may be considered a
type of analogical change.

See also *Reanalysis*.

Feature strength

Within the Minimalist Program, the differences among languages are accounted for in terms of feature strength. For example, finite Infl in French or Spanish has a strong V-feature, but in English finite Infl has a weak V-feature. Thus, Spanish -*mos* in *comemos* is strong, but Ø in English *we ate* is weak. Strong features must be checked overtly through movement. Weak features, instead, must be checked covertly.

See also *Covert Movement, Extended Projection Principle*, and *Overt Movement*.

Focus

A piece of information which is particularly relevant or new, or which is being contrasted with some other piece of information (**focus of contrast**). In a sentence, focus can be identified by means of a wh-question. In (1), several constituents may be focused:

(1) a. *the teacher told my mom about my bad grade*
    b. *who told my mom about my bad grade?* (focus: *the teacher*)
    c. *what did the teacher tell my mom about?* (focus: *my bad grade*)
    d. *whom did the teacher tell about my bad grade?* (focus: *my mom*)

Focus may be indicated by means of special constructions, such as cleft sentences:

(2) **it was the teacher** *who told my mom about my bad grade*

or focus particles:

(3) *the teacher told **even my mom** about my bad grade*

Example (3) makes it clear that focus must not be identified with comment; rather, it is some part of the information that is specially relevant, often a part of the comment, as in (3), where the topic is *the teacher*, and the comment (i.e. what is being said about the topic) is *told even my mom about my bad grade*, while the focused part of the information is *even my mom*.

Lambrecht (1994: 202) defines focus as "the semantic component of a pragmatically structured proposition whereby the assertion differs from the presupposition." Presupposed information is shared between the speaker and the hearer, that is, it is topical, or old. Focal information is new. Because comment is defined as new information, it may be tempting to identify focus with comment, and this has actually been done in several sentence-based approaches (as opposed to discourse-based approaches). For example, in S. C. Dik's Functional Grammar, Focus is one of the pragmatic functions of constituents within a sentence and roughly corresponds to comment or rheme. Sentence-based approaches require a topic and a focus for all sentences, and pay little attention to the context.

The expression *even my mom* in (3) is also called **narrow focus**. A focus that corresponds to the whole comment is called **broad focus** or **predicate focus**. Entire sentences may be focal too (**sentence focus**) in case they report events, as in:

(4) a. *what happened?*
    b. *I got stuck in a traffic jam*

Focus of contrast, or contrastive focus, involves two contrasted constituents:

(5) *the teacher told **my mom** about my bad grade (not my dad)*

In English, focus of contrast is often indicated only by stress.

Limiting one's analysis to single sentences can make it difficult to distinguish between topic and focus: the topic of (1a) is normally considered to be *the teacher*, but the same constituent can be focus as shown by the wh-question test (even if a more normal answer to (1b) would simply be *the teacher* or *the teacher did*).

Full Interpretation

Within the Minimalist Program, **Full Interpretation** is a principle of representational economy, which requires all the features of Phonetic Form (PF) and Logical Form (LF) to be legible at the relevant interfaces. The syntactic structure to which the semantic and phonetic interface rules apply should consist only of interpretable features. If the structure contains **uninterpretable** features, then the derivation will crash, because it will not be able to assign a complete interpretation to its constituents in the structure. It follows from Full Interpretation that uninterpretable features must be eliminated from syntax before the semantic and phonetic interface rules apply. This is the job of syntactic operations: to eliminate uninterpretable features. Economy considerations select the derivations which are built in an optimal way.

See also *Interpretable features* and *Uninterpretable features*.

Gapping

The leaving out of the verb in two or more coordinated clauses, as in:

(1) *John ate the potatoes and Mary the meat*

In (1) the verb *ate* applies to both *John* and *the potatoes* on the one hand, and *Mary* and *the meat* on the other, but only appears in the first clause.

Depending on the language, gapping can operate rightward, as in English, or leftward, as in Japanese:

(2) *Kuniko wa hon o,   Taroo wa sinbun   o   yomu*
    Kuniko TOP book OBJ Taroo TOP newspaper OBJ read
    "Kuniko reads a book, Taroo a newspaper." (Japanese, Japanese)

In general, it is thought that rightward gapping is typical of VO languages, while leftward gapping is typical of OV languages. In Turkish (OV), however, gapping can operate in both directions:

(3) a. *Ali armut iyor Veli ise   elma*
       A. pear   eats V.   instead apple
    b. *Ali armut Veli ise   elma iyor*
       A. pear   V.   instead apple eats
       "Ali eats a pear and Veli an apple." (Turkish, Turkic, Altaic).

See also *Coordination reduction* and *Word order*.

Goal

a) Within the Minimalist Program (Phase Theory), a **goal** is an element that matches with a **probe** in the Agree operation. The goal has interpretable features and the probe has noninterpretable features. Once all the noninterpretable features of an item are checked (i.e. erased), it becomes inactive.

b) A semantic role.

Government

A government relation is a type of dependency relation in which a certain item determines the syntactic function of another item and selects its morphological features.

Not all scholars agree on the definition of government and not all definitions of government actually fit all instances of putative government relations. According to Moravcsik (1995: 708) "Constituent A governs constituent B if the syntactic function of B depends on A." Other definitions highlight the fact that government only obtains when the governor obligatorily requires a governed element to fill its valency. In this case, the governor is conceived of as having an empty slot (Ch. Lehmann 1983, 1985). Moravcsik's definition is not concerned with the fact that the governor obligatorily selects the morphological features of the governed item, while this is considered a basic condition for government by most other authors.

The relation between a preposition and its complement is considered a typical government relation. In (1) the preposition *at* is said to govern the NP *train station*, because a preposition cannot stand without its complement, and because it is the preposition that determines the function of the NP:

(1) a. *the girl was waiting **at the train station***

A governed constituent is part of a larger constituent, headed by the item that governs it; governed constituents cannot be left out:

(1) b. * *the girl was waiting **at***

A verb is said to govern its complements, as in:

(2) *pántes   ánthrōpoi   toû   eidénai   orégontai   phúsēï*
     all:NOM.PL man:NOM.PL ART.GEN know:INF.AOR pursue:PRS.3PL nature:DAT
     "All humans naturally pursue knowledge." Aristotle, *Metaphysics* 980a (Classical Greek, Indo-European)

In (2), the verb *orégontai* 'they pursue' is bivalent, and requires a second argument; the second argument *toû eidénai* 'knowledge' is marked genitive, because the verb obligatorily takes the genitive (such verbs are said to govern the genitive, while most bivalent verbs in Greek take the accusative). The syntactic function of the governed constituent is determined by the governor, which also selects its morphological form (case marking).

However, it is not always so clear that government relations determine the morphological form of the governed item. Compare:

(3) a. *ich fahre in der   Stadt*
     I   drive in the:DAT town
     "I drive inside the town."
   b. *ich fahre in die   Stadt*
     I   drive in the:ACC town
     "I drive into town."
   c. **ich fahre in*
     "I   drive in."
     (German, Germanic, Indo-European)

The complement of a preposition is a governed item, but some prepositions can take NPs with different cases. In this case, the governed constituent is obligatory, as shown in (3c), and its syntactic function is determined by the governor, but the selection of morphological features must be accounted for in some other way.

Note further that there are apparent exceptions to obligatoriness of government. Consider sentence (4a):

(4) a. *John ate pasta*

In a sentence such as (4a) the transitive verb *eat* is said to govern its direct object, *pasta*. However, sentence (4b):

(4) b. *John ate*

is by no means ungrammatical. This depends on the fact that several transitive verbs (such as *eat, read, paint*) can indicate an accomplishment, as in (4a), that is, a state of affairs that implies a change of state, or an activity, as in (4b), which does not imply any change of state. If *eat* indicates an accomplishment, then the direct object is indeed obligatory.

Another apparent exception is constituted by example (5a) as opposed to (5b):

(5) a. *John is in his office*
    b. *John is in*

We wrote above that the complement of a preposition is an obligatory item. In fact, there is a difference in the use of the preposition *in* in (5a) and in (5b). In (5a) we find a PP, *in his office*, while in (5b) *in* is not itself a PP, but rather an AdvP. However, it is true that some prepositions, such as *at*, cannot occur alone building an independent AdvP. This may mean that there are varying degrees of obligatoriness even in government relations.

Government relations (in the sense of obligatory head—complement relations) are typical of configurational languages, as opposed to nonconfigurational ones, in which modification relations (nonobligatory) predominate.

In Government and Binding Theory, the theta-role of the **internal argument** of the verb phrase, usually the object, is determined by the verb. The theta-role of the **external argument**, typically the subject, is instead determined by the combination of the verb and its internal argument. Theta-roles must be assigned under **government** in this framework. Government is defined in terms of **c-command**, as in (6):

(6) A governs B if and only if
    (i) A is a governor
    (ii) A c-commands B and B c-commands A

In this definition, government is assigned under sisterhood as is shown in the structure in (7), in which the subject is internally generated in VP:

(7)
```
                            VP
                           / \
                        John  V'  ← V' assigns theta-role to the subj
                             / \
                            V   DP
                            |   |
V assigns theta-role to the object→  loves  Mary
```

In the structure in (7), V and V' are the governors of their sister constituents. However, before the subject-internal hypothesis was generalized, the subject was generated in the specifier (Spec) of IP. In this case, the governor for the theta-role assignment of the subject was the whole VP mediated by inflectional node (Infl) as shown in (8).

(8)

Later on, in the same framework, the theta-role of the subject was assigned by Spec-head agreement of the subject *John* by I⁰, as shown in (9):

(9)

```
                              IP
                            / \
                       John   I'
                            / \
     Spec/head agreement→ I°  VP
                            / \
                             V'
                            / \
                       loves  Mary
```

Within the Minimalist Program, the theta-relations must be established upon lexical insertion by the operation called Merge. Moreover, in this framework government is being eradicated as a primitive relation in grammar.

See also *Argument, C-command, Configurational vs. nonconfigurational language, Dependency relation, Merge, Modification, State of affairs* and *Theta-role*.

Governing Domain

Within Transformational Generative Grammar, anaphors, pronouns, and referential expressions corefer with their antecedent under certain structural configurations. These configurations must contain the coreferring element and a governor. More formally, it can be said that α (alfa) is the governing domain for β (beta, the coreferring element) iff α is the smallest IP (sentence) containing β and a governor of β. For example, consider (1):

(1) **Ann**$_i$ *loves* **herself**$_i$

In (1) the sentence contains *herself*, which is the coreferring object, and the governor, which is the verb *loves*. Thus, the whole sentence is the governing domain.

Governor

An item that governs another item. In Transformationl Generative Grammar government takes place under mutual c-command of the governor and the governee or by agreement of the phrase that is in the Spec of IP (Inflectional Phrase) and the head of IP.

See also *C-command* and *Government*.

Grammatical relation

A relation borne by a constituent with respect to the predicate of a sentence, to another constituent, or to the whole sentence. Grammatical relations include **subject** and **direct object**, also called core grammatical relations, **indirect object**, **oblique**, **complement**, and **adverbial** or **adjunct** (the terminology may vary). Core relations are those that belong to the nuclear predication, display more relevant morphosyntactic properties, and are assigned to constituents required by the verbal valency; their coding is relevant to the typology of alignment. Indirect object is sometimes included among core relations, sometimes not, partly depending on its coding, and partly because the way in which it is coded does not have a role in determining the alignment type of a specific language, which is rather determined by the way in which subject and object are coded.

In Lexical Functional Grammar, grammatical relations are called **grammatical functions**, while in S. C. Dik's Functional Grammar the term **syntactic functions** is used in very much the same way. In Relational Grammar, the grammatical relations subject, direct object, indirect object, and oblique are considered primitives, not to be further defined; the same is true of grammatical functions in Lexical Functional Grammar.

See also *Adjunct, Adverbial, Alignment, Complement, Direct object, Indirect object, Oblique, Subject,* and *Valency*.

Grammatical/ungrammatical

Grammatical or well-formed sentences or constructions conform to the rules of grammar and are accepted by native speakers. Ungrammatical sentences or constructions do not conform to the rules of grammar and are not accepted by native speakers. Ungrammatical sentences or constructions are marked with a preceding asterisk *. Grammatical sentences or constructions are also said to be well formed.

A well formed sentence is for example:

(1) *John eats apples*

Sentence (2) is syntactically ungrammatical:

(2) **John eat apples*

Sentence (2) is syntactically ungrammatical because there is lack of agreement between the subject and the verb.

In Transformational Generative Grammar, sentences are interpreted in semantic terms as well. Thus, they can be semantically grammatical or semantically ungrammatical. Sentence (3) is semantically ungrammatical:

(3) **the table eats stones*

Sentence (3) is semantically ungrammatical because a verb such as *eat* does not select (in a literal sense) an inanimate subject argument such as *the table*. This sentence, however, is syntactically well formed. Chomsky (1957) made famous the sentence *colorless green ideas sleep furiously* as an example of a syntactically grammatical sentence, which is semantically ungrammatical.

Note however that there is a fundamental difference between syntactically ungrammatical and semantically ungrammatical sentences. Indeed, a sentence like (3) can be given an acceptable interpretation if metaphor and metonymy are involved: for example, we can imagine a situation in which someone dressed up as a table at a Halloween party is eating stone-like candies. On the other hand, sentences which are syntactically ungrammatical, such as (2), can under no circumstances be considered acceptable. For this reason, in semantically oriented theories only syntactically ungrammatical sentences are considered real instances of ungrammaticality.

See also *Embedding*.

Grammaticalization

(a) The fact that a certain category or function is overtly encoded in a certain language, that is, that it is indicated by means of specific forms. Definiteness is grammaticalized with English NPs (English has a definite and an indefinite article), while it is not grammaticalized with Japanese NPs (Japanese has no articles); gender is highly grammaticalized in the Romance languages, in which all nouns belong to one of two genders, and trigger gender agreement with articles, adjectives, pronouns, and partly with compound verb forms, whereas it is grammaticalized only to a limited extent in English (it only appears on personal and possessive pronouns in the singular).

(b) A change, often defined as a process, by which a lexical item becomes a grammatical item. For example, the English indefinite article *a(n)* derived out of the numeral *one* through a grammaticalization process. As in this case, grammaticalization may have the consequence of creating new categories (articles did not exist in Proto-Germanic). Typically, before grammaticalization occurs, certain items occur in frequent collocations, which later constitute the basis for grammaticalization: for this reason, it is sometimes held that "today's morphology is yesterday's syntax," a statement formulated by Givón.

Often, through grammaticalization, free lexical items may become affixes: for example, the English suffix *-ly* of manner adverbs, whose cognates are found in other Germanic languages (e.g. German *-lich*), derives from a Proto-Germanic noun **lika* 'body', 'form'. Some inflectional endings can also be shown to derive from free lexemes, and many scholars would support Gabelentz' (1891) statement, according to which "Alle Afformativen waren ursprünglich selbständige Wörter" ("all bound morphemes were once independent words").

The idea that grammaticalization operates in languages has a long tradition, reaching back to Wilhelm von Humboldt, and research on this issue has its origin in Franz Bopp's *Agglutinationstheorie,* or agglutination theory. The term 'grammaticalization' was first used by Meillet in his seminal article of 1912. More recently, the study of grammaticalization processes has enjoyed a major revival, also based on data from non-Indo-European languages.

In some recent studies, the concept of grammaticalization has been broadened to include all cases whereby "lexical items and constructions come in certain linguistic contexts to serve grammatical functions or grammatical items develop new grammatical functions" (Hopper and Traugott 1993: xv and Traugott 1988), that is, not limited to morphosyntactic change. Following this approach, and focusing on semantic-pragmatic change in grammaticalization, grammaticalization is shown to often proceed along the following cline:

propositional > textual > expressive

This cline has been reformulated as three tendencies which involve (increasing) pragmatic strengthening, and in which the tendency toward expressiveness/subjectivity is the most prominent. In this framework, morphologization, that is, reduction and obligatorification of morphemes, may occur in grammaticalization, but it does not necessarily have to. Many examples of the extension from propositional to expressive function can be found in the use of connectives or adverbs. Consider for example English *indeed,* which can function as a sentential adverb, as in (1):

(1) *it was clear from the beginning that he would indeed be late*

or have an expressive function, as in (2):

(2) *I thought he was being extremely silly.*
    Indeed!

Another issue about grammaticalization is constituted by directionality. It is questionable that grammaticalization processes are indeed reversible, that is, that **degrammaticalization** processes also occur. In spite of existing evidence for degrammaticalization, it is often said that grammaticalization is unidirectional.

See also *Auxiliary*.

Grounding

Grounding is a property of discourse, and thus a feature of textuality, and refers to the communicative status of information. Information can be **foregrounded** if it is presented as focal and relevant, or **backgrounded** when it is either shared information, or presented as additional and less relevant. Typically, foregrounded information is encoded in main clauses, while subordinate clauses (mainly adverbial) convey backgrounded information.

Head

A head is an item that determines the category of the lowest phrase of which it is the nucleus. The items which depend on a head are called dependents. A head is usually a governor, and it selects some morphological features of the dependent. The expression in (1) is a noun phrase, because its nucleus is the noun *boy*; the attributive adjective *tall* and the attributive relative clause *who's coming toward us* are its dependents:

(1) *the tall boy who's coming toward us*

In (2) the head *Tag* selects nominative case, masculine gender, and singular number of the modifier *schöner*:

(2) *ein schöner*   *Tag*
     a   beautiful:NOM.M.SG day
     "a beautiful day" (German, Germanic, Indo-European)

(Note however that in the DP hypothesis the heads of the phrases in (1) and (2) are the determiners *the* and *ein*.)

This definition, that goes back to Bloomfield (1933), is not without problems. Not all head-dependent relations are the same: in some, the head requires the dependent (government), in others it does not (modification). Zwicky (1985) lists a number of conditions for headhood; some other conditions are given in Hudson (1987). Most problematic in this respect is the subject—VP relation, in which head properties appear to be distributed between the two: on the one hand, the VP is the governor, but on the other, it is the subject that selects agreement features (see Corbett, Fraser, and McGlashan 1993 for discussion).

In Government and Binding Theory, a phrase is a projection of a *head* or *nucleus*. For example, a verb phrase or VP is the projection of the head V. This is diagrammed in (3):

(3)   VP
                            / \
                        Spec   V'
                              / \
                             V ← *head or nucleus*

In the Minimalist Program, a head of a phrase is a syntactic element selected by **Merge** to form a syntactic structure.

In the terminology used in Bartsch and Vennemann (1972), the term **operand** is used, virtually as an equivalent of head.

See also *Dependency relation, Merge, Movement,* and *Selection.*

Head vs. dependent marking

Languages can be classified based on their tendency to mark a dependency relation between words or constituents on the head of the construction or on its modifiers or dependents. In the English NP *Mary's book*, *book* is the head and *Mary's* the dependent; the dependency relation is marked on the dependent by means of the clitic *'s*. The preposition *of* in *the door of the house* also marks the same type of relation on the dependent (the prepositional phrase *of the house*). In this respect, English is said to be a dependent marking language.

In head marking languages, instead, dependency relations are marked on the head:

(1) *a   tanító   könyv-e*
       the teacher book-POSS.3SG
       "the book of the teacher" (Hungarian, Finno-Ugric, Uralic)

In (1) the head noun *könyv* 'book' bears a third person possessive marker *-e* that refers to the dependent *a tanító* 'the teacher', which in turn has no markers. Another type of head marking strategy is the so-called **construct state**, typical of the Semitic languages:

(2) *pəne   ha 'areṣ*
       'face-CONSTR the earth
       "the face of the earth" (Biblical Hebrew, Semitic, Afro-Asiatic)

In (2) the dependency relation is coded on the head noun through accent shift (the normal form of the word for 'face' would be *panim*, which changes to *pəne* in the construct state).

Some languages mark dependency relations both on the head and on the dependent; they are called **double marking languages**. An example is Turkish:

(3) *Ahmed-in   hanım- ı*
Ahmed-GEN wife-POSS.3SG
"Ahmed's wife" (Turkish, Turkic, Altaic).

In (3) the head noun *hanım* is marked through the possessive suffix *-ı*, while the dependent bears the genitive suffix *-in*.
Another example of dependent marking is the occurrence of a case affix or a preposition on a complement of a verb:

(4) *b-ərešit   bara'   elohim et ha-ššamaim   wə   et   ha-'areṣ*
in-beginning create:PF God   OBJ the-heavens and OBJ the-earth
"In the beginning God created the heavens and the earth." *Genesis* 1.1 (Biblical Hebrew, Semitic, Afro-Asiatic)

In (4) the direct object marker **et** indicates the corresponding grammatical relation on the relevant NPs. The direct object is a dependent of the verb that governs it.
Languages may be head marking in this respect as well and mark the direct object (and other grammatical relations) on the verb as shown in:

(5) *zuhaitz-a ikusten d-u-t*
tree-ART   see   3SG-have-1SG
"I see the tree." (Basque, isolate)

In example (5), both the subject and the direct object are marked by affixes on the verb.
See also *Head*.

Host

A word or constituent with which a clitic item forms a unit, either phonologically (phonological host) or syntactically (syntactic host).
See also *Clitic*.

Hypotaxis see *Subordination*.

Immediate constituents

The constituents into which a superordinate construction can be divided, without leaving a further superordinate level in between. In (1):

(1) *the friend who came to my home yesterday bought me a wonderful present*

the two constituents *the friend who came to my home yesterday* and *bought me a wonderful present* are immediate constituents of the sentence, because there is no further level of constituency between them and the whole sentence.

See also *Constituent* and *Sentence*.

Inclusiveness Condition

Within the Minimalist Program, the Inclusiveness Condition disallows the possibility of introducing lexical elements absent in the numeration after the building process of a sentence has started. More formally this condition states what is included in (1):

(1) The LF (Logical Form) of sentential objects must be built only from the features of lexical items in N (Numeration).

Incorporation

A process by which a constituent—the object or some other complement or adverbial—adjoins to the verb and forms a compound word, retaining its original function, but not definiteness, as shown in example (1):

(1) a. *ni-c-qua   in   nacatl*
       1SUBJ-3OBJ-eat the flesh
       "I eat the flesh."
    b. *ni-naca-qua*
       1SUBJ-flesh-eat
       "I eat flesh." (Nahuatl, Uto-Aztecan, Central Amerind)

According to Sapir (1911), the difference between (1a) and (1b) lies in the fact that "the former means 'I eat the flesh' (a particular act), the latter 'I eat flesh, I am a flesh-eater'." In general, the function of incorporation is to background a scarcely individuated argument, as shown by the fact that arguments that rank high in animacy or definiteness usually do not undergo incorporation.

Incorporated forms are affixes, or clitics, or parts of compound words. Incorporation is mostly typical of polysynthetic languages, in which several arguments and adverbials can be incorporated into the verb, so that the compound verb form corresponds to a complete predication.

Isolated instances of incorporation are also known from more familiar languages, such as object incorporation (*baby*) in English *to baby-sit*. (Note that the English example shows that the incorporated noun is necessarily indefinite.) In Italian, adverbial modifiers that indicate location can be incorporated into verbs that express the action of putting something into a container: *imbottigliare* 'to bottle', *incorniciare* 'to frame', *inscatolare* 'to box', which can be seen as corresponding to *mettere in bottiglia, in cornice, in scatola* 'put into (a) bottle, frame, box'.

Indirect see *Semantic macro-role* and *Semantic role*.

Indirect object

The indirect object is the third argument of trivalent verbs such as *give* or *tell*, in addition to subject and direct object. Verbs that take an indirect object are a semantically quite homogeneous group, thus indirect objects mostly have human referents. In languages with cases, the indirect object is typically coded by the dative case. For this reason, the name 'dative' is sometimes used in place of 'indirect object', as in the case of the English **dative shift** construction:

(1) a. *Paul gave a present* ***to Susan***
    b. *Paul gave* ***Susan*** *a present*

In (1b) the indirect object is 'shifted', that is, it is placed before the direct object, and does not take the preposition *to*, but is encoded through its position only, in much the same way as the direct object. As is well known, such indirect objects can be passivized:

(1) c. ***Susan*** *was given a present by Paul*

Because they can take two arguments with (at least partial) direct object properties, verbs such as *give* are also called **ditransitive** or **bitransitive** (however, it must be noted that in some terminologies 'ditransitive' is a synonym of 'trivalent').

See also *Argument, Direct object, Transitivity,* and *Valency.*

Interpretable features

Within the Minimalist Program, **interpretable features** have an effect on semantic interpretation. For example, **Phi-features (Φ-features)** are interpretable. Phi-features are: person, number, and gender. Interpretable features are motivated by semantic and morphological facts. Interpretable features participate in multiple checking relations. Uninterpretable features are deleted after checking. The agreement relation of subjects and verbs ensures that a subset of Phi-features on subjects agrees with the features of the verbs. Uninterpretable or [–interpretable] features acquire their value in the course of the derivation. The operation Agree assigns values to unvalued features for morphological reasons and at the same time it deletes uninterpretable features due to Logical Form (LF) requirements. Only [+interpretable] features are fully specified in the lexicon by **Lexical Redundancy Rules**.

See also *Lexical redundancy rules* and *Uninterpretable features.*

Island constraint

An island is a domain that does not allow extraction. For example, **wh-island** is a constraint that blocks wh-movement in (1), while complex NP constraint blocks wh-movement out of an NP island in (2):

(1) **what$_j$ did Ann wonder who$_i$ would eat t$_i$ t$_j$?*
(2) ***who$_i$ did Mary make the claim that she saw t$_i$ at the theater?*

The restrictions on extractability are often designated as **Island conditions**. Thus, the example in (1) is a case of **wh-island Condition**, and the example in (2) is case of **Complex Noun Phrase Condition**. Most of the islands were discovered by Ross (1967).

Kernel sentence see *Classical Transformational Generative Theory* and *Sentence*.

Last Resort Condition

In the Minimalist Program, **Last Resort** is a condition on movement. It is one of the Global Conditions, together with Procrastinate (elements in the sentence move the least possible) and Greed (elements in the sentence move for their own benefit only). According to the Last Resort Condition, transformations must be driven by the need to check a feature. This condition allows the elimination of **unintepretable features.**

See also *Uninterpretable features*.

Lexical redundancy rules

Lexical redundancy rules state general properties of lexical entries. In the Minimalist Program, lexical redundancy rules divide formal features into two types: **interpretable** or **[+interpretable]** and **uninterpretable** or **[–interpretable]** features. Usually, the Phi-features of a verb are [–interpretable] and the Phi-features of the arguments of a verb are [+interpretable].

See also *Interpretable features* and *Uninterpretable features*.

Light verb

Light verbs are thematically incomplete verbs which must combine with a complement (noun or verb) to qualify as a predicate. Light verbs have little semantic content, but they usually provide aspect, mood or tense to the predicate through inflection. The semantics and the argument structure of the compound light verb + complement are determined by the head or primary component of the compound, which may be a verb or a noun. Thus, the meaning and argument structure of light verbs heavily depend on the meaning of their complements. In English, light verb constructions usually have nouns as complements, for example *take a nap* 'to nap', *give a kiss* 'to kiss', *take a walk* 'to walk', *have a rest*, 'to rest'. Some researchers such as Dixon (1991) analyze the complement of the light verbs *give a*, *take a,* and *have a* as verb roots, rather than nouns. In Japanese, light verbs such as *suru* 'do' combine with a noun to form a predicate. From a historical point of view, light verbs have lost some of their original semantics through bleaching, and they can become auxiliary verbs, clitics, and even affixes.

Chomsky (1995) suggests that the light verb is a functional category present in VP structures. Within the Minimalist Program, a light verb is formalized as a lower case light **v⁰** head that projects a light **vP** phrase and has a VP lexical complement. The verbal structure of a ditransitive sentence such as (1) has a light verb structure as shown in (2):

(1) *John gave a ball to Mary*

(2)

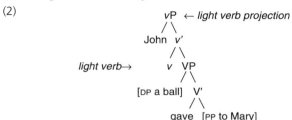

When the light verb has a strong verbal feature, the content verb head V (*gave* in (2)) adjoins to the head of the light verb vP as in (3):

(3)

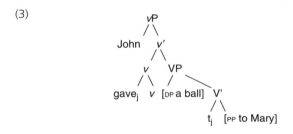

Some **serial verb** constructions, such as the one in (4), can be analyzed as involving an overtly realized light verb (*yñá*), as shown in (5):

(4) *Aémmaá yñá adwuáma maá Kofä*
    Amma do   work   give Kofi
    "Amma works for Kofi." (Akan, Kwa, Niger-Congo)

(5)
```
                    vP
                   / \
            Aemmaá   v'
                    / \
                  yña   VP
                       / \
                adwuáma   V'
                         / \
                       maa   Kofä
```

The light verb structure has been generalized to all sentence types as an extension projection of VP because it allows to better formalize ditransitive, unaccusative, unergative, and transitive structures as well as the external subject.

See also *Coverb* and *Serial verb*.

Locality

In Transformational Generative Grammar it is crucially assumed that syntactic relations are local. That is, whether syntactic relations are base generated or the result of movement, their length of distance is limited. Within the Government and Binding Theory, binding, government, and minimality are centered on locality conditions. In the Minimalist Program, Chomsky (1995) states that all relations between elements should be local, for example, Spechead agreement, head to head relations, the internal domain, the checking domain. The minimal domain (formed from the conjunction of the internal domain and the checking domain) is used to define the distance of movements, that is, locality.

Logical Form (LF)

In the Government and Binding framework, Logical Form or LF is an interface level, together with PF or Phonetic Form, D-structure (Deep structure), and S-structure (Surface structure). Logical Form, as a level of syntactic representations, is subject to the principles of syntax such as the Projection Principle and the Empty Category Principle. It includes the information required to assign semantic interpretation to a sentence. Some researchers claim that Binding Theory applies at LF. In the Minimalist Program it has been proposed that some pleonastic or meaningless elements must be eliminated at the level of LF because they have no semantic interpretation. LF and PF are the grammatical inputs to the Conceptual-Intentional and Articulatory-Perceptual systems. They are obligatory levels of natural languages since they represent phonetic form and meaning.

See also *Articulatory-Perceptual systems* and *Conceptual and Intentional properties*.

Logophor

A term used to account for cases in which an anaphor corefers with an element outside its binding domain in a grammatical sentence, violating principle A of Binding Theory in examples such as (1):

(1) *John thinks that there is a picture of himself in the White House*

In example (1) *John* and *himself* logophorically corefer outside their binding domain since each of them belongs to a different binding domain and the sentence is grammatical.

More in general, a logophor is an anaphora with no proper antecedent in the sentence, but rather with a discourse antecedent.

See also *Binding* and *Binding domain*.

Matrix

The governing clause of another clause. A matrix clause is not the same as a main clause: a main clause is independent, while a matrix clause can itself be the dependent of another superordinate clause.

See also *Subordination*.

Merge

Within the Minimalist Program, **Merge** is a recursive structure-building or grammatical operation that puts lexical items together into phrasal structures that comply with X-bar theory. It combines at least two lexical items in order to form a constituent. The lexical items are positioned in the **Numeration**. Merge proceeds from bottom to top. Theta-role assignment and movement take place under Merge.

See also *Numeration, Theta-role*, and *X-bar theory*.

Modification

A type of dependency relation which, contrary to government, is not obligatory. In a relation of modification, an item, called the **modifier**, modifies another item, which is the head of the construction, by restricting its reference. In (1) both the attributive adjective *pretty* and the relative clause *who came yesterday* are modifiers of the head noun *girl*:

(1) the **pretty** girl **who came yesterday**

Modifiers are not obligatory, as shown by the fact that they can be left out, and still leave a grammatical construction: *the girl*. In this respect, modifiers contrast with governed items, which cannot be left out. For example, the complement of a preposition, which is a governed item, cannot be left out: *at noon* / **at*.

See also *Dependent* and *Government*.

Modifier see *Modification*.

Move alfa or Move α

In the Government and Binding theory, **move** α is a term for movement. It is used to refer to any type of movement from one place to another place in a syntactic tree. In this framework, even if movement is free, there are restrictions to the positions to which each element can be moved. Movement is constrained by general, not by rule-specific principles.

See also *Movement*.

Movement

In Transformational Generative Grammar since the publication of *Aspects* (Chomsky 1965) up till the Minimalist Program, movement transformations were assumed to relate the two levels of syntactic representation (D-structure and S-structure) to each other. Elements which originate in some position at D-structure are moved elsewhere at S-structure. Schematically, this looks like the figure in (1):

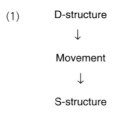

(1)   D-structure
              ↓
          Movement
              ↓
          S-structure

This means that expressions that appear in one position at D-structure can appear in another position at S-structure. Only heads (X°) and maximal projections (XP) can be moved. They move to specific landing sites. For example, a head of a projection must move to another head position. This is called **head-to-head-movement**. In English the head of the Inflectional Phrase (IP) moves to the head of the Complementizer Phrase (CP) in questions, as is shown in (2) and (3):

(2) DS: *you **will** go* → SS: ***will** you go?*
(3) *[$_{CP}$**will**$_i$ [$_{IP}$ you **t**$_i$ go?]]*

A Maximal Projection XP, such as wh or NP, is moved to a Spec position, which is a landing site for XP.

In the Government and Binding Theory, movement is free, but principles that regulate **traces** constrain the overgeneration produced by free movement due to **Move** α.

In the Minimalist Program, movement has a different function, due to the eradication of the two levels of D-structure and S-structure. However, due to **Procrastinate**, movement occurs only if it is necessary and as late as possible. Movement is driven by the need to check features. If features are strong, they must be checked by overt movement. If features are weak, they need to be checked covertly, at Logical Form. Moreover, movement can apply while building a sentence through **Merge.** Movement is the conjunction of the operations copy/move and Merge. Thus, whatever principles apply to Merge alone, hold when movement (Merge and copy/move) takes place.

See also *Copy, Covert movement, Merge, Move alpha*, and *Overt movement*.

Node

Nodes are sets of points that form a Phrase Marker or tree. Each pair of nodes in a Phrase Marker is related by **precedence** or **dominance**. Every node carries a label. A node *cannot* both precede and dominate another node. Consider the following phrase marker in (1):

(1)

In (1) the nodes have the labels S, NP, Aux, and VP. S (sentence) dominates (in fact immediately dominates) NP, Aux, and VP, and NP precedes Aux, which precedes VP. A node is a **mother** of another node if it immediately dominates it. A node is the **daughter** of another node if it is immediately dominated by that node. A set of nodes are **sisters** if they are immediately dominated by the same mother node. Thus, in (1) S is the mother of NP, Aux, and VP; NP, Aux, and VP are daughters of S; NP, Aux, and VP are sisters.

NP-Movement

This operation moves a DP/NP element from a theta-position to an A-position for it to be assigned Case. Such movement occurs in passive constructions, in raising constructions (to subject and object), with VP internal subjects and unaccusative verbs. This movement leaves in situ a coindexed NP trace or copy that forms a chain together with the moved head. The NP trace is an anaphor; thus it is subject to principle A of Binding Theory. The following constructions are instances of NP movement:

(1) *[ₗₚ the thieves, were [ᵥₚ captured tᵢ*
    by the police]]   (passive)
(2) *[ₗₚ John, seems [ₗₚ tᵢ to have*
    travelled around the world]]   (raising to subject)
(3) *[ₗₚ Silvia believed himᵢ [ᵥₚ tᵢ to have*
    a fortune]]   (object raising)

(4) $[_{IP}$ Mary$_i$ $[_{VP}$ t$_i$ loves John]]   (VP internal subject)
(5) $[_{IP}$ Gianni$_i$ è $[_{VP}$ arrivato t$_i$]]   (unaccusative verb subject)

See also *Raising* and *Voice*.

NP-trace see *Binding, Copy,* and *Trace*.
Nominative-accusative languages see *Alignment*.

Nucleus

(a) A part of a construction that determines its status: a head is the nucleus of a phrase or constituent.
(b) The nucleus of a predication is the inner part of the core, and it is constituted by the verb. Some authors use nucleus as synonym of core.

See also *Core, Head, Sentence,* and *Valency*.

Null argument

An argument of a predicate that can be omitted but is in some way recoverable. Frequently occurring null arguments are null subjects and null objects. Languages that allow null arguments are called **null subject/null object languages**, or **pro-drop languages**. Various Romance languages, such as Italian and Spanish, are null subject languages:

(1) *vado   a casa*
     go:PRS.1SG to home
     "I go home." (Italian, Romance, Indo-European)

Portuguese is both a null subject and a null object language:

(2) *vi   uma   roupa bonita e   Ø comprei*
     see:1SG.PRET a   dress pretty and buy:1SG.PRET
     "I saw a pretty dress and bought it." (Portuguese, Romance, Indo-European)

Null subject language see *Null argument*.

Numeration

In the Minimalist Program the **Numeration** contains the lexical atoms or constituents that will feed the **computational system**. It is the starting point where certain lexical items are put together specifying the number of instances that each particular lexical item will be used in the computation (derivation). It is abbreviated as **(LI i)**, which means *Lexical Item* and *index*. For example the items in (1) have the numeration shown in (2):

(1) *the boy ate the apples*
(2) N = {*the$_1$, boy$_1$, ate$_1$, apples$_1$ <tense$_1$>*}

See also *Computational system*.

Object see *Direct object.*

Oblique

(a) The grammatical relation borne by an adjunct, or by an argument other than subject or direct object, especially when overtly marked. In English, indirect objects are considered obliques when they are marked by the preposition *to*, as in (1):

(1) *I gave a book* **to my brother**

while they are considered core arguments in the dative shift construction, in which they are marked by word order only, in much the same way as subjects and direct objects (i.e. core arguments):

(2) *I gave* **my brother** *the book*

(b) Oblique case: a case other than the nominative or vocative.

See also *Argument, Grammatical relation*, and *Sentence.*

Operand see *Head.*

Operator

A quantifier or a wh-phrase that A-bar binds a variable (x) at Logical Form, as in (1b) and (2b):

(1) a. *John hates someone*
    b. *LF:* **someone x***, John hates* **x**
(2) a. *who does John hate?*
    b. *LF:* **for which x***, John hates* **x**

In semantics an operator is prefixed to a formula to produce a new formula. Negation operates on a truth value of the proposition.

In the terminology used in Bartsch and Vennemann (1972), operator corresponds to dependent.

Overt movement

In Government and Binding theory, **overt movement** takes place from D-structure to S-structure. That is, **overt movement** is movement in syntax, for example wh-movement and I movement in a sentence such as (1):

(1) $[_{CP}$ **what**$_i$ **will**$_j$ $[_{IP}$ you t_j $[_{VP}$ eat t_i ?$]]]$

In the Minimalist Program, strong features must be checked by **overt movement** before the grammar splits into Phonetic Form (PF) and Logical Form (LF).

See also *Covert movement, Feature strength*, and *Movement*.

P2 (Second position)

P2 or second position is a position in a sentence which is relevant for the placement of certain elements, typically clitics; in V2 (verb second) languages it is the position of the finite verb.

Depending on the language, P2 indicates either the position after the first accented word, or after the first accented constituent. The relevance of P2 was first acknowledged by Wackernagel in 1892, when he described what later became known as 'Wackernagel's Law' in a number of Indo-European languages, notably Old Indic and Homeric Greek. In such languages, clitics are placed in P2, and P2 is most often the position after the first accented word, which means that the occurrence of clitics may split up constituents. Later the same placement rule for clitics has been detected in some non-Indo-European languages, such as Warlpiri (Hale 1973) and Tagalog (Anderson 2005).

P2 clitics are usually pronouns, modality particles, or auxiliaries, whose structural host is most often the verb; furthermore, sentence particles and conjunctions may also occur in P2, which is the leftmost accessible position for enclitics (such items have the whole sentence as their host, and are placed at its left border, see Luraghi 1990). The finite verb of main clauses was unaccented in some ancient Indo-European languages, most notably Old Indic; Wackernagel took this as evidence for the V2 phenomenon as being related to prosodic features of the verb.

The occurrence of P2 clitics inside constituents has been taken as evidence for nonconfigurationality in the relevant languages. Indeed, the fact that some Indo-European languages exhibit an increasing tendency for P2 to be located after the first constituent, rather than after the first accented word, can be taken as evidence for the emergency of constituency.

P2 is also relevant for the position of the verb in V2 languages, such as German, where P2 is located after the first constituent, rather than after the first word (which is consistent with the fact that German and related V2 languages are configurational).

It is questionable that the occurrence of clitics in P2 and the V2 phenomenon are related to each other, as Wackernagel thought (see Anderson 2005: 177–225).

See also *Clitic, Configurational vs. nonconfigurational languages,* and *V2*.

Parameter

Notion in the theory of Universal Grammar (UG) and language acquisition. Parameters specify certain options that are not specified in UG. The values of parameters are not genetically fixed. Thus, language acquisition becomes a process of parameter setting.

Linguistic diversity is characterized in terms of the values of parameters, for example the null subject parameter. Certain languages such as Italian and Spanish may have sentences with no overt subject, while other languages such as English must have an overt subject, even in cases in which this is non-referential (dummy subject). Parameter theory, thus, provides an explanation for systematic syntactic variation between languages and imposes restrictions on the number of choices which the language learner has to make.

See also *Null argument* and *Pro or little pro*.

Parameter setting

In Transformational Generative Grammar it is proposed that a child, during language acquisition, sets certain language specific options (parameters) available in UG (Universal Grammar). For example, the head parameter, which explains sentence word order, can be head-first, as in English, or head-last, as in Japanese. That is, in English the head of a construction precedes its complement, as in (1), where the verb precedes its complement. In Japanese, the head of a construction follows its complement, as in (2), where the verb follows its complement:

(1) *Taroo*   *read*   *the book*
               HEAD   COMPLEMENT
(2) *Taroo ga*   *hon o*   *yonda*
    Taroo SUBJ   book OBJ   read
               COMPLEMENT   HEAD

"Taroo read the book." (Japanese, Japanese)

Parameter setting restricts the options that a language learner has to make. In the Minimalist Program morphology is the main locus of parametrization. Variation depends on the lexicon, which is language-specific and has to be learned. However, the computational system is innate and it does not have to be learned. Languages vary with respect to having certain particular functional categories and certain weak or strong features in the lexicon.

See also *Parameter* and *UG*.

Parataxis

The term 'parataxis' derives from Greek *paratássein* 'to place side by side', and refers to the placing together of syntactically independent sentences. Parataxis contrasts with subordination, also called 'hypotaxis', from Greek *hupotássein* 'to place below, to subordinate'. Paratactically constructed sentences may or may not include connectives (syndetic parataxis o asyndetic parataxis). The latter is illustrated in (1):

(1) *veni,*   *vidi,*   *vici*
come:PRET.1SG see:PRET.1SG conquer:PRET.1SG
"I came, I saw, I conquered." Suetonius, *De Vita Caesarum, Iul.* 37.1
(Latin, Italic, Indo-European)

As example (1) and (2a) illustrate, paratactically ordered clauses are iconically ordered, that is, they must mirror the order of the events, whereas subordination allows noniconic order as shown in (2b):

(2) a. *I read the recipe and baked the cake ≠ I baked the cake and read the recipe*
b. *I read the recipe before baking the cake = before baking the cake I read the recipe*

Note that coordinated sentences are usually treated as instances of parataxis, as opposed to subordination, even though, strictly speaking, they cannot be said to be paratactically constructed, since they are connected by a coordinator, and consequently build a single syntactic unit.

See also *Coordination* and *Subordination*.

Parsing

In computational linguistics, analysis of sentence and constituent structure.

Participant

A referential entity which takes part in an event in the real world. Participants are typically referred to by NPs. In example (1):

(1) *Little Red Riding Hood met the wolf*

the NPs *Little Red Riding Hood* and *the wolf* refer to two participants, a girl named 'Little Red Riding Hood' and a wolf, which are involved in an event or state of affairs referred to by the verb *met*. The role of participants in an event is linguistically mirrored by the semantic roles of NPs.

See also *Semantic role* and *State of affairs*.

Part of speech

Parts of speech or **syntactic categories** are classes of lexical items that display the same morphosyntactic behavior. They can be divided into open classes, such as nouns and verbs, and closed classes. Open classes can be enlarged (new nouns or new verbs can be created without causing a change in the grammar of a language), while closed classes cannot, unless a change in the grammar also occurs. Closed classes are constituted by items that have mostly grammatical function, such as pronouns, articles, prepositions, subordinators, etc.

Other possible definitions of parts of speech may be discourse based, or may reflect their referential properties.

While the parts of speech system of the Indo-European languages is often taken for granted, it is far from being universal: typologically different languages may present quite different parts of speech systems.

Commonly found lexical classes are the following:

Noun (also called substantives). Nouns may inflect for number and case and be organized in noun classes (or genders); they prototypically indicate static entities, such as concrete objects or living beings, and are prototypically referential; their most frequent syntactic function is to serve as arguments of predicates and to head constituents. Nouns can be definite or indefinite; in some languages this feature is mirrored by the fact that they may occur with articles. In Cognitive Grammar, nouns and other nominal categories are "symbolic structure[s] whose semantic pole profiles a thing" (Langacker 1987: 491). In a discourse definition of parts of speech (e.g. Hopper and Thompson 1984, Thompson 1988, Croft 1991), nouns "specify what we are talking about" (Croft 1991: 109). A distinction must be made between common and proper nouns, the latter being personal names, names of cities and countries, names of particular landmarks, etc. Proper nouns differ from common nouns in that they have unique reference. Based on their semantic properties, nouns can be divided into concrete (*table, book*) and abstract (*love, departure*), mass (*milk, water*) and count (*book, boy*), animate (*boy, mother*), and inanimate (*table, stone*).

Verb.   Verbs may inflect for tense, aspect, modality, voice, and some agreement categories, such as person, number, and gender; prototypically, they indicate dynamic entities, such as actions or processes, but can also indicate states; their usual syntactic function is to serve as predicates of clauses. In Cognitive Grammar a verb is "a symbolic structure whose semantic pole profiles a process" (Langacker 1987: 494). In discourse-based approaches, verbs specify what we are saying about something. Verbs have valency: they may be transitive, intransitive, or ditransitive. Based on their lexical aspect, or *Aktionsart,* they may indicate various types of events or states of affairs, such as states (*know, love*) or activities (*walk, sleep, smoke*).

Adjective.   Adjectives may inflect for the same categories as nouns, including gender (typically, in languages that have systems of nominal classification, gender is inherent in nouns, while it is inflectional in adjectives). Adjectives may indicate degrees of comparison. They prototypically indicate qualities, and most frequently serve as attributes of nouns. Another frequent function of adjectives is to serve as predicates. For this reason they are sometimes grouped with verbs in functionally based classifications of parts of speech, while in morphologically based ones they are considered part of nominals (nouns and pronouns).

Pronoun.   The word pronoun indicates that items in this word class usually 'stand for nouns': in fact, pronouns have the same distributional properties of noun phrases but do not have a lexical meaning. Their reference is indicated either by a noun that they stand for (called antecedent), in which case they are said to be anaphoric, or by extra-linguistic factors when they refer to an entity external to the text and function as deictics. Pronouns may be inflected for number, case, and gender; personal pronouns, which are partly deictic (*I, you*), partly anaphoric (*he*) also indicate person.

Adverb.   Adverbs modify verbs, adjectives, and clauses; they may inflect for degrees of comparison. Semantically there are several types of adverbs: manner adverbs (*slowly, eagerly*), adverbs of place (*there*), adverbs of time (*yesterday*), etc.

Determiner. Determiners determine or specify nouns in various ways. There are different types of determiners: articles, demonstrative adjectives, quantifiers, possessive adjectives. Articles are a device that languages may use for indicating definiteness of nouns: *the cat* (definite) vs. *a cat* (indefinite). Articles may agree with nouns and inflect for the same inflectional categories, as in the Romance languages. Numerals can be used as determiners, as in *two books*.

Preposition. Prepositions are particles that must necessarily take a noun or a pronoun as their complement and indicate the noun's grammatical relation or semantic role, as *to me* (*to* is the indirect object marker), *in the box* (*in* indicates location). They owe their name to the fact that they come before nouns and pronouns, as in English and most other Indo-European languages; however, several languages have **postpositions** (as Turkish *kız ile* 'girl with' = 'with a girl'), that is to say, particles that occur after nouns or pronouns. A cover term for both pre- and postpositions is **adposition**.

Conjunction. Conjunctions indicate that a certain unit is connected with another unit, and belong to several types: coordinative, subordinative, and sentence connectors. Coordinative conjunctions have the function to connect two syntactic units of the same type and indicate that they build a single unit with the same function; subordinative conjunctions or subordinators indicate the subordinate status of a given clause (like *if*, *that*, etc.); sentence connectors, such as *thus* or *however*, connect sentences and indicate their status in discourse.

Numeral. Numerals indicate numbers. In spite of numbers being infinite, numerals constitute a closed class, because languages usually exhibit some form of recursivity for their formation (as in *twenty*, *twenty one*, *thirty*, *thirty one*, and so on).

Classifier. Classifiers are lexical items found in certain languages, such as Chinese and Japanese, which help classify NPs based on their reference, often in connection with quantification. In (1):

(1) *3-nin   no seito*
     three-CLASS of student
     "three students" (Japanese, Japanese)

nin is the classifier for human beings, and it occurs when human beings are counted. An English parallel is constituted by measure words, such as *bottle* in *two bottles of beer*, or *head* in *ten heads of cattle*.

Other parts of speech include auxiliary verbs, negators, interjections, particles (the latter often being employed as a catch-all category). Open classes in English are nouns, verbs, adjectives, and adverbs, but this is not true of the same classes in all languages: for example, in some languages adjectives constitute a closed class (see Dixon 1977).

The term 'part of speech' is a calque of Latin *partes orationis*, which in turn is a translation of Greek *méroi toû lógou*, and betrays its origin as being function based: indeed, the earliest division of parts of speech was between *ónoma* and *rhêma*, roughly nouns and predicates, and the words *lógos* and *oratio* referred to discourse. In this classification, used by Plato and Aristotle, nouns were defined as what is being talked about, and predicates as what is being said about nouns, in much the same way as in today's functional definitions (indeed, Aristotle's *Rhetorics* was not a treatise on grammatical description, but rather on the structure of discourse). The definition at the beginning of this article, based on morphosyntactic properties of lexical classes, has been worked out later by grammarians with a Greek and especially Latin background; for this reason it presents idiosyncratic features connected with the Indo-European languages. Modern linguistic typology tries to switch back to discourse-based definitions in an attempt to work out a model that can also account for non-Indo-European languages, which may have very different parts of speech systems.

See also *Animacy, Auxiliary, Coordination, State of affairs, Transitivity,* and *Valency*.

Passive see *Voice*.

Percolation

Mechanism that copies the properties of a head to the node that immediately dominates it. For example, in a compound word such as *understand*, the feature [+abl] (ablaut) in *stand* percolates to the compound *understand*, as shown in (1):

(1)
```
                    V
                [+abl] ← percolation
                /  \
              P     V
           under  stand
                  [+abl]
```

The past of *stand* is *stood*, the same way that the past of *understand* is *understood*.

Periphery

The part of a sentence that does not belong to the core or nucleus of the predication. All constituents that are not required by the verbal valency are peripheral constituents. For example in (1):

(1) *Jane ate apples **in the park***

the constituent *in the park* is peripheral.
   See also *Adjunct, Adverbial*, and *Nucleus*.

Phase

In the Minimalist Program, phase is a part of a derivation where convergence (well-formedness) is inspected. Each sentence has two phases, vP and CP. Once a phase has been checked, its role in the syntactic derivation is finished; it does not participate in other syntactic computations, complying with the **Phase Impenetrability Condition**.
   See also *Convergence* and *Phase Impenetrability Condition*.

Phase Impenetrability Condition (PIC)

This condition does not allow reconsidering the situation of a phase after it has been inspected, excluding the head and its edges, as is shown in (1):

(1) In a phase A with head H, the domain of H is not accessible to operations outside A, only H (head) and its edge are accessible to such operation. (Chomsky 2001)

Consider example (2):

(2) [$_{CP}$ Who [do you think [$_{CP}$ ~~who~~ left]]?

   In (2) the Spec of the lower CP is an edge that allows moving *who*, the subject of the verb *left* to the next upper phase.

Phonetic Form (PF)

In the Government and Binding framework, Phonetic Form (PF) is an interface level, together with Logical Form (LF). PF is the information that is required to assign phonetic interpretation to a sentence. Within the Minimalist Program, PF and LF are the inputs to the Conceptual-Intentional System and the Articulatory-Perceptual System. They are obligatory levels of natural languages since they represent phonetic form and meaning.

See also *Articulatory-Perceptual System* and *Conceptual and Intentional properties*.

Phrase

Phrases are groups of words or constituents that form a syntactic unit other than a sentence or a clause. There are various types of phrases, depending on their head: noun phrase (NP) as in *happy **girl***, verb phrases (VP) as in ***drink** milk*, adjective phrases (AP) as in *very **nice***, adverbial phrases (AdvP) as in ***slowly***, and prepositional (PP) as in ***for** you*.

Within Transformational Generative Grammar, lexical and functional heads project into phrases. Lexical phrases have semantic content; they are projections of nouns, verbs, adjectives, and adverbs. Functional phrases do not have semantic content; they are projections of complementizer, agreement, tense. Lexical and functional phrases such as CP (complementizer phrase), IP (inflectional phrase), DP (determiner phrase), VP (verb phrase), NP (noun phrase) etc. have the same X-bar structure:

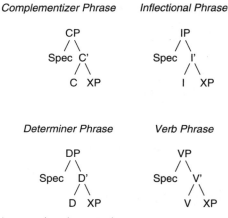

(For DP projection as a head, see DP.)

See also *Constituent, Phrase structure rules,* and *X-bar theory*.

Phrase Structure rules (or constituent structure rule)

The basic notions of category and constituency in sentences are given by phrase structure rules (PS rules). Phrase structure rules specify the constituents of a sentence in terms of rewriting rules. For example, the phrase structure rules in (1) generate a sentence such as:

(1) *the girl will eat the apples very fast*
   (1)

$$S \rightarrow \quad NP\text{-}Aux\text{-}VP$$

$$VP \rightarrow \quad V\text{-}NP\text{-}AdvP$$

$$AdvP \rightarrow \quad Deg\text{-}Adv$$

$$NP \rightarrow \quad Det\text{-}N$$

(Adv=Adverb, AdvP=Adverbial Phrase, Aux=Auxiliary, Deg=Degree, Det=Determiner, N=Noun, NP=Noun Phrase, S=Sentence, V=Verb, VP=Verb Phrase.)

The Phrase Structure rules specify a structure to be diagrammed. The resulting diagram is called a **phrase marker** or tree. The diagram in (2) is the abbreviated phrase marker of sentence (1) (the triangles indicate there is missing structure):

(2)

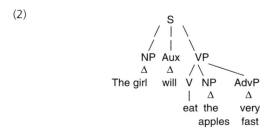

PS rules were commonly assumed in early versions of Transformational Generative Grammar. However, they project a flat structure because they do not allow to distinguish the position of complements from the position of adjuncts in the tree, as being different levels of structure. Thus, the strings *eat the apples very fast* and *eat the apples* would come from the same node (VP).

The separation is possible only with an X-bar structure, which adds more layers to the VP node and allows separating formally the verb and the object from the adverbial phrase or adjunct by means of two V-bars. Thus, Phrase Structure rules were abandoned and substituted by X-bar phrases in Transformational Generative Grammar.

See also *X-bar theory*.

Pivot

In Role and Reference Grammar, the pivot is the privileged syntactic constituent which triggers various morphosyntactic processes, for example, it governs anaphora. In languages such as English, the subject functions as pivot, while in others the pivot is a constituent with a specific semantic role (e.g. actor), rather than a certain grammatical relation. Pivots of the former type are syntactic pivots, while pivots of the second type are semantic pivots.

See also *Subject*.

Postposition see *Part of speech*.

Pragmatic function

The function determined by the communicative status of a constituent. In S. C. Dik's Functional Grammar, focus, topic, theme, and tail are said to be pragmatic functions of constituents.

For Croft (1991), pragmatic functions are externally motivated functions of syntactic categories. Following this approach, the pragmatic function of nouns is reference, the pragmatic function of verbs is predication, and the pragmatic function of adjectives is modification.

Predicate

A predicate is an item that indicates a property of an entity or a relation among entities. In (1):

(1) *Claudia **is tired***

the predicate *to be tired* indicates a property of Claudia. In (2):

(2) *the boy **ate** the apple*

the predicate *eat* indicates a relation between the boy and the apple.

A predicate is said to have a valency, and the items required by its valency are called the predicate's arguments: thus in (1) the NP *Claudia* is an argument of the predicate *be tired*, and in (2) the NPs *the boy* and *the apple* are arguments of the predicate *eat*. Based on the number of arguments they take, a distinction can be made among one-place predicates, two-place predicates, etc. The predicate's valency is also called **predicate frame** or **argument structure**, depending on the theoretical approach.

Predicates are not only verbs or phrases that contain verbs; they may also be other parts of speech. For example, prepositions are also predicates. In the NP:

(3) *the cat **on** the mat*

on is a predicate that indicates the relation between the cat and the mat.

According to another current definition, the predicate is one of the two main parts of a sentence or predication, and it is defined as what is being said (or predicated) about the subject. In this sense, the predicate in (2) is the whole VP *ate an apple*, because this is what is being said about the subject *the boy*.

English predicates in the latter sense are VPs: they either contain a verb (verbal predicates) or a nominal form, called the predicate noun (sometimes also subject complement) and a form of the verb *be*, called copula. In several other languages nouns and other nominals, such as adjectives, can function as predicates without a copular form. These are true nominal predicates:

(4) *omina   praeclara   rara*
    all:N/A.PL distinguished:N/A.PL rare:N/A.PL
    "All distinguished things are rare." Cicero, *Laelius* 21.79 (Latin, Italic, Indo-European)

In some languages both nouns and adjectives can function as predicates without the copula, while in others, such as Chinese, adjectives do not require a copula while nouns do.

See also *Argument, Copula,* and *Valency*.

Predication

A construction containing an item that is being talked about and a second item that tells something about the first. A sentence is a predication.

In subject-prominent languages, the item that is being talked about is usually the subject, while in topic-prominent languages it is the topic. What is being said about the subject/topic is called the predicate.

See also *Predicate, Sentence, Subject,* and *Topic.*

PRO or big PRO

In Transformational Generative Grammar the nonovert or null subject of nonfinite verbs, such as infinitives and gerunds, is syntactically represented in a sentence. This nonovert or null subject is called PRO (big PRO). Within the Binding Theory framework, PRO has the features [+anaphor, +pronominal]; however, these features have been questioned lately within the Minimalist Program. When PRO has an antecedent in the immediately dominating clause, it is said that PRO is referentially dependent or controlled by such antecedent, usually a DP/NP subject or object. In sentence (1) *Mary* is the antecedent or controller of PRO:

(1) *Mary$_i$ went to the store PRO$_i$ to buy a book*

In (1) Mary is the subject of the main and the subordinate clause. When PRO does not have an antecedent—typically when the clause with the nonfinite verb is in subject position or when it is in an indirect question—it is said that PRO is not controlled. In these cases, PRO has an arbitrary or generic interpretation, and it is called PRO$_{arb}$, as in example (2):

(2) *PRO$_{arb}$ to play ball in the classroom would be inappropriate*

In the subject clause in (2) the PRO$_{arb}$ has the generic meaning 'anyone' or 'everybody' and has an independent theta-role (agent). In (1), for example, *Mary* is the goer (to the store) and the buyer (of the book), which are two different roles that *Mary* undertakes. The presence of a theta-role is one of the differences with the subjects of **raising verbs**, such as *seem*, that have only one theta-role. Within the Government and Binding Theory, PRO was said to be ruled by the PRO Theorem (PRO must be ungoverned). However, since its syntactic configuration is not different from that of a subject of a finite verb, as is shown in (3a) and (3b), the PRO Theorem was not justified.

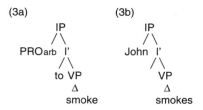

Chomsky and Lasnik (1993) solved the issue by claiming that PRO must be Case-marked by a null case, which is assigned by a nonfinite I, the head of Inflectional Phrase (IP), in terms of Spec/head agreement. This change has been adopted within the Minimalist Program framework. Thus, Government is removed from Universal Grammar (UG) and PRO is explained within a unified and homogeneous account of subjects (see Landau 2001).

Pro or little *pro*

Pro or little *pro* is a phonetically empty subject pronoun in a sentence with a finite verb. It is usually interpreted by virtue of rich agreement on the finite verb or on the auxiliary as shown in Figure 1:

(1)   IP
                                            /   \
                                        pro$_i$ I'
                                        [3pl]   /\
                                              I$_i$ Δ
                                            [3pl]

Little *pro* occurs mostly in languages that have rich agreement, such as Spanish or Italian, which are called **Pro-Drop Languages** or **Null Subject Languages**. Little *pro* is found in examples such as (1):

(1) a. *I bambini$_i$ erano stanchi. Adesso pro$_i$ dormono.*
       "The kids were tired. Now, (they) sleep." (Italian, Romance, Indo-European)
    b. *Los niños$_i$ estaban cansados. Ahora, pro$_i$ duermen.*
       "The kids were tired. Now, (they) sleep." (Spanish, Romance, Indo-European)

There are two main types of *pro*: referential *pro* and nonreferential or expletive *pro*. A referential *pro* makes reference to an element present in the context as *i bambini/los niños* 'the children' in (1). Nonreferential *pro* or expletive *pro* is a dummy element that does not have reference at all. It corresponds to English *it* as is shown in (2):

(2) *pro*$_{expl}$ *llueve*
       rain:3sg
       "It is raining." (Spanish, Romance, Indo-European)

The justification of the expletive *pro* in a sentence such as (2) is the Extended Projection Principle (EPP), which states that every sentence must have a subject.

Within the Government and Binding framework of Chomsky (1981) *pro* was considered to be an empty constituent with the features [−anaphor +pronominal]. However, in the framework of the latest generative model, the Minimalist Program (Chomsky 1995, 2001), the status of referential *pro* is problematic because it is said that agreement morphology is interpretable. Thus, the agreement morpheme is a referential element and *pro* is superfluous. In this case, in Null Subject Languages the Theta Criterion (each argument has a theta-role, and every theta-role is assigned to an argument) would be met morphologically rather than syntactically, since agreement would bear the theta-argument.

Pro-drop see *Null argument.*
Proclitic see *Clitic.*

Procrastinate

In the Minimalist Program, **Procrastinate** is a principle which favors covert syntax over overt syntax when there is a choice. In this framework, movement occurs only when it is necessary, and as late as possible due to economy reasons. Covert movement is more economical because movement can be procrastinated only when weak features are involved. Strong features are uninterpretable at Phonetic Form. Thus they must be deleted before Spell-Out. This conception of movement is opposite to the Government and Binding framework, where movement was optional.

See also *Movement*.

Projection Principle

Within Transformational Generative Grammar, the Projection Principle states that:

(1) Lexical information is syntactically represented (at all levels)

This means that the properties of lexical items—mainly the thematic structure of the predicate—must be preserved categorically at all syntactic levels: D-structure, S-structure, and LF (Logical Form). As stated by the Theta Criterion, the thematic structure of lexical items must be projected in the syntax. For example in a sentence such as (2), the arguments *table* and *John* must be present at all levels of representation (D-structure, S-structure, and LF):

(2) *John hit the table*

If one argument is missing, as in (3), there is a violation of the subcategorization properties of the verb, the Theta Criterion, and the Projection Principle:

(3) **John hit*

Thus, the sentence is ungrammatical.
See also *Government* and *Valency*.

Pronoun see *Part of speech*.

Promotion

In Relational Grammar, the fact that at a lower level a certain constituent receives a grammatical relation which ranks higher on the scale *subject > direct object > indirect object* than the relation that the same constituent has at a deeper level. For example, in the passive the direct object is promoted to subject with respect to the active.
See also *Demotion*.

Raising

In raising constructions an argument that belongs to a subordinate clause is realized as a syntactic constituent of a higher clause, as in (1):

(1) *John$_i$ seems **t**$_i$ to have traveled around the world*

In (1), *John* is the **semantic subject** of the lower verb *have traveled,* and the **syntactic subject** of the upper verb *seems*. This type of movement is possible with some verbs called **raising verbs,** such as *seem* in English or *parecer* 'to seem' in Spanish and Portuguese. In (1) the subject DP/NP *John* must raise from the subordinate clause to the subject position of the main verb *seems* because it cannot be Case-marked as (Nominative) subject by the nonfinite verb *to have traveled* in the subordinate clause due to lack of Agreement of the infinitive.

When the subject of the lower clause does not raise because it is Case-marked by a finite subordinate verb, the subject of the raising verb must be an expletive *it* or *there* in English or an expletive little *pro* in Spanish or Portuguese because the raising verb does not have a theta-role to assign to its argument. This is shown in (2a) and in (2b):

(2) a. ***it** seems that John has traveled around the world*

     b. ***pro** parece que Juan ha viajado alrededor del mundo*
       "It seems that John has traveled around the world." (Spanish, Romance, Indo-European)

In (2a) and (2b) the finite verb *has traveled/ha viajado* assigns a theta-role to its subject argument *John/Juan*, and the agreement features in the inflection of this verb Case-mark this argument with nominative Case. The agreement features of the upper verb *seems/parece* Case-mark the expletive subject as nominative, but these raising verbs cannot assign a theta-role to their subject argument.

Raising structures are **voice transparent** as is shown in (3a) and (3b):

(3) a. *John seemed to examine the students*
     b. *the students seemed to be examined by John*

In (3) the embedded clause can be in active or passive voice without changing the meaning of the entire sentence. In fact, sentences (3a) and (3b) are paraphrases of each other. However, if the main verb of the sentence is not a raising verb, the meaning of the sentences changes drastically with the change of voice, as shown in (4a) and (4b):

(4) a. *John hoped to examine the students*
    b. *the students hoped to be examined by John*

The examples in (1)–(4) show that the semantic roles of the subjects in the lower sentences are determined uniquely by the verb in the embedded clause, and that the verb *seems/parece* does not assign a semantic role to its subject.

ECM (Exceptional Case Marking) verbs are also often analyzed in terms of raising (subject to object raising). This means that in this construction the subject of the subordinate clause raises to the object position of the verb in the main clause in order to receive Accusative Case, as in (5) *her* raises to the object position of *believe*:

(5) *John believes **her** to be smart*

(However, this analysis is controversial in Transformational Generative Grammar.)

Reanalysis

Reanalysis is one of the basic processes involved in syntactic change (and in language change in general). It consists of a change "in the underlying structure of a syntactic pattern," and "does not involve any modification of its surface manifestation" (Harris and Campbell 1995: 50). Specific kinds of reanalysis are **rebracketing** and **restructuring**.

An example of reanalysis is the creation of auxiliary verbs. Consider example (1) from Latin:

(1) *nihil   opust   nobis   ancilla   nisi   quae   texat*, . . .
    nothing need:3SG 1PL.DAT slave:NOM if+not REL.NOM.F spin:SBJ.PRS.3SG

> *habeat*   *cottidianum familiae coctum*   *cibum*
> have:SBJ.PRS.3SG daily:ACC   family:DAT cook:PART.ACC food:ACC
> "We don't need a servant, unless she spins, and has every day meals
> ready for the family." Plautus, *Mercator* 396–398 (Latin, Italic,
> Indo-European)

The verb of the second sentence is *habeat* 'has'; the participle *coctum* is a predicative adjunct connected with *cibum* 'food'. The structure is as follows:

(2) [$_{VP}$ [$_V$ habeat] [$_{NP}$ [$_{ADJ}$ coctum] [$_N$ cibum]]]

In Proto-Romance, the participle was reanalyzed as building a compound verb form with the verb *have*, which became an auxiliary. The structure thus became the following:

(3) *[$_{VP}$ [$_{VP}$ [$_{AUX}$ habeat] [$_V$coctum]] [$_{NP}$ cibum]]
      (In (3) the asterisk * indicates a reconstructed form.)

The result is constituted by the compound verb forms of the Romance languages:

(4) *ho   cucinato la   cena   per tutti*
      I.have cooked the dinner for everybody
      "I cooked dinner for everybody." (Italian, Romance, Indo-European)

Rebracketing see *Reanalysis*.

Recursion or recursivity

Recursion or recursivity is a property of languages that allows speakers to create an infinite number of sentences using a finite set of rules. For example, embedding is recursive because an embedded clause can contain another embedded clause, and this process can be repeated in principle an infinite number of times. Potentially, recursivity is infinite. However, this property of language is limited by human short-term memory and perception.

In Government and Binding theory **D-structure** is built by recursion of XP phrases. Within the Minimalist Program, the operation **Merge** builds phrasal structures recursively, eradicating D-structure.

See also *Embedding, Merge,* and *X-bar theory*.

Relative clause

A type of attributive clause. A relative clause functions as a modifier of a head noun, such as:

(1) *I met a girl **who was running in the street***

As shown in (1), relative clauses are often marked by a relative marker, in this case the relative pronoun *who*. The relative pronoun refers to an antecedent, *a girl* in (1), which is said to be relativized. Relative pronouns typically inflect for case (as in *who, whom, whose*), but relative markers do not necessarily have inflection, as English *that*.

Relative pronouns can be targets of gender and number agreement:

(2) *ja   ne videla   čeloveka,   c   kotorym   ja   gavorila*
1SG.NOM NEG see:PAST.SG.F man:ACC.M with REL.INSTR.M 1SG.NOM speak:
PAST.SG.F
"I couldn't see the man with whom I was speaking." (Russian, Slavic, Indo-European)

In many languages in which the relative pronoun does not have independent case marking, the relative clause contains a **resumptive pronoun** (or resumption), that is, a pronominal form coreferential with the relativized constituent which indicates its function within the relative clause:

(3) *ha-'areṣ ašer atta šokeb   'al-**eha** lə-ka   ettənenn-**ah***
ART-earth REL you lie:PF.2SG.M   on-it   to-you give:IMPF.1SG-it
"I will give you the land on which you are lying." *Genesis* 28.13
(Hebrew, Semitic, Afro-Asiatic)
(4) *ar-raajul alladi daxala   fi l-bayt   alladi ra'aytu- **hu**   huwa*
the-man REL   go.inside:PF.3SG in the-house REL see:PF.2SG-3SG.F   he
ax- i
brother-POSS.1SG
"The man who went into the house that you saw is my brother."
(Classical Arabic, Semitic, Afro-Asiatic)

In (3) the pronominal clitic ***eha*** in the relative clause is coreferential with the noun phrase *ha-'areṣ* 'the earth', which is the head of the relative clause;

similarly, in (4) the pronominal clitic *hu* in the relative clause is coreferential with the head of the clause *bayt* 'house'.

Relative clauses can also be made without any marker or any relative word:

(5) *the girl I saw was running in the street*

In (5) *I saw* is a relative clause which is marked as such only by its position. Relative clauses that do not present relative words are sometimes called **contact clauses**, following Jespersen (1933: 360).

In English, any type of constituent can be relativized, but this is not necessarily so in all languages: in some, only (some) core constituents can be relativized. Typological comparison has led to work out an accessibility hierarchy for relativization, which later turned out to be relevant for other syntactic phenomena as well:

subject > direct object > indirect object > oblique > genitive > object of comparison

The meaning of the scale is the following: if in a certain language a given constituent can be relativized, then all constituents on its left can also be relativized (so if e.g. oblique can be relativized, then indirect object, direct object, and subject can also be relativized).

Relative clauses may follow their head as in English or precede it, as in Japanese:

(6) *kanojo wa jibun no okane de   katta   yoofuku ga daisuki   desu*
    3SG.F TOP self GEN money with buy:PAST dress   SUBJ agreeable be
    "She likes the dress she bought with her own money." (Japanese, Japanese)

In (6) the relative clause precedes the head noun *yoofuku* 'dress'. Note that there is no subordinator: the relative clause is marked as such by its position alone. Both the position before the head and the absence of overt markers are features of relative clauses in OV languages, such as Japanese.

Some languages may have relative clauses that contain their head. They are called **internally headed relative clauses** as in the following Ancient Greek example:

(7) *eis dè   hề̀n   aphíkonto   kômēn   megálē   te ên*
    to PTC   REL.ACC.F arrive:AOR.MID.3PL village:ACC.F large:NOM.F PTC be:IMPF.3SG
    "The village which they reached was a large one." Xenophon,
    Anabasis 4.4.2 (Classical Greek, Indo-European)

Here the head of the relative clause, *kômēn* 'village', which should be the subject of the main clause, is in the accusative as the relative pronoun and is placed inside the relative clause.

Relative clauses can be **restrictive** as in (8a) or **nonrestrictive**, as in (8b):

(8) a. *the students **who didn't attend the class** failed the exam*
    b. *the students, **who didn't attend the class**, failed the exam*

In (8a) it is said that only some of the students, namely those who didn't attend classes, failed the exam: the relative clause is restrictive, because it narrows down (restricts) the reference of the head. The information conveyed by the relative clause is essential to the identification of the referent. In (8b), on the other hand, it is said that all students failed the exam, and some referentially nonessential piece of information is added in the relative clause. The reference of the NP *the students* in (8b) would still be the same if we were to leave out the relative clause.

See also *Agreement, Apposition, Modification*, and *Subordination*.

Restructuring see *Reanalysis*.
Resumption see *Relative clause*.

Rheme

In Functional Sentence Perspective, the rheme is what is being said about a theme, and is equivalent to comment in other terminologies.

See also *Comment, Theme*, and *Topic*.

Right- vs. left-branching, see *Branching*.

Scope

Part of the sentence (or text) on which an operator (wh-element, negation, quantifier etc.) performs its characteristic action. If one operator is within the scope of another operator, their relative scope, which can be wide scope or narrow scope, determines their order of operation. For example in (1), Op1 has wide scope over Op2 and Op2 has narrow scope over Op1:

(1) Op1 [. . . Op2 [. . .] . . .]

In an ambiguous sentence such as (2), (2b) *every man* has wide scope over *woman* and in (2c), *a woman* has wide scope over *every man*:

(2) a. *every man loves a woman*
    b. *for every man there is such a woman such that he loves her*
    c. *there is a woman such that every man loves her*

In Transformational Generative Grammar, c-command plays a crucial role in determining the scope or interpretation of the operator. That is, the scope of a quantifier, such as *every, who,* or *no*, is everything which it c-commands at LF (Logical Form). In the Government and Binding framework, a variable must be bound by an operator. For example, an empty element, such a quantifier trace or a wh-trace, must be A-bar bound by the operator, which is the quantifier or the wh-element.

See also *C-command, Operator*, and *Variable*.

Scrambling

The variation of the order of words in sentences of nonconfigurational languages such as Latin is called scrambling. Also, in the study of Germanic languages scrambling is used to refer to word order variation of argument phrases with respect to adverbial phrases, as shown in (1) and (2):

(1) *dass Hans wahrscheinlich <u>mit diesem   Geld</u> die Torte gekauft hat*
    that Hans   probably   with this   money the cake   bought has
    "that Hans bought the cake with this money probably"

(2) *dass Hans mit diesem Geld wahrscheinlich die Torte gekauft hat*
    that Hans   with this   money probably   the cake bought has
    "that Hans bought the cake with this money probably" (German,
    Germanic, Indo-European)

In (1) the adverb *wahrscheinlich* precedes the prepositional phrase, but in
(2) the same adverb follows the prepositional phrase. Usually nonspecific
indefinite noun phrases cannot scramble in Germanic languages.

In Generative Transformational Grammar, scrambling is a process that
reorders phrases (maximal projections) internally within clauses moving them
further to the front of the clauses (Radford 1988).

Selection see *Subcategorization*.

Semantic macro-role

In Role and Reference Grammar, actor, undergoer, and indirect are semantic
macro-roles of arguments within the nuclear predication and of adverbial
modifiers. Actor is the semantic macro-role of arguments that usually are
chosen as subjects of transitive verbs, while undegoer is the semantic macro-
role of arguments that are usually chosen as direct objects. The notion of
macro-role is defined in a way as to capture some significant syntactic and
semantic correlates across argument types. In this perspective, the semantic
macro-role actor, in a language such as English, includes agent, experiencer,
possessor, and other semantic roles (or micro-roles) of arguments that are
usually syntactic subjects, while the semantic macro-role undergoer includes
patient, theme, recipient (in dative shift constructions), and so on. The indirect macro-role includes semantic roles such as beneficiary, recipient, and
addresse.

See also *Semantic role*.

Semantic role

Semantic roles (also called thematic roles, semantic relations, semantic functions, case roles or deep cases, depending on the theoretical framework) of
constituents are determined by the semantic relation they bear to the predicate,

which in turn is a generalization based on the role of participants in given events. For example, in (1) *Mary* bears the role agent, *bread* bears the role patient, and *knife* bears the role instrument, indicated by the preposition *with*:

(1) *Mary cuts the bread with a knife*

The earliest predecessors of semantic roles are 'deep cases', introduced in the 1960s in the framework of Case Grammar, later a branch of Generative Semantics. Since then, the number of semantic roles is a matter of discussion. Since the number of possible events in the world is potentially infinite, and any event can be slightly different from any other, the only possible solution seems to be to try and single out a relatively small number of semantic roles, based on the fact that they are grammaticalized (i.e. expressed with specific grammatical means) in a number of languages, and consider semantic roles as prototypical categories, that is, categories whose members are characterized by the fact that they share at least some of the features of the prototype.

A rough list of the most frequently assumed semantic roles includes the following:

Agent: the entity, usually a human being, that intentionally brings about a state of affairs, typically an action, as in **Paul** *ate an apple*;

Actor: Agent and some agent-like roles in Role and Reference Grammar; the term was introduced by Bloomfield (1933) and is also used, as distinct from agent, in Systemic Functional Grammar;

Patient: the entity most directly affected by a state of affairs, as in *the dentist treated* **Mary**;

Recipient: a participant, usually a human being, who is the goal of a transaction, as in *I gave a book* **to Mary**;

Addressee: a participant, usually a human being, who is the goal of an event of communication, as in *I told a story* **to my sister**;

Experiencer: a living being who experiences a process signified by a verb of sensation, perception, or mental activity, as in **Paul** *likes pears*;

Possessor: the entity, most often a human being, that possesses another entity, as in **John's** *book*.

Beneficiary (also called benefactive):   a participant, usually a human being, who profits from a state of affairs, as in *I bought a present* **for you**; a variant of beneficiary is malefactive;

Indirect: in Role and Reference Grammar, a semantic macro-role that covers beneficiary and related semantic roles;

Cause: an entity (often a state of affairs) that brings about a state of affairs unintentionally, as in *The child is shivering* **with fear**;

Force: an inanimate entity that exerts control on a state of affairs (i.e. a type of cause), as in *The village was destroyed* **by an earthquake**;

Reason: an entity (often a state of affairs) that motivates an agent to bring about a state of affairs, as in *I stayed home* **because I wanted to watch TV**;

Purpose: the end for which an agent brings about a state of affairs, as in *They were fighting* **for liberty**;

Instrument: an entity, usually inanimate, which is manipulated by an agent in order to bring about a state of affairs, as in *Susan cuts the bread* **with a knife**;

Means: an entity which helps an agent bring about a state of affairs without direct manipulation or with a lesser degree of manipulation than the one needed for an instrument, as in *It is doubtful that you can spread democracy* **through force**;

Intermediary: a human being through which an agent brings about a state of affairs, as in *I did this* **through John**;

Comitative: a participant involved in a state of affairs together with another, more central participant, as in *Jennifer went to the movies* **with her father**;

Locative (or location): the place where a state of affairs is brought about, as in *Mary lives* **in Philadephia**;

Direction: the place which is the final goal of motion, as in *The train goes* **to Rome**;

Source: the place from which a motion originates, as in *I have just arrived* **from Rome**;

Path: the place through which a moving entity moves, as in *The boys were wandering* **through the forest**;

Time: the temporal setting of a state of affairs, as in *I came home* **at five o' clock**;

Goal: (a) = direction; (b) in S. C. Dik's Functional Grammar and in Systemic Functional Grammar: patient (*goal* is also used in this latter sense by Bloomfield 1933);

Theme: (a) a participant which is not actively involved in a state of affairs, as in **the book** *is on the table*, (b) the second argument of perception verbs, as in *I am watching **TV***, (c) a participant that undergoes a change of place, as the direct object of verbs of transaction (*I gave **a book** to Mary*) or the subject of motion verbs (***Jennifer** went to Philadelphia*);

Undergoer: Patient and some patient-like roles, see *Semantic macro-role*;

Stimulus: a participant which generates a feeling or sensation in an experiencer, as in *Mary is afraid **of dogs***.

See also *Semantic macro-role* and *Theta-role*.

Sentence

A sentence is a unit consisting of at least one independent clause, or of several clauses, at least one of which is independent. A sentence which consists of a single clause is called **simple sentence**. A sentence consisting of subordinated clauses with a main clause is called a **complex sentence**. A sentence consisting of several coordinated clauses is called a **compound sentence**. Because sentences may consist of a single clause, the word 'sentence' is sometimes used to mean 'clause'.

Halliday (2004: 192) defines a sentence as "CLAUSE COMPLEX: a Head clause [sc. the main clause] together with other clauses that modify it," and draws a parallel between sentences and constituents (called 'word complexes').

Transformational Generative Grammar assumes that, due to recursivity in language, there is no need to distinguish between sentences and clauses. Thus, sentences and clauses have been formalized as the same category S (Sentence) in the first works and as IP (Inflectional Phrase) in later works.

Verbal and nominal sentences. In most languages the predicate of a sentence or clause contains a verb or verb phrase. For example:

(1) *John eats artichokes*

However, there are languages in which sentences can have predicates without a verb. They are called nominal sentences (or **small clauses** in Transformational Generative Grammar) because they have a subject (usually a NP), and a predicate NP or AP. An example is Spanish:

(2) *el chocolate, caliente*
    the chocolate hot
    "Chocolate [must be] hot." (Spanish, Romance, Indo-European)

Typically, a verbal sentence has a subject (usually a NP), and a predicate (a VP). The predicate of a simple sentence such as (1) is the finite verb with the direct object, that is, the VP. Certain subordinate clauses have a predicate formed by a nonfinite verb and an object, such as *to buy a book* in (3), in which the subject is not overtly expressed:

(3) *Mary went to the store Ø to buy a book*

The subject of the subordinate clause is implicit. It need not be expressed because it is coreferential with the subject of the main clause. In Transformational Generative Grammar this implicit subject is called 'big PRO' and it is said that it is controlled by the subject of the main clause.

Sentence types. There are several types of sentence: declarative sentences, which make a statement, such as (1), interrogative sentences, which request information, such as (4):

(4) *what did John eat?*

imperative sentences, which make a demand or a request, such as (5):

(5) *eat your dinner!*

and exclamatory sentences, which convey an emotional reaction, such as (6):

(6) *how nice is this car!*

Broadly speaking, the three basic sentence types, declarative, interrogative, and imperative, correspond to statements, questions, and commands (Lyons 1977: 745). Statements can be true or false, while orders and commands cannot. This is shown by the fact that declarative sentences can be negated. Thus sentence (1) is true if and only if its negated counterpart:

(7) *John doesn't eat artichokes*

is false. This does not hold for questions and commands. If we negate (5), we do not falsify it, but simply give a different order:

(8) *don't eat your dinner!*

In most functional approaches to syntax, a simple sentence is conceived of as having a **layered structure**, which includes an inner layer (the core), that is, the predicate and its arguments, and an outer layer, the periphery, which contains nonarguments (or adjuncts):

Predicate + Arguments	Non-arguments

From Van Valin and LaPolla (1997:25).

A sentence may be viewed as a unit of information. In this perspective, it is said to have an **information structure**, and to contain a theme and a rheme, or a topic and a comment (a topic and a focus in S. C. Dik's Functional Grammar).

In early Transformational Generative Grammar a simple sentence may become a more elaborated sentence through a transformation. For example **kernel sentence** (9) becomes sentence (10) by applying wh-movement rules:

(9) *John ate an apple*
(10) *who ate an apple?*

See also *Clause, Core, Periphery, Predicate, Predication*, and *Subject*.

Serial verb

Serial verbs are strings of two or more verbs occurring in the same clause with no coordination markers, sharing the same subject and possibly the same object, and agreeing in tense, aspect, mood, and polarity. Serialized verbs indicate simultaneous events, or events that immediately follow each other. Serial verb constructions vary as to their morphology: in certain languages, they contain strings of fully inflected verbs, while in others, only the first or the last verb in a series displays inflection. Serialized verbs may all express their own lexical meaning, as in:

(1) *yñ-sōreá-eà   ntñám kō-ō   fäe*
1PL-get.up-PAST quickly go-PAST home
"We got up quickly and went home." (Akan, Kwa, Niger-Congo)

or they may have a unitary meaning which is not compositional. In the latter case, serialized verbs have a function which is typical of prepositions in other languages. For example, the verb 'give' often corresponds to the preposition 'to' (recipient) or 'for' (beneficiary):

(2) *Aémmaá yñá adwuáma maá Kofä*
Amma   do   work   give Kofi
"Amma works for Kofi." (Akan, Kwa, Niger-Congo).

In grammatical descriptions of Chinese, serial verbs are called 'coverbs'. See also *Auxiliary, Coverb*, and *Light verb*.

Sisterhood

Sisterhood is a relation between two nodes in a tree. Node A and node B are sisters if there is a node C (their mother) that immediately dominates both A and B.
See also *Node*.

Small Clause

In the Government and Binding framework a small clause is a construction that lacks a verb. It consists of a subject NP/DP and a predicate adjective phrase, noun phrase, or a prepositional phrase. Formally, a small clause is an XP with a subject in its Spec (or adjoined to the XP), where its head, is, among others, a N (noun) a PP (prepositional phrase), or an A (adjective), as in (1):

(1) a. *we elected **Silvia president***
    b. *I want **John out of the boat***
    c. *I consider **Carlos intelligent***

In (1), *Silvia president, John out of the boat* and *Carlos intelligent*, are small clauses.

Spell-Out

In the Minimalist Program, **Spell-Out** is an operation that splits the **computation** in two parts, leading to Phonetic Form (PF) and Logical Form (LF). The computation that precedes Spell-Out is overt syntax, which is the result of **Merge** and **Move**, after having selected the sentential elements from the Numeration (N). The position of Spell-Out in this model can be diagrammed as shown in (1):

(1)   **LF**

                  ↑ *select, merge and move*

         Spell-Out → **PF**

                  ↑ *select, merge and move*

        N = {A$_i$, B$_j$, C$_k$,}

In some recent versions of the Minimalist Program, Spell-Out applies at LF, which sends the information to PF after some computations. This is shown in (2):

(2)   **PF**

               ↑   *Spell-Out*

              LF

               ↑   *select, merge and move*

        N = {A$_i$, B$_j$, C$_k$,}

See also *Logical Form, Merge, Movement, Numeration,* and *Phonetic Form.*

Split-ergativity see *Alignment.*
S-structure see *Surface Structure.*

State of affairs

A state of affairs is "the conception of something that can be the case in some world" (Dik 1997: 51). States of affairs in the world are indicated by predications:

(1) *John kissed Mary*

Example (1) refers to a state of affairs in which a person called John performed the action of kissing another person called Mary at some moment prior to the time of utterance. The referential entities involved in states of affairs are called **participants**.

In some terminologies, 'state of affairs' is a synonym of 'event' and/or 'situation', or even of 'process', whereas in other terminologies events, situations, and processes are considered types of states of affairs.

States of affairs can be classified based on a number of parameters. In the first place, a distinction is made between dynamic and nondynamic states of affairs. The latter are usually called **states**, as in (2):

(2) *Bill is tall*

In some approaches, a distinction is made between uncontrolled non-dynamic states of affairs, as (2), and controlled ones, which are then called **positions**, as in (3):

(3) *Bill keeps his ties in a drawer*

Van Valin and LaPolla (1997) use the word **situation** to refer to states; for others, as in Comrie (1985), 'situation' is a synonym of 'state of affairs'. Dik (1997) considers 'situation' a cover term for states and positions, that is, for nondynamic states of affairs. In Systemic Functional Grammar, the word 'process' is used as a cover term for all types of states of affairs.

Dynamic states of affairs are of various types. For example, they can be controlled or not controlled, depending on whether they are brought about by a controlling entity (usually an agent), or they occur spontaneously. The former are called **actions**; an example is (1). Uncontrolled, dynamic states of affairs are often called **processes**, as in (4):

(4) *time goes by*

(but note that in some terminologies controlled events may also be called processes, as in *John walks, swims, runs*).

A parameter that crosscuts the distinction between controlled and uncontrolled states of affairs is the parameter of telicity. In this respect, states of affairs are divided into atelic and telic. Atelic states of affairs do not indicate any change of state; they include states, as in (2), and **activities**, as in (5) and (6):

(5) *I play guitar*
(6) *the door squeaks*

Activities are referred to both by transitive and intransitive verbs; example (6) shows that activities are not necessarily controlled. Telic states of affairs involve a change of state or a change of position; they can have one or more participants, and are divided into **achievements** and **accomplishments**. Achievements are punctual telic predicates; they indicate events that are often spontaneous, as in (7):

(7) *the ice melted*

although this is not necessarily the case, as shown in (8):

(8) *she arrived late*

Accomplishments are similar to activities, in that they are not punctual (they indicate events with an internal structure), but, similar to achievements, they are telic, i.e. inherently bounded, as in:

(9) *I ate a giant cheeseburger*

This classification was first put forward by Vendler (1957) in his description of *Aktionsart*, or 'manner of action'. *Aktionsart* corresponds to the English term **lexical aspect**. According to Dik (1997) *Aktionsart* can be considered a synonym of state of affairs. Van Valin and LaPolla (1997:92) treat the two as different, but in their system, Vendler's four *Aktionsarten* correspond to the four possible types of states of affairs included in their classification: situation = state; event = achievement; process = accomplishment; action = activity. Note that, following this approach, the concept of 'action' does not necessarily imply the occurrence of an agent that acts voluntarily: intentionality is not viewed as a relevant parameter for the classification of states of affairs. (In this classification, 'event' indicates a telic, momentaneous state of affairs; in Dik 1997 it is a cover term for processes and actions, i.e. dynamic states of affairs, whereas many others, e.g. Croft 1991, use it as a synonym of 'state of affairs'.)

It can be remarked that in Vendler's classification there is a fundamental difference between states of affairs that imply a change of state or position (accomplishments and achievements) and those that do not (states and activities). Based on this distinction, Pustejovsky (1995) proposed a three-fold classification, which includes states, processes (Vendler's activities), and transitions (Vendler's accomplishments and achievements). In Pustejovsky's system, the difference between events that involve two participants and events that only involve one is not relevant, while the feature of change of state (or change of position) is highlighted.

According to Croft (1991) events (= states of affairs) include causative (*the rock broke the window*), inchoative (*the window broke*), and stative (*the window is broken*), while subtler distinctions can be subsumed under these categories.

In Functional Systemic Grammar, the main types of processes (i.e. of states of affairs) are material, mental, and relational. Material processes, or processes of doing (Halliday 1994: 102) involve change of state; they can be events (i.e. spontaneous events), or actions; mental processes, or processes of sensing, are states of affairs expressed by verbs of perception, cognition, and affection; relational processes, or processes of being, are indicated by copular sentences and can be attributive or identifying. To these, behavioral, verbal, and existential processes can also be added (see Halliday 1994 for further reference).

State of affairs is often abbreviated **SoA**.

See also *Semantic role* and *Transitivity*.

Strong Feature

In the Minimalist Program there are Strong Features and Weak Features. Strong Features have Strength (for example, phonetic verbal morphology as in Spanish). A Strong Feature must be checked in overt syntax, before Spell-Out. Strong features induce movement.

See also *Spell-Out,* and *Weak Feature*.

Subcategorization

In Transformational Generative Grammar, the internal arguments required by a verb are encoded in distributional frames or **subcategorization frames**. Thus, a verb **selects** or **subcategorizes** for its internal arguments.

For example, the verb *watch* selects or subcategorizes for a DP/NP complement, as shown in (1):

(1) *John watched TV.*

The subcategorization frame of the verb *to watch* is as follows:

(2) watch: V, [___ DP/NP]

See also *Argument* and *Valency*.

Subjacency Condition

The Subjacency Condition is a condition on movement. In the Government and Binding framework the Subjacency Condition states that movement is not allowed across more than one bounding node. The bounding nodes are NP and IP in English, as shown in (1) and (2), and NP and CP in Italian and Spanish.

(1) *John talked to a girl that passed the bar-exam*
(2) * [$_{CP}$ which exam$_i$ did John talk to [$_{NP}$ a girl [$_{CP}$ that [$_{IP}$ passed t$_i$]]]]

Example (2) shows that it is impossible to move a constituent from the well-formed relative clause in (1) because it violates subjacency (it is moved across NP and IP).

In Italian the example in (3) is grammatical, while the equivalent example in English is not grammatical:

(3) *tuo fratello a cui mi domando che storie abbiano raccontato era molto preoccupato*
   tuo fratello, [$_{CP}$ a cui $_j$ [$_{IP}$ mi domando [$_{CP}$ che storie$_i$ [$_{IP}$ abbiano raccontato t$_i$ t$_j$]]]], era molto preoccupato (Italian, Romance, Indo-European)
(4) **your brother, to whom I wonder what stories they have told, was very worried*

In this case, the difference between English and Italian is due to the fact that in Italian long movement of *a cui* 'to whom' is allowed. This is so because in Italian it is acceptable to transgress two IP nodes and only one CP, as shown in (3). However, this is not possible in English, as shown in (4).

Subjacency has been reinterpreted in terms of phase recently.
See also *Movement, Phase* and *Phase Impenetrability Condition.*

Subject

A constituent that has certain (morpho)syntactic properties in a sentence, like triggering verb agreement and controlling zero anaphora in coordination reduction, as in (1):

(1) **John** always kiss**es** Mary and **Ø** embrac**es** the kids

This definition, which fits English and most Indo-European languages, originates from the Greco-Roman grammatical tradition, and has been shown to be problematic for typologically different languages.

Keenan (1976) lists a number of properties typical of subjects but not necessarily occurring together in all languages. This list constitutes a set of parameters that can be used to determine the degree of subjecthood of certain constituents in languages that do not conform to the model of Western grammatical description. It includes coding properties (case marking and agreement), and behavioral properties (binding of reflexive pronouns, coordination reduction, Equi NP deletion, raising, high ranking on certain accessibility scales such as the relativization scale).

Coding properties are most typical of inflectional languages, in which the subject is marked by a certain case: depending on alignment, typical cases marking the subject are the nominative, the ergative, or the absolutive. In English, only certain pronouns have case distinctions: *I* (subject) vs. *me* (non-subject). Verb agreement, too, has a limited range in English, but is pervasive in many other languages, such as for example Italian or Spanish.

Coordination reduction as shown in (1) mostly involves the constituent marked by the nominative case in nominative/accusative languages. In ergative languages, we find two groups. In the first group, coordination reduction involves the constituent in the ergative with transitive verbs, and the constituent in the absolutive with intransitive verbs:

(2) *Gela   gavida   saxlidan*
    Gela:ABS AOR-go.out home-ABL
    "Gela left home."

(3) *Gelam   dainaxa Maria   da   gavida   saxlidan*
   Gela-ERG AOR-see Maria:ABS and   AOR-go.out home-ABL
   "Gela saw Mary and Ø left home." (Georgian, Kartvelian)

In (3) the null subject of the second clause is coreferential with the NP *Gelam*, that is, Ø is controlled by the NP in the ergative.

In the other group of languages (much less numerous) coordination reduction always involves the constituent in the absolutive in both transitive and intransitive sentences. Thus, in the first group of languages subjects display different case marking depending on transitivity/intransitivity of the verb, while in the second the constituent in the absolutive has subject properties both with transitive and with intransitive verbs.

Accessibility scales can help identify the subject in languages in which other morphosyntactic parameters offer few clues, since subjects rank the highest on such scales.

In languages in which word order is not free, or at least not completely free, the position of the subject is often specified. In English, for example, declarative and interrogative sentences differ in this respect because subjects of declarative sentences usually precede the finite verb, while subjects of interrogative sentence follow it, as is shown in (4) and (5):

(4) *I have never read this book*
(5) *have **you** ever read this book?*

In German, as well as in the Scandinavian languages, the subject either precedes the finite verb or follows it but precedes other postverbal constituents in main clauses (these are V2 languages).

Often, the constituent chosen as subject of a sentence is its topic, although this is not necessarily the case, especially with emphatic subjects. In nominative-accusative languages, the subject of transitive verbs is normally the agent. When the patient is chosen as subject, since this is a less usual choice, it is marked on the verb through passive morphology:

(6) *John kisses Mary/Mary is kissed by John*

Arguments bearing other semantic functions can also be chosen as subject, based on what S. C. Dik calls the **Semantic Function Hierarchy** (Dik 1997: 267):

Agent > Patient > Recipient > Beneficiary > Instrument > Locative > Temporal

Languages also differ as to whether the subject must be obligatorily realized or not. In languages in which the subject is obligatory, such as English or French, it can be omitted only under certain very restricted conditions, such as in cases of coordination reduction, as in example (1); otherwise it must always be expressed. Nonreferential subjects, that is, those that do not refer to any entity, also have to be expressed, as in:

(7) *it's five o'clock*

The pronoun *it* in (7) is called an 'expletive' or 'dummy' subject, and it is nonreferential.

The majority of the world's languages do not have obligatory subjects: they are null subject languages. In such languages, the subject is normally omitted when it is recoverable from the context, or through verb morphology; the equivalent of sentences such as (7) does not allow overtly expressed subjects, as in Italian in (8):

(8) *sono   le cinque*
    be:PRS.3PL ART five
    "It's five o'clock." (Italian, Romance, Indo-European)

Linguistic theories assign a special status to the subject. In Transformational Generative Grammar, the subject NP (i.e. the NP immediately dominated by S) is one of the two basic constituents of a sentence, the other being the predicate VP, and, under the Extended Projection Principle, every sentence is conceived of as having a subject. In functional approaches, the subject is considered the privileged syntactic argument (Role and Reference Grammar), or the pivot of a sentence, that is, the starting point for the predication.

In some languages, it is the topic rather than the subject that receives this special status. These are called **topic-prominent** languages (as opposed to **subject-prominent** languages).

See also *Pivot, Topic,* and *Valency.*

Subordination

Subordination is a process by which complex sentences are built by putting together clauses which stand in a hierarchical relation with each other.

A complex sentence is constituted by a main clause, that is, a clause that could also occur alone, and a number of subordinate clauses, which can be governed by the predicate of the main clause (complement clauses), modify the main clause (adverbial clauses), or modify a NP (attributive clauses).

A subordinate clause can also be called a dependent clause. A clause that has a dependent clause is called a matrix. Subordination can obtain at various levels: a dependent clause can itself be the matrix of another dependent clause, as shown in (1):

(1) *Paul told me that he would come only if it didn't rain*

In (1) *Paul told me* functions as main clause for the complex sentence, and it is the matrix of the complement clause *that he would come*; the latter is the matrix of the adverbial conditional clause *if it didn't rain*.

Subordination is also called **hypotaxis**, from Greek *hupotássein*, 'to place below'. Because they are dependent, subordinate clauses are in some way 'less' sentences than main clauses. This special status can be described by saying that subordinate clauses are **de-sententialized** (Ch. Lehmann 1988). Traces of desententialization include obligatory choice of mood, occurrence of nonfinite verb forms, fixed word order, and incorporation into the main clause. Subordinate clauses, especially adverbial ones, also have a lesser relevance from the point of view of the information structure of sentences, since they usually carry backgrounded (or less relevant) information.

In contrast to main clauses, subordinate clauses do not have independent illocutionary force.

See also *Adverbial clause, Attributive clause, Clause, Complement clause, Parataxis,* and *Relative clause.*

Suffix copying see *Agreement.*

Superiority Condition

The Superiority Condition states that if a transformation, such as *wh-movement*, is applicable to one of two constituents of the same category, such as the subject NP and the object NP, the transformation will apply to the constituent that is placed in a superior position (i.e. higher) in the tree structure, that is, the subject.

See also *Wh-movement*.

S-Structure (Surface Structure)

In Transformational Generative Grammar until Minimalism, S-structure represents the superficial syntactic structure of sentences. It is related to D-structure by a set of movement rules known as transformations. In fact, S-structure is a second level of representation where the constituents of a sentence acquire or check their functional properties, such as Case and Agreement, and attain their word order features. Following X-bar theory, a wh-question or partial question has a D-structure such as in (1a), which is diagrammed in (2a) and an S-structure (1b), which is diagrammed in (2b):

(1) a. *will you eat what?*
    b. *what will you eat?*

(2)   a.

```
                 CP                          b.              CP
                / \                                         / \
            Spec   C'                                  what_i   C'
                  / \                                          / \
                 C   IP                                    will_k  IP
                    / \                                           / \
                Spec   I'                                     you_j  I'
                      / \                                           / \
                     I   VP                                      t_k   VP
                 [+Tense] / \                                         / \
                  future DP  V'                                     t_j  V'
                   |    Δ  / \                                          / \
                  will you V  DP                                       V   DP
                       ↑  eat Δ                                       eat  t_i
                       
                      θ  →  what
                  D-structure                              S-structure
```

In the D-structure (2a), the verb assigns the theta-role **theme** to the internal argument or object *what* and the theta-role **agent** to the external argument or subject, *you*. The head I of the Inflectional Phrase IP hosts the future tense marker *will*. In the S-structure (2b), the constituents in D-structure have been moved. They bear the required grammatical features and they have the right word order. The letter *t* stands for **trace.** Each trace is co-indexed with the moved element; different subscripts *(i, j, k)* show their connection.

Within the Minimalist Program, the linguistic levels of representation are restricted to only the ones that are required by conceptual necessity. These are the A–P-system (Articulatory Perceptual) and the C–I system (Conceptual Intentional). Thus, D-structure and S-structure are levels that can be eradicated in this framework

See also *D-structure, Movement,* and *Trace.*

Tail See *Afterthought.*

Theme

In Functional Sentence Perspective, theme is the equivalent of topic, and it is opposed to rheme. In S. C. Dik's Functional Grammar, a distinction is made between theme and topic. While the topic is an element that syntactically belongs into a sentence, a theme is a left-dislocated constituent, which is syntactically external as in (1):

(1) *as for Paris, the Eiffel Tower is impressive*

In (1) there are said to be both a topic (*the Eiffel Tower*), and a theme *(as for Paris)*. The particle -wa in Japanese, usually considered a topic marker, is considered a marker of theme constituents within this approach.

See also *Rheme* and *Topic.*

Theta-role (θ-role)

Theta-roles are the equivalent of semantic roles.

In Transformational Generative Grammar the semantic relations between verbs and their arguments are designated in terms of theta-roles. A theta-role is the semantic role that a NP/DP plays in a sentence, such as agent, patient, or theme, experiencer, beneficiary, and so on. There is no agreement about what the specific theta-roles in syntax are or what their specific labels are.

Following the Theta Criterion, the verb theta-marks its arguments. Within the Minimalist Program, theta-roles are checked during the Merge operation.

See also *Merge, Semantic role,* and *Theta Criterion.*

Theta Criterion

In Transformational Generative Grammar, the Theta Criterion states that:

a. Each argument is assigned one and only one theta-role.
b. Each theta-role is assigned to one and only one argument.

The Theta Criterion is assumed as a principle of Universal Grammar (UG), which means that all languages have it. It requires a biunique relation between argument and theta-role features (bi-uniqueness condition). Within the Government and Binding framework, the theta-roles are assigned by the verb or the predicate to theta-positions at Deep Structure. Consider (1):

(1) *children love chocolates*

In (1) the verb *love* assigns the **theme** theta-role to *chocolates* in VP. Then, the predicate *love chocolates* assigns the theta-role **experiencer** to the subject *children*. This is diagrammed in (2):

(2)
```
                          VP
                         / \
               Children   V'
                         / \
                 ↑      V   DP
                       love chocolates
                 ↑            ↑
                 ←     θ     →
```

The Theta Criterion applies to all syntactic levels (D-structure, S-structure, and Logical Form (LF)). Within the Minimalist Program, the theta-relations must be established upon lexical insertion (Merge) while building the sentence, and cannot be established by movement of constituents.

Tobler-Mussafia Law see *Clitic*.

Topic

The topic or theme is what is being talked about in a sentence. In (1) *John* is the topic of the sentence:

(1) **John** *didn't go to the movies yesterday*

What is said about the topic is called **comment**. The concept of topic refers to the information structure of a sentence or a discourse, rather than to its syntactic or grammatical structure, but topics may have grammatical properties. In English, the topic often coincides with the grammatical subject, as in (1), but this is not always the case. In (2) *ice cream* is the topic, but not the subject:

(2) **ice cream**, *I like*

The constituent *ice cream* is left-dislocated, that is, it is placed to the left of the clause, the normal position for topic in English, and it is said to be topicalized. Topicalization may be signaled by intonation, as in English, or by some overt marker, as in Italian in (3):

(3) **il gelato** *l' ho   mangiato tutto io*
    the ice cream it have:1SG eaten   all   I
    "The ice cream, I ate it up all by myself." (Italian, Romance, Indo-European)

In (3), which is spoken with normal intonation, the object NP *il gelato* is topic, and it is coreferential with the clitic *l(o)* attached to the verb. The clitic does not appear when the object follows the verb, that is, when it is not topicalized.

The topic is a piece of information which the speaker chooses as a starting point to which some new information is added. In order to do so, the speaker must assume that the hearer already has some notion of the topic. The fact that (1) is about John implies that the speaker and the hearer share the information that John exists, and is a possible topic of discourse. The comment, in its turn, conveys some piece of new information that the speaker assumes the hearer does not know, and that s/he wants to transmit to the hearer. For this reason, topic is often considered synonym of old information, even though shared information is a more fitting definition.

A distinction must be made between the topic of a single sentence, and the topic of discourse. Within a single sentence, topic is considered one of the pragmatic functions of arguments in S. C. Dik's Functional Grammar. The notion of discourse topic takes wider stretches of discourse into account, and is connected with various phenomena of discourse cohesion, such as anaphoric processes.

Once established, a topic is often referred to with phonologically reduced expressions, such as an anaphoric pronoun or zero.

Some languages have special topic markers, as the particle *wa* in Japanese:

(4) *Taroo* **wa** *sensee ga kinoo   shikatta*
    Taroo TOP teacher SUBJ yesterday scold:PAST
    "Taroo, the teacher scolded yesterday." (Japanese, Japanese)

In some languages, called topic-prominent, it is the topic, rather than the subject, that governs anaphoric processes:

(5) *nèi kuài   tián dàozi zhǎngde hěn dà suǒyi Ø hěn zhìqían*
    that piece land rice   grow   very big so   very valuable
    "That piece of land (topic), rice grows very big, so **it** (the land) is very valuable." (from Li and Thompson 1976: 469) (Mandarin, Sinitic, Sino-Tibetan)

In a discourse there may not be a single topic: in this case one speaks of different degrees of topicality of participants. A new topic may be established and then continued for a stretch of discourse: in this case, discourse exhibits some degree of **topic continuity**; the topic which is being continued is called an **active topic**. Once established, a topic may be abandoned for another topic, and become **inactive**; later, it may be reestablished.

See also *Anaphora, Comment*, and *Subject*.

Tough Movement

Type of movement in the derivation of sentences headed by predicates like *tough* and *easy*, as in (1):

(1) *John is tough to please*

In this construction the subject *John* seems to be thematically related to the object position, "for someone it is tough to please *John*," "it is tough to please *him.*"

At first sight, the object of *please* is moved to the subject position as an instance of NP-movement. However, this analysis violates principle A of Binding Theory, which applies to NP traces (they are anaphors). Moreover there is no justification for NP-movement (or A movement), since the object of *please* is a Case assigning position. Within the Government and Binding framework, Chomsky (1981) suggested that there is a type of wh-movement (A-bar movement) with a Null Operator coindexed with *John* as shown in (2):

(2) John$_i$ is [tough [$_{CP}$ Ø$_i$ [PRO to please t$_i$]]]

In (2) the empty Operator that represents the object moves to the Spec of CP, close to the predicate *tough*. The empty Operator forms a complex predicate with the adjective *tough*. The subject *John* receives a theta-role from *tough* and the empty Operator.

Trace see *Copy*.
Trace Theory see *Copy Theory*.
Transformation see *Movement*.

Transitivity

A syntactic property of certain verbs, called transitive. Transitive verbs are those which require a direct object, as *see* in (1):

(1) *I can't see anything*

Verbs which never occur with a direct object are called **intransitive**. Some transitive verbs, such as *see*, can also occur without an object, and thus be used as intransitives:

(2) *I can't see*

while some others cannot:

(3) a. *Mary resembles her mother*
    b. **Mary resembles*

Transitive verbs have at least two valencies, that is, they are at least bivalent; verbs with a higher valency are also transitive. On the other hand, avalent (valency Ø) and monovalent (valency 1) verbs are intransitive. In nominative-accusative languages, transitive verbs typically have both active and passive voice; passive is an operation that involves valency reduction with respect to active voice.

In some languages, both the second and the third argument of transitive verbs may exhibit (partial) direct object properties, as in the English **dative shift** construction:

(4) a. *Paul gave me this present*
    b. *I was given this present (by Paul)*
    c. *this present was given to me (by Paul)*

Both the NP *me* and the NP *this present* can be passivized. For this reason, such verbs are also called **ditransitive** or **bitransitive**. (Note however that in some terminologies, ditransitive is a synonym of trivalent, independent of the morphosyntactic properties of the third argument.)

According to Hopper and Thompson (1980), transitivity is a semantic property of sentences, and verbal transitivity is only one of its constituting features. In this sense, transitivity is a scalar notion, and sentences and predicates can be more or less transitive. For example, verbs of sensation, such as *see*, which do not imply a change of state on the side of the patient, are less transitive than verbs of action, such as *eat* or *cut*, which do. Parameters of transitivity are given below in Table 1.

In Functional Systemic Grammar, transitivity is defined as a system within the experiential mode of the ideational metafunction, and determines the

Table 1 The components of transitivity (adapted from Hopper and Thompson 1980)

	High	Low
A. PARTICIPANTS	2 or more participants, A and O	1 participant
B. KINESIS	action	nonaction
C. ASPECT	telic	atelic
D. PUNCTUALITY	punctual	nonpunctual
E. VOLITIONALITY	volitional	nonvolitional
F. AFFIRMATION	affirmative	negative
G. MODE	realis	irrealis
H. AGENCY	A high in potency	A low in potency
I. AFFECTEDNESS OF O	O totally affected	O not affected
J. INDIVIDUATION OF O	O highly individuated, i.e. O is: (i) proper (ii) human, animate (iii) concrete (iv) singular (v) count (vi) referential, definite	O nonindividuated, i.e. O is: (i) common (ii) inanimate (iii) abstract (iv) plural (v) mass (vi) nonreferential

In this table, A = agent, O = direct object.

configuration of processes (= states of affairs in this terminology), participants and circumstances (Halliday 1994: 144–158). This conception of transitivity is similar to the one assumed by Hopper and Thompson, since, rather than as a property of the verb, it views transitivity as a dynamic set of variables which is concerned with the overall linguistic representation of an event.

In some languages, two types of intransitive verbs can be detected, sometimes called **unergative** and **unaccusative**. Unergative verbs display features that are similar to some features of transitive verbs, while unaccusative verbs do not. For example, in Italian both unergative and transitive verbs select the auxiliary *have* for the past tense, while unaccusative verbs select the auxiliary *be*:

(5) *Paola ha mangiato la torta*
Paola has eaten the cake
"Paola ate the cake." (Italian, Romance, Indo-European)

(6) *Mario ha telefonato a suo fratello*
Mario has telephoned to his brother
"Mario called his brother on the phone." (Italian, Romance, Indo-European)

(7) *i bambini sono andati a scuola*
the children are gone to school
"The children went to school." (Italian, Romance, Indo-European)

Mangiare 'eat' in (5) is transitive and selects the auxiliary *avere* 'have'; *telefonare* 'telephone' in (6) and *andare* in (7) are both intransitive and never occur with a direct object, but *telefonare* selects the auxiliary *avere*, while *andare* selects the auxiliary *essere* 'be'. This phenomenon is called **split intransitivity**. Usually, intransitive verbs that behave like transitive verbs refer to activities, while other intransitive verbs refer to achievements, that is, they indicate a change of state or a transfer in space on the side of the subject. For this reason, the subject of unaccusative verbs is similar to the patient of transitive verbs (it is an undergoer, in the terminology of Role and Reference Grammar), while the subject of unergative verbs is similar to the subject of transitive verbs (it is an actor).

See also *State of affairs* and *Valency*.

Tree diagram see *Node* and *Phrase structure rules*.

Unaccusative See *Voice* and *Transitive*.

Uniformity Condition

In the Minimalist Program, the Uniformity Condition states that the operations available in the Covert Component (after Spell-Out), should also be available in the Overt Component (before Spell-Out), that is, they are symmetrical.

See also *Spell-Out*.

Uninterpretable features

Within the Minimalist Program, **uninterpretable features** or **[-interpretable] features** are features that do not have an effect on semantic interpretation. Uninterpretable features must be eliminated from the system through movement operations before they reach Logical Form (LF). Otherwise the **Full Interpretation Principle** would be violated, and the derivation would crash at LF. The checking operation that results from movement has the goal to eliminate uninterpretable features. Uninterpretable features are checked only once, since they are eliminated after checking. For example, Case features are uninterpretable when they appear with a verb, so they must be checked by a NP that will eliminate them from the verb. Thus, they are checked only once.

See also *Interpretable features, Last Resort Condition*, and *Lexical redundancy rules*.

Universal Grammar (UG)

In Transformational Generative Grammar, Universal Grammar or UG is the system of principles, conditions, rules and properties of all human languages. Following this approach, Chomsky (1965, 1986) claims that human languages are governed by a small set of principles of UG, which limits the class of possible grammars that human beings can develop. Evidence that sustains this hypothesis comes from the linguistic properties of the languages of the world and from the way children acquire language. Despite the deficiency of data to which they are exposed, children attain the complex system of language in a short time. There are three aspects that are essential for language acquisition:

a. The speech children hear from their environment includes incomplete sentences, pauses, slips of tongue etc. This is called "poverty of stimulus."
b. The available data are finite, but children are able to produce and understand an infinite number of novel sentences. This proves the "creativity of human language."
c. Speakers have knowledge of their language even if they have not been exposed to all its structures as children. They have judgments concerning complex sentences, paraphrase, ambiguity relations, and ungrammatical sentences. This is called "native language intuition."

It is assumed that UG is innate. This explains why children acquire languages so quickly. In reality, the kinds of errors that children make while acquiring language reflect innate constraints, such as regularizing irregular forms of language, for example: *I eated* as opposed to *I ate*. Empirical studies of language acquisition have confirmed that children do this.

In the early 1960s, Noam Chomsky proposed that children learn language the same way they learn to walk. For Chomsky, the speed and precision of language acquisition leaves no real alternative but to conclude that children somehow have an innate linguistic ability before they have experience with language. Thus, when they are exposed to their language (or languages, if they are multilingual), they are able to acquire the complexities of the language or languages they are exposed to. This is due to the fact that their ability to speak is part of their biological endowment, not part of their culture. Universal Grammar, therefore, is part of the knowledge that resides in the human brain. The science of linguistics tries to ascertain what linguistic aspects are parts of UG and what aspects of particular languages are not part of UG.

Some linguists focus on the study of social circumstances and on their significance for language. They focus on what Chomsky calls **E-language** or **external language**. Other linguists study language as an internalized system that represents what is in the mind or brain of a particular individual or a set of individuals. They focus on what Chomsky calls **I-language** or **internalized language**.

In 2002 Marc Hauser, Noam Chomsky, and Tecumseh Fitch claimed that a distinction should be made between the **faculty of language in the broad**

sense (FLB) and the **faculty of language in the narrow sense** (FLN). The faculty of language in the broad sense includes a Sensory-Motor System, a Conceptual-Intentional System, and the computational mechanisms for recursion, providing the capacity to generate an infinite range of expressions from a finite set of elements. The faculty of language in the narrow sense includes at least recursion, which is the primary component of the faculty of language.

In 2001 a team of British researchers claimed to have isolated a gene, the gene FOXP2, that may be directly involved in the development of speech and language. When mutated, this gene causes abnormal development of brain structures that control facial movement and certain verbal abilities. This is the first time that a single gene has been linked to an inherited speech disorder. There is need for further research in order to determine the exact relation between genetics and speech. Nevertheless, this discovery seems to support and give empirical evidence to Chomsky's claim that the language faculty (or UG) is innate.

V2 (or Verb Second) languages

V2 (or verb-second) languages are languages in which the finite verb of the main clause obligatorily occurs in second position (or P2), while the subject is either in initial position, or in the position immediately following the verb. The most consistent language of this type is Modern High German. In such languages, initial position can be taken by any constituent:

(1) a. *Hans war   gestern   nicht bei mir*
       Hans be:PRET.3SG yesterday not   at 1SG.DAT
    b. *gestern   war   Hans nicht bei mir*
       yesterday be:PRET.3SG Hans not   at 1SG.DAT
    c. *bei mir   war   Hans gestern   nicht*
       at 1SG.DAT be:PRET.3SG Hans yesterday not
       "Hans was not with me yesterday." (German, Germanic, Indo-European)

With compound verb forms, it is normally the finite auxiliary that occurs in V2, while the nonfinite form of the main verbs occurs in final position, as in:

(2) *ik heb dit boek gelezen*
    I have this book read
    "I read this book." (Dutch, Germanic, Indo-European)

All Germanic languages (except Gothic) have been V2 during at least some stage in their history, and most of them still are, even though not as consistently as German. French and some of the Northern Italian varieties have had at least a partial V2 stage during the Middle Ages. Outside the area of influence of Germanic, V2 appears to be a very limited phenomenon (it has been reported from Kashmiri). According to some Indo-Europeanists, Germanic inherited V2 from Proto-Indo-European, where it is sometimes held to be a product of Wackernagel's Law (see P2).

V2 has been widely studied in Transformational Generative Grammar, in which it is described as due to verb movement in languages whose underlying order is SOV.

See also *P2* and *Word order*.

Valency or valence

A property of predicates, most typically verbs, based on the number of arguments required, which determines the syntactic configuration in which they occur. Verbs can be avalent (valency Ø), monovalent (valency 1), bivalent (valency 2), or trivalent (valency 3), while the existence of tetravalent verbs is a matter of disagreement.

Valency is a notion connected with the interface between syntax and semantics, and consequently it may have a double nature, depending on whether we consider it a primarily syntactic or a primarily semantic notion, as can be easily shown on the example of avalent verbs. Avalent verbs do not require any arguments; typically, they refer to spontaneous events in which no participant is involved. Weather verbs are avalent and in null subject languages they do not require any overtly expressed or understood constituent to form a grammatical sentence as is shown in (1):

(1) *nevica*
snow:PRS.3SG
"It is snowing." (Italian, Romance, Indo-European)

Languages like English require an expletive subject, which however does not refer to an argument. This example demonstrates the difference between **syntactic** and **semantic valency**: English weather verbs are syntactically monovalent, even if they are semantically avalent (in other words, English has no syntactically avalent verbs).

A monovalent verb requires a single argument, which is usually selected as subject, as in (2) and (3):

(2) *Paul runs*
(3) *the water boils*

The explanation for the valency of the verbs *run* and *boil* in the above examples is that the event of running requires at least one participant, in this case a mover (someone who runs); similarly the event of boiling requires a patient (something boiling).

Bivalent verbs (sometimes called divalent) are verbs that require two arguments, most notably transitive verbs, which have a subject and a direct object, as in (4):

(4) *I bought a book*

Many transitive verbs can occur with or without a direct object, as the verb *paint*:

(5) a. *John was painting*
   b. *John was painting a picture*

This phenomenon is described in different ways depending on the theoretical framework: the verb *paint* can be said to have two different valencies, or two predicate frames, or it can be said to represent two homophonous verbs, a unergative one in (5a), and a transitive one in (5b).

Trivalent verbs are verbs of giving or verbs of communication that take three arguments: subject, direct object, and indirect object, as in (6):

(6) *my mom gave me a birthday present*

The existence of tetravalent verbs is disputed. Verbs that indicate commercial transactions are sometimes said to be tetravalent, as in (7):

(7) *Mary paid John 25 euros for the book*

Note, however, that, apart from the subject, the other NPs in this sentence are certainly not equally obligatory: in other words, these verbs may be semantically tetravalent, but not syntactically.

Nonverbal predicates also have valency. The valency of most adjectives is 1 (but it can be higher, as in *similar*):

(8) *ona   krassivaja*
    3SG.NOM.F pretty:NOM.SG.F
    "She is pretty." (Russian, Slavic, Indo-European)

In S. C. Dik's Functional Grammar, the valency of a verb is called **predicate frame**, and predicates are divided into one-place (=monovalent), two-place (bivalent), etc.

The term **argument structure** is also used in the place of valency, mostly in the United States, following the terminology of Lexical Functional Grammar (Bresnan 2001).

The term 'valency' was first used by Tesnière who borrowed it from chemistry. As seen above, it has both semantic and syntactic implications. This two-fold nature of valency is its most problematic aspect that also renders it difficult to determine syntactic valency for higher than bivalent (transitive) verbs: this is because morphosyntactic tests (verb agreement, passivization) are most revealing only with monovalent and bivalent verbs.

In Cognitive Grammar, valency is considered a semantically based scalar notion with syntactic implications. From this perspective, sentences like (7) are not problematic since the event of paying usually involves all four participants; however, there is a higher degree of argumenthood for the subject than for all other constituents.

See also *Applicative, Causative, Transitivity*, and *Voice*.

Variable

An item bound by a quantifier, as in:

(1) *Mary likes something*
    [there is an x such that Mary likes x].

An empty element such as a wh-trace or the trace of a quantifier which must be A-bar bound by an Operator is a variable.

See also *Binding Theory* and *Operator*.

Visibility Condition

The Visibility Condition is linked to the Case Filter in Transformational Generative Grammar. In fact, the Case Filter is reduced to the Visibility Condition. The Visibility Condition states that a syntactic element must be Case-marked for it to be Theta-marked. In other words, a predicate can only assign a theta-role to DP/NP that is visible. In order to be visible, a DP/NP must be Case marked with abstract Case. This condition applies at Logical Form (LF) as well. For example, in sentence (1):

(1) *he hit the ball*

the theta-role agent which is assigned to *he* is visible at LF after *he* has checked its abstract (nominative) Case.

See also *Case* and *Case Filter*.

Voice

A property of verbs, also called **diathesis**. In English, transitive verbs have **active** and **passive** voice:

(1) *the police captured the thieves*
(2) *the thieves were captured by the police*

In languages like English, the active form of transitive verbs is morphologically the same as the only form of intransitive verbs, showing the more basic character of the active with respect to the passive. The English passive requires an auxiliary (*be*) but several other languages have morphological passive, such as Latin: *laudo* 'I praise' (act.) vs. *laudor* 'I am praised' (pass.).

With respect to the active, the passive has reduced valency: passive verbs are intransitive. The direct object of an active sentence is the subject of the corresponding passive sentence, and it remains the only argument of the verb. The agent, which would be the subject (i.e. an argument) in the active, is an adverbial in the passive, and need not be expressed: indeed, one of the reasons for using the passive seems to be that the agent can be left out.

In Relational Grammar, the passive is conceived of in terms of agent demotion and patient promotion. The agent, which is the subject in an underlying stratum, is demoted and becomes a chômeur (jobless), leaving the subject position empty, while the patient, which is the object in the underlying stratum, is promoted to subject.

In S. C. Dik's Functional Grammar, voice depends on the perspective or vantage point from which a state of affairs is presented: if it is the agent's vantage point, then active voice is chosen, if it is the patient's, we will have passive voice.

Besides active and passive, another commonly found voice is the **middle** voice, as in Classical Greek: *epoíesa* 'I did' (act.), *epoioûmai* 'I did (for myself)' (mid.), *epoiéthē* 'I was done' (pass.).

The middle voice essentially indicates affectedness: it can occur with intransitive verbs, especially when they indicate change of state, or with active verbs, in which case it indicates special involvement of the agent in the action.

In addition, the middle voice often has impersonal meaning. This is also true of the passive in some languages that do not have a morphological middle, as Latin:

(3) *itur*
go:PRS.P.3SG
"You (impersonal) go." (Latin, Italic, Indo-European)

Middle voice in the Romance languages is expressed by verbs with the reflexive particle:

(4) *mi   sono mangiato tutta   la   torta*
REFL am   eaten   all   the cake
"I ate up the whole cake." (Italian, Romance, Indo-European)

In (4) the verb form *mi sono mangiato* 'I ate' contains the reflexive particle *mi*, which does not have reflexive meaning, but rather indicates special involvement of the agent: it implies that the action of eating was performed deliberately and with pleasure.

Another diathesis, found in ergative languages, is the **antipassive**. The antipassive owes its name to the fact that it is the agent, and not the patient, that remains the only argument of the antipassive. In the antipassive, the agent takes the absolutive case and the patient, if expressed, takes the dative or another case (but this is not always the case in all languages: in some, both arguments remain and take the absolutive case). As an example, consider (5a) and (5b):

(5) a. *anguti-up arnaq   kunik-taa*
        man-ERG   woman.ABS kiss-PART.3SG/3SG
        "The man kissed the woman."
    b. *angut   kunik-si-vuq   arna-mik*
        man.ABS kiss-AP-IND.3SG woman-INSTR
        "The man is kissing a woman." (from Spreng in press) (Inuktitut, Inuit, Eskimo-Aleut)

In (5a) the agent *anguti-up* 'man' is in the ergative, and the patient *arnaq* 'woman' in the absolutive. In the antipassive construction in (5b), the agent *agut* is in the absolute, while the patient *arna-mik* is in the instrumental case.

Some languages have an **applicative** voice, which is a voice that increases the valency of verb to include some oblique constituents. Applicatives are similar to causatives, because they increase the verbal valency. As causative, applicative is often derivational.

In Transformational Generative Grammar, especially in the Government and Binding framework, passive voice is conceived of in terms of theta-role assignment and NP movement (although it must be said that in earlier stages of the theory the relation between active and passive was conceived of as a specific passive transformation).

See also *Alignment, Applicative, Causative, NP-movement,* and *Valency.*

Wackernagel's Law See *Clitic* and *P2*.

Weak Features

In the Minimalist Program Weak Features are features that lack strength and hence are checked at Logical Form rather than in the syntax. For example, in English, which has poor agreement morphology, the agreement features in the verb are weak and hence they are covertly checked at LF. However, in Italian and French, which have rich agreement, the agreement features of the verb are strong features and must be checked in overt syntax, inducing verb movement. Due to Procrastinate, Weak Features must be checked in covert syntax.

See also *Covert Syntax, Procrastinate*, *Spell-Out* and *Strong Features*.

Weight (of constituents)

Internal **categorial complexity** of constituents is often called their 'weight'. The word weight is used because higher complexity usually corresponds to a larger amount of phonological material: clitics, which are typical **light** constituents, are often monosyllables, while complex constituents which contain heads and modifiers consist of several words, hence many more syllables. Complex constituents are said to be **heavy**.

See also *Clitic, Constituent,* and *Word order*.

Wh-in situ

In some languages, such as Chinese and Japanese, wh-words appear in their based generated positions. In (1):

(1) *tā shì   shéi*
    he COP who
    "Who is he?" (Chinese, Sinitic, Sino-Tibetan)

the wh-word *shéi* is moved covertly, in order to have the meaning of the question "Who is he?".

In such a case wh-movement is covert, at Logical Form (LF). In other languages, such as English and French, there is overt and covert movement. For example, consider French (2) and (3):

(2) **qu'** *est que tu veux?* (wh-movement)
   what is that you want
(3) *tu   veux* **quois**? (wh-in situ)
   you want what
   "What do you want?" (French, Romance, Indo-European)

In (2) *que* has been moved, in (3) *quois* is in situ. In order to interpret the question in sentence (3), the wh-word *quois* moves covertly to the specifier of CP at LF.

However, when sentences have two wh-words one movement is overt, at S-structure, and the other movement is covert, at LF. Consider (4):

(4) *I wonder* **who** *bought* **what**

In (4), after *who* was moved overtly, *what* rises covertly to the Operator position (i.e. CP position) and adjoins to the embedded clause at Logical Form.

Wh-movement

Movement that transfers an element (usually a wh-word) to an A-bar position, mostly the Specifier of CP. The movement leaves a trace or a copy forming a chain, as shown in (1):

(1) $[_{CP}$ **what**$_i$ **will**$_j$ $[_{IP}$ John t_j eat t_i]]

In (1) the wh-word *what* is moved to the Spec of CP and the auxiliary verb moves to the head of CP. The wh-element always lands in an A-bar position. In example (1) wh-movement is overt at the syntactic level. In some cases, when there are two wh-elements, one wh-word moves overtly, and the other wh-word stays in situ, as in (2):

(2) *I wonder which wine Ann bought* **for whom**

In (2) *which wine* has been moved to the Specifier of CP and *whom* stayed in its base generated position. The movement of the wh-elements could be changed as in (3):

(3) *I wonder* **for whom** *Ann bought* **which wine**

However, when one of the wh-words is the subject, wh-movement obeys the Superiority Condition, as shown in (4) and (5):

(4) *I wonder* **who** *bought* **what**
(5) * *I wonder* **what** *bought* **who**

In some languages, such as Chinese and Japanese, wh-questions have all wh-elements in situ, as in example (6):

(6) *Taroo wa nani o   kakimashita ka*
     Taroo TOP what OBJ bought   INT.PTC
     "What did Taroo buy?" (Japanese, Japanese)

When the wh-word is an argument, its trace will receive Case. However, since wh-words move to an A-bar position, the trace of the wh-element will behave as a variable. Thus, wh-traces are subject to principle C of the Binding Theory.

Wh-movement applies in relative clauses as well.

See also *Binding Theory, Chain, Relative Clause, Superiority,* and *Wh-in situ.*

Word order

The term 'word order' can refer to the order of single words either within a sentence or within a phrase; most often, though, it refers to the order of constituents in a sentence. There are essentially two traditions in word order research: one focused on its pragmatic function, and the other focused on the syntactic correlates of word order.

The pragmatic function of word order has been the matter of study at least starting with Weil (1844), whose seminal research was later expanded by members of the Prague School in the framework of the Functional Sentence Perspective. According to FSP, initial and final positions are most relevant to the communicative structure of sentences. They are the positions of the theme (initial) and the rheme (final); the linguistic material that may occur in between them is called transition as in (1):

(1) *Mary   went to school on a bike*
     theme transition   rheme

The order theme—transition—rheme is the one that occurs most frequently, but the opposite order, rheme—transition—theme may also occur in special circumstances. It is called emotive order.

Already Weil noted that freedom in word order varies across languages: in particular, he compared Latin and Classical Greek, in which word order is comparatively free, with French and English, in which it is largely obligatory. Fixed position of certain constituents in languages such as English serves the purpose of marking grammatical relations which, in a language like Latin, are encoded by case. Compare (2) and (3):

(2) *the mother loves the child* ≠ *the child loves the mother*
(3) *mater   amat   puerum = puerum amat   mater*
     mother:NOM love:3SG child:ACC   child:ACC love:3SG mother:NOM
     "The mother loves the child." (Latin, Italic, Indo-European)

The degree of freedom in word order in a specific language is not necessarily connected with the availability of case-marking, or with the need to distinguish the subject from the direct object. For example, the subject of intransitive verbs, even though it cannot be mistaken for a direct object, still has to precede the verb in English, while it frequently follows it in Italian and other null subject languages:

(4) *arriva   il   treno*
     arrive:3SG ART train
     "The train comes." (Italian, Romance, Indo-European)

According to German scholar Otto Behagel, categorial complexity of constituents, or constituents' 'weight', influences their position in the sentence. Light constituents, that is, simpler ones, precede constituents that are heavier, and display a higher degree of internal categorial complexity. This tendency is known as Behagel's Law, or the Law of Growing Members (*Gesetz der wachsenden Glieder*), and combines with Wackernagel's Law, according to which clitics tend to come early in the sentence (clitics are typical light elements). Behagel's Law has a foundation in discourse principles: constituents with lower complexity, such as anaphoric pronouns, normally convey shared information, while new information is generally coded by means of more complex constituents, as remarked by Hawkins (1983: 98–99).

The publication of Greenberg's 1963 paper on basic word order and its correlates gave rise to what is now known as 'word order typology'. Greenberg analyzed the order of S(ubject), V(erb), and (direct) O(bject) in a sample of 30 genetically unrelated languages, and found three main word order types:

i) VSO, as in most Semitic and Celtic languages;
ii) SVO, as in English or French;
iii) SOV, as in Turkish or Japanese.

The basic order of constituents correlates with some other word order features: languages of type (i) and (ii) usually have prepositions, while languages of type (iii) most often have postpositions; in languages of type (i) and (ii) modifiers usually follow their head, while the reverse is most often true in languages of type (iii), and so on. The main generalizations found by Greenberg on basic word order are as follows:

	VSO	SVO	SOV
1.	NA	NA	AN
2.	NGen	NGen	GenN
3.	NRel	NRel	RelN
4.	Prep	Prep	Postp
5.	VO	VO	OV

(N=head noun, Rel=relative clause, Gen=nominal modifier, V=verb, O=direct object, Prep=preposition, Postp=postposition.)

VSO and SVO languages largely behave in the same way: for this reason, they are sometimes referred to simply as VO languages. Note that the position of adjectival modifiers has been shown not to be relevant for word order typology by Dryer (1988), based on a sample of over 600 languages: consequently, correlations in line 1 do not hold.

Even without considering the order of nouns and adjectives, the regularities remain striking. Consequently, scholars have set out to explain why they hold. Bartsch and Vennemann (1972) suggest that this owes to the *natural serialization principle*, which states that the reciprocal order of head and dependent in languages tends to be uniform: VO languages favor the order head-dependent, while OV languages favor the order dependent-head (operator and operand in Bartsch and Vennemann's terminology). An alternative to the natural serialization principle is the *cross-category harmony principle*, proposed by Hawkins (1983).

In some languages, subordinate clauses do not have the same order found in main clauses. It is the case of German, in which main clauses have the finite verb in second position, while subordinate clauses have the order SOV:

(5) *die Kinder* **essen** *gern* *Schokolade*
the children eat with.pleasure chocolate
"Children like chocolate." (German, Germanic, Indo-European)

(6) *die Kinder, die gern Schokolade* **essen**, *gehen gerade*
the children that with.pleasure chocolate eat go presently
in die Schule
in the school
"The children, who like chocolate, are going to school." (German, Germanic, Indo-European)

In (5) the verb *essen* 'eat' is in second position; in the subordinate clause in (6) the same verbs occurs in final position. According to some theories, the subordinate clause reflects the underlying order (SOV).

It appears that the extent to which grammatical and pragmatic factors influence word order varies from language to language. For this reason, Thompson (1978) suggested that languages should be better divided into those that have pragmatic word order vs. those that have grammatical word order. This grouping leaves a number of questions unanswered: for example, why does the position of the finite verb have very little freedom in certain case-marking languages, such as Turkish, while it is completely free in others, such as Classical Greek? (A possible answer is that Classical Greek was in a transition from SOV to SVO, but note that languages are virtually always in a stage of transition.)

In general, the position of the finite verb seems to be more relevant for word order than the position of any other accented constituent, in the sense that it obeys comparatively more constraints. Within the Transformational Generative Framework, Richard Kayne (1994) has suggested that all languages have the universal SVO order, and that the different word orders fund in languages are due to movement (transformations) of their constituents.

WP-trace see *Binding, Copy, Movement*, and *Trace*.

X-bar theory

X-bar theory has been developed as a result of Chomsky's proposal in Chomsky (1970). This theory brings together the common features in the structure of phrases discovered at the time. In X-bar theory, all phrases are headed by either a lexical or a functional head. That is, they are endocentric phrases. The lexical or functional head of any phrase is a zero projection (X^{o}, X meaning 'any head'). A complement XP combines with X^{o} to form an X' (X-bar) projection. Adjuncts combine with X' (X-bar) projections to form more X' (X-bar) projections. The specifier (or Spec) combines with the topmost X' (X-bar) to form the X" or XP projection.

Specifiers are positions where subjects are generated or positions where elements land that are moved in a tree. Specifiers differ from complements in that they are not sisters of the head, but rather sisters of the phrase formed by the head and the complement, which optionally may have one or more adjuncts. Many different functions such as subject, determiner, or modifier, are assigned to this position, depending on the category of X^{o}. For example a Spec may have the Determiner of a NP, the Degree element of an AP, the subject of an IP, or the modifier (adverb or even auxiliary) of a VP. Within the VP-internal Subject Hypothesis, the Spec, VP is the D-structure position of the verb's external argument.

Within the Minimalist Program the subject is merged in the light verb *vP*, that is, in the specifier of *vP*.

Ignoring optional adjuncts and attributes, all phrases have the schematic structure indicated in the XP (x-phrase) in (1):

(1)
$$
\begin{array}{c}
\text{XP} \\
\diagup \diagdown \\
\text{Spec} \quad \text{X'} \quad \leftarrow \textit{X-bar} \\
\diagup \diagdown \\
\textit{head} \rightarrow \text{Xo} \quad \text{ZP} \leftarrow \textit{complement}
\end{array}
$$

Within the X-bar theory, this schematic structure is repeated recursively to form complex constituents, as shown in (2):

(2)

```
            XP
           / \
        Spec  X'
             / \
           Xo  ZP
              / \
           Spec  Z'
                / \
               Zo
```

However, the order of constituents with respect to the head of the projection is not universally fixed. There are languages that are head-first, such as English, or head-last such as Japanese. Within Transformational Generative Grammar, it is proposed that the X-bar format applies to both phrases and clauses. This would ease the process of language acquisition for children.

The distinction between finite and nonfinite clauses depends on the [+/–Tense] features of the node Infl (inflection). Thus, if the inflection node has [+Tense], the sentence is finite, such as *Mary likes apples*, but if the inflection node has [–Tense], the sentence is nonfinite, such as *to go home* in (3):

(3) *Mary wants **to go home***

Since in X-bar theory it is assumed that a sentence is headed by Infl, it follows that the sentence is an (endocentric) projection of IP (Inflectional Phrase), like other phrasal categories. Moreover, the type of sentence—interrogative or declarative—depends on the complementizer that introduces the clause. Thus, the complementizer, such as *whether* or *that*, determines the type of clause or IP that follows or complements C. Since the complemetizer is a head, it projects as a Complementizer Phrase or CP. Considering all these facts from the X-bar theory perspective, a sentence such as (4):

(4) *the girl liked the apples*

has the X-bar structure depicted in (5):

(5)

```
                    CP
                   / \
               Spec   C'
                     / \
                    C   IP
                       / \
                   Spec   I'
                         / \
                        I   VP
                   [+Tense] / \
                     past  DP  V'
                           Δ  / \
                       the girl V  DP
                            liked Δ
                               the apples
```

In (5), the subject, an external argument, is generated in the Spec of VP, following the VP-internal subject hypothesis. According to this hypothesis, the external argument is a sister of V'. The external theta-role (experiencer) is assigned compositionally by the verb together with its sister constituent (DP in this case).

Adjuncts are attached to X'. Thus, the sentence in (6), which has the adjunct *in the morning* would have the structure in (7):

(6) *the boy ate the toast in the morning*

(7)

```
                    CP
                   / \
               Spec   C'
                     / \
                    C   IP
                       / \
                   Spec   I'
                         / \
                        I   VP
                   [+Tense] / \
                     past  DP  V'       ← adjunct
                           Δ  / \
                       the boy V'  PP
                             / \  Δ
                            V  DP in the morning
                          eat   Δ
                              the toast
```

More recently, within the Minimalist Program, X-bar phrase structure has undergone several changes. The subject merges in the Spec of vP, a light verb pharse. The light verb vP projection has a lexical VP complement. The light vP phrase is introduced to solve the constituency problem of double object constructions (e.g. *to give*). Then, the vP projection is generalized to capture the meaning of light verb constructions such *as take a bath = to bath*, where the meaning of the light verb phrase vP depends on the meaning of its VP complement. Finally the light vP is generalized as a constituent of all verb phrases.

While in X-bar theory subjects (such as *the boy* in (5)) and modifiers (such as *in the morning* in (5)) are adjuncts to bar (X'), in the Minimalist Program modifiers are *adjunts* to XP and subjects are constituents dominated by XP . Moreover, the preformed clausal skeleton of X-bar theory is partially abandoned as a consequence of dropping D-structure (Deep Structure), even if the X-bar general scheme is maintained. Each sentence is built from bottom to top by means of the operation Merge and copy/move.

See also *Construction, Constituent, Copy, Light Verb, Merge, Numeration*, and *Phase*.

Key Thinkers

Section 1

Bloomfield, Leonard
(1887–1949)

Leonard Bloomfield is the leading figure in American linguistics during the first half of the twentieth century. He became a key figure in the development of structuralist descriptive linguistic theories with the publication of his book *Language* (1933), which, up to the publication of the first works of Transformational Generative Grammar in the sixties, was the most widely used textbook in American universities. In this book, which is a revised version of his 1914 *Introduction to the Study of Language*, Bloomfield treats linguistics as a science with its own methods and goals, focusing on language itself. He followed the scientific models of his time: deductive positivism and behaviorism, after a brief period in which he embraced mentalism, and followed the theories of Wilhelm Wundt, the father of experimental psychology. Bloomfield was the founder of the Linguistic Society of America and the main stream journal of American linguistics, *Language*. In addition he initiated the annual summer institutes of linguistics of the LSA.

Bloomfield was born in Chicago in 1887, but he moved with his family to Wisconsin when he was nine years old. There he was in contact with the Menomini people and their language, which explains his interest in the Menomini (Algonquian) language later on in his life, for example, his well-known 1939 article 'Menomini morphophonemics'. He received his BA in 1906 from Harvard and his Ph.D. in 1909 from the University of Chicago, after attending the graduate program of the University of Wisconsin. After his Ph.D., he spent a year in Germany studying with the Indo-Europeanists Leskien and Brugmann. In Germany he met students, such as Nikolaj Trubeckoj, who later would become important linguists. He was a Germanist at the University of Cincinnati, the University of Illinois, Ohio State University, and the University of Chicago before moving to Yale University in 1940 as a Sterling professor of linguistics, on Prokosh and Sapir's death. At Ohio State, he met the behaviorist Albert Weiss, who largely influenced his thought. In Chicago, Bloomfield was a colleague of Sapir with whom he had an uneasy friendship.

In his work, he insisted on the necessity of developing linguistics as a science conceived as a 'cumulative' and 'impersonal' discipline. Using the inductive method, his explanations were based on observable events analyzed by principles of mathematics and logic only. He argued against mentalistic and cognitive explanations of language. Thus, he eliminated meaning from his framework because he believed that a scientific study of meaning had to include all the details of encyclopedic knowledge. As a structuralist antimentalist that Bloomfield was, he thought that the structural properties of languages could be studied without reference to meaning. In his book *Language* (1933: 184), he separates syntax from morphology, and defines syntactic constructions in terms of free constituents as "constructions in which none of the immediate constituents is a bound form."

In his work of American Indian languages, Bloomfield used the methodology of comparative reconstruction establishing a comparative grammar of Algonquian languages, such as Menomini, Cree, Fox, and Ojibwa.

Further reading

Bloomfield, Leonard 1914. *Introduction to the Study of Language*. New York: Henry Holt and Company.

Bloomfield, Leonard 1926. 'A set of postulates for the science of language'. *Language 2*, 152–164.

Bloomfield, Leonard 1928. *Menomini Texts*. New York: G. E. Stechert, agents.

Bloomfield, Leonard 1933. *Language*. New York: Henry Holt and Company.

Bloomfield, Leonard 1939. 'Menomini morphophonemics'. *Travaux du cercle linguistique de Prague 8*, 105–115.

Bloomfield, Leonard 1957. *Eastern Ojibwa: Grammatical Sketch, Texts, and Word List*. Ann Arbor: University of Michigan Press.

Bloomfield, Leonard 1962. *The Menomini Language*. New Haven CT: Yale University Press.

Fought, John G. 1999. 'Leonard Bloomfield's linguistic legacy: Later uses of some technical features'. *Historiographia Linguistica 26*, 313–332.

Hall, Robert Anderson (ed.) 1987. *Leonard Bloomfield: Essays on His Life and Work*. Amsterdam: Benjamins.

Sebeok, Thomas A. 1966. *Portraits of Linguists: A Biographical Source Book for the History of Western Linguistics, 1746–1963*. Bloomington: Indiana University Press.

Chomsky, Noam
(b. 1928)

Noam Chomsky was born in Philadelphia, Pennsylvania in 1928. He studied philosophy and linguistics at the University of Pennsylvania in 1945, where he worked under C. West Churchman, Nelson Goodman, and Zelling Harris. Harris's teachings were fundamental for Chomsky's development of transformational grammar. He earned his Ph.D. in 1955 from the University of Pennsylvania, after staying in Harvard for four years as a Junior Fellow. His 1955 dissertation, later published as *The Logical Structure of Linguistic Theory* (1975) shaped many of his ideas on linguistics. Since 1955 he has taught at MIT, where he was appointed full professor in the Department of Modern Languages and Linguistics in1961. He was nominated Ferrari P. Ward Professor in 1966 and Institute Professor in 1976. His contributions in different fields of knowledge have been recognized with an enormous number of awards in various disciplines.

Chomsky's books *Syntactic Structures* (1957) and *Aspects of the Theory of Syntax* (1965) provided the basis for a new formal generative approach to linguistics and for the beginning of cognitive science. These books provided a new framework for thinking about human language and mind to linguists, philosophers, and psychologists.

Chomsky criticized structural linguistics procedures and the relevance it was given to the corpus or data collection. In the 1950s, the aim of most structural linguistic models was to discover rigorously a set of procedures for linguists to extract mechanically from a corpus the phonemes, the morphemes, and syntactic structures it contained. In structural linguistics the study of meanings had little place. Meanings were thought to be patterns of behavior determined by stimulus and response. Thus, they were not the subject matter of linguistics. Structuralism in linguistics derived from the behavioral approach of science and it was a consequence of the philosophical assumptions of positivism.

Once the corpus as the subject matter of linguistics was questioned, the notion of mechanical discoveries was rejected. In the two books mentioned above, Chomsky suggests, instead, that linguistic science must advance hypothesis, and *evaluate* them by testing them against evidence provided by native speakers. One of his main achievements in syntax was to show that the surface syntax of sentences was different from their underlying or deep structure. In fact, structural linguists working too close to the surface were unable to explain structural ambiguity of sentences such as *flying planes may be dangerous*. Such a sentence means either that 'for someone to fly planes may be dangerous' or that 'some artifacts that fly may be dangerous'. Furthermore, structural linguistics was unable to account for some internal relations of sentences such as *John is easy to please* and *John is eager to please*, which at the surface look as if they had exactly the same grammatical structure. However, despite their superficial similarity, in the first sentence *John* is understood to be the direct object of the verb *to please*. It means 'it is easy for someone to please John'. In the second sentence *John* is understood as the subject of the verb *to please*. It means 'John is eager to please someone'. This difference in the *syntax* of the sentences had to be accounted for, but there was no mechanism to explain such facts within the structuralist framework. Chomsky argued that the goal of syntax should be to construct a theory of syntax that would account for the following three main aspects:

1. The infinite number of sentences of a natural language.
2. The strings of words that were sentences and the strings of words that were not sentences.
3. A theory that would provide a description of the grammatical structure of each sentence, including their internal grammatical relations and their ambiguities.

In order to account for these three aspects, the description of a natural language would be a formal generative device which would contain a finite set of grammatical rules that generate the infinite set of sentences of a language, but they would not generate ungrammatical sentences. This grammar would provide a description of the syntactic structure of each sentence as well. Such a device was named *generative grammar*. Chomsky claimed that since any speaker could produce and understand an infinite number of sentences that he or she had never heard or produced before, the proper study of linguistics must be the speaker's underlying knowledge of the language. Within the production of language, he distinguished between *competence,* the speaker-hearer's knowledge of his or her language, and *performance,* the speaker-hearer use of language in a concrete situation.

In his 1959 review of B. F. Skinner's *Verbal Behavior*, Chomsky showed that no behaviorist account based on a stimulus-response model of language acquisition could possibly explain the rapidity and ease with which children acquire language. He employed three main arguments to support his claims: *nativism, poverty of the stimulus,* and *linguistic creativity*. Regarding nativism, he maintained that children must possess an innate ability as part of their biological endowment that enables them to produce and understand language. Regarding the poverty of stimulus, he claimed that children learn the very complex properties of their language despite the reduced, irregular and incomplete utterances that they are exposed to. Finally, regarding linguistic creativity, he maintained that children are able to understand and produce an infinite number of sentences, which they have never encountered before. This shows that they may have an innate recursion mechanism as part of their innate ability to acquire language. Thus, language speakers are less at the mercy of environmental factors than behaviorists argued. That is why stimulus-response models could not explain language acquisition properly.

Much of the developments of generative grammar in the 1970s and 1980s were efforts to formulate constraints on the generative and the transformational components of grammar. For example, X-bar theory attempted to reduce phrase structure rules into a structural scheme for all phrases and move-Alfa tried to reduce all movements to this single rule whose applicability was restricted by general principles of grammar. However, starting from 1981, Chomsky began to combine the innate principles of UG (Universal Grammar) to *parameters*, the components of languages whose values were not genetically fixed. At this point, language acquisition became a process of parameter setting and linguistic diversity was explained in terms of different choices of the values of the parameters associated with the principles of UG. Within this framework, the construction of rule systems was not the central task of linguistics. The focus of linguistics was instead to uncover the principles of UG and account for linguistic variation through the identification of parameters.

Within the Minimalist Program framework (1995–to date), Chomsky has proposed that the language faculty is a perfect device. Representations and derivations are as minimal as possible given the fact that they have to interact with the *articulatory-perceptual system* (its phonetic aspect) and the *conceptual-intentional system* (meaning). The derivation of sentences begins with a set of items drawn from the lexicon into the numeration. Lexical items include features, such as <tense>. Lexical elements are merged one by one to form successively larger and larger syntactic objects. At a certain point (*spell-out*) the derivation splits: semantic operations continue without overt phonological realization to produce LF (Logical Form). On the other hand, Phonological operations continue without affecting the meaning of the derivation. The last principle of UG is *full interpretation,* which requires every element of PF and LF receive appropriate interpretation. Movements occur as a last resort, in a least effort manner.

Chomsky's proposals have always been controversial and revolutionary in Kuhn's sense, as Newmayer (1986) has shown. Besides his work in linguistics, Chomsky is well known in other fields such as philosophy, politics, cognitive sciences, and psychology, fields in which he has published several books and articles. As political analyst and activist, he has been inspirational for hundreds of left wing individuals and groups due to his radical and non-conventional points of view on politics.

Further reading

Barsky, Robert 1997. *Noam Chomsky. A Life of Dissent*. Cambridge MA: The MIT Press.

Chomsky, Noam 1959. 'A review of B. F. Skinner's verbal behavior'. *Language 35*, 26–58.

Chomsky, Noam 1965. *Aspects of the Theory of Syntax*. Cambridge MA: The MIT Press.

Chomsky, Noam 1966. *Topics in the Theory of Generative Grammar*. The Hague: Mouton.

Chomsky, Noam 1972. *Language and Mind*. 3rd edn. New York: Harcourt, Brace & World.

Chomsky, Noam 1981. 'Principles and parameters in syntactic theory'. In *Explanation in Linguistics*. London: Longman.

Chomsky, Noam 1986. *Knowledge of Language*. New York: Praeger.

Chomsky, Noam 1988. *Language and Problems of Language: The Managua Lectures*. Cambridge MA: The MIT Press.

Chomsky, Noam 1995. *The Minimalist Program*. Cambridge MA: The MIT Press.

Chomsky, Noam 1996. *Class Warfare*. London: Pluto Press.

Kuhn, Thomas 1970. *The Structure of Scientific Revolutions*. Chicago: Chicago University Press.

Newmeyer, Frederick 1986. 'Has there been a "Chomskyan revolution" in linguistics?'. *Language 62*, 1–18.

Otero, Carlos (ed.) 1993. *Noam Chomsky: Critical Assessments*. London/ New York: Routledge.

Dik, Simon Cornelis
(1940–1995)

Dutch linguist, famous for developing the theory of Functional Grammar. Dik studied classics in Amsterdam, the city to which he moved during his childhood from his native Delden, and where he spent most of his life. Already during the early years of his study he developed an interest for general linguistics. In the 1960s he was one of the early critics of Transformational Generative Grammar, which had recently been exported to the Netherlands. In 1968 he defended his dissertation on *Coordination; its implications for the theory of General Linguistics*, and shortly thereafter he was appointed the chair of general linguistics at the University of Amsterdam, which he occupied until short before his death.

In 1978, Dik launched his theory of Functional Grammar, in which he combined formal and functional principles, viewing the sentence as a syntactic, semantic, and pragmatic object, in a theory that conceived of language primarily as a communication tool. Dik's later publications mostly constitute refinements of the theory. His last book was the first volume of *The Theory of Functional Grammar* (1989), whose second volume was published posthumously in 1997, edited by Kees Hengeveld.

Functional Grammar became especially popular in the Netherlands, Belgium, and Spain, while in several other countries some individual scholars also work in the Functional Grammar framework. Among functional approaches to syntax, Functional Grammar was among the first to offer a high degree of formalization because Dik's intention was to provide scholars with a paradigm which could be an alternative to Transformational Generative Grammar. Some of his former students and collaborators have developed refinements of Functional Grammar, such as the Functional Procedural Grammar of Jan Nuyts, the Functional Discourse Grammar of Kees Hengeveld, and the Incremental Functional Grammar proposed by Lachlan Mackenzie.

However, nowadays, in spite of growing interest for functional approaches, neither Dik's Functional Grammar nor its developments seem to have reached a position of dominance within functionalism, such as to give it a status comparable with that of Transformational Generative Grammar. This is largely due to the fact that Dik's theory of Functional Grammar has never really had followers in the United States, where partly similar functional approaches have developed, virtually in a totally independent manner.

Further reading

Anstey, Matthew and John Lachlan Mackenzie (eds.) 2005. *Crucial Readings in Functional Grammar*. Berlin: Mouton de Gruyter.

Dik, Simon C. 1968. *Coordination: Its Implications for the Theory of General Linguistics*. Amsterdam: North Holland.

Dik, Simon C. 1997a. *The Theory of Functional Grammar*. Vol. 1: *The Structure of the Clause*. Second, revised edn. Edited by Kees Hengeveld. Berlin: Mouton De Gruyter.

Dik, Simon C. 1997b. *The Theory of Functional Grammar*. Vol. 2: *Complex and Derived Constructions*. Edited by Kees Hengeveld. Berlin: Mouton De Gruyter.

Hengeveld, Kees and John Lachlan Mackenzie 2006. 'Functional discourse grammar'. In Keith Brown (ed.), 668–676.

Kooij, Jan G. 2001. 'Simon Cornelis Dik'. *Jaarboek van de Maatschappij der Nederlandse Letterkunde*, 62–66.

Mackenzie, John Lachlan and María Á. Gómez-González (eds.) 2004. A *New Architecture for Functional Grammar*. Berlin: Mouton de Gruyter.

Greenberg, Joseph Harold
(1915–2001)

American linguist. Joseph Greenberg remains one of the most influential scholars in linguistic typology and language universals. He studied at Columbia, Yale, and Northwestern University, where he received his Ph.D. in anthropology. After the Second World War, he got a position at the University of Minnesota, where he remained for two years, before moving to the Department of Anthropology of Columbia University. He taught at Columbia from 1948 to 1962, then moved to Stanford where he remained for the rest of his life. At Stanford, Greenberg was professor of anthropology, helped to found the Linguistics Department and organized the African Studies Center. He was the first linguist to become a member of the National Academy of Sciences.

Already in his early years, Greenberg showed a major interest for languages, and managed to learn as many as he could. His interest for classification is already present in his first article, devoted to the classification of African languages (1949). In this and other early works, Greenberg distinguished features of genetic classification from typological features and features connected with anthropological and cultural factors. His classification of African languages was partly based on mass comparison; its final version, which appeared in the 1950s, was highly innovative, and remains one of his most important achievements.

Greenberg's first contribution to typology appeared in 1954, and is a refinement of Sapir's work on morphological typology contained in *Language* (1921). His most significant contribution to syntax, which is also a milestone for linguistic typology, is his 1963 paper "Some universals of grammar with particular reference to the order of meaningful elements." In this paper, Greenberg made extensive use of implicational universals (expressed in the form "if a language has x, then it also has y"); based on a sample of 30 genetically unrelated languages, he found 45 such universals, that concerned the order of constituents in the simple sentence and inside phrases.

As Croft remarks in his obituary, Greenberg's paper appeared at a time when Transformational Generative Grammar had moved the focus of linguistic research to syntax, and Chomsky was arguing that linguists should seek language universals. However, while in the Chomskyan tradition universals are sought deductively, based on the analysis of individual languages (and often limited to the analysis of English), Greenberg's perspective was the opposite: he sought universals through an inductive method, based on comparison across languages.

Upon its publication, Greenberg's paper had a major impact on linguistics, and word order universals were incorporated in numerous theories. It also had a big impact on historical syntax, especially due to the work of W. P. Lehmann. For about two decades, syntactic change was virtually conceived of as uniquely conditioned by change in word order patterns, an assumption which was certainly too far fetched with respect to Greenberg's intentions, but still contributed to generate major interest in historical syntax.

Greenberg's impact on linguistic theory cannot be overestimated. In fact, according to Newman, quoted in the obituary published in the *New York Times*, "next to Chomsky, you have to say Greenberg is clearly the most important linguist we have had over the last 50 years, in terms of the quality, quantity and scope of his work." Greenberg's seminal works in typology opened new paths of research and contributed to establish what is today known as the functional-typological approach to language, which combines West Coast Functionalism with cognitive linguistics, and presently constitutes the most significant alternative to Transformational Generative Grammar.

Further reading

Croft, William 2001. 'Joseph Harold Greenberg'. *Language 77*, 815–830.

Greenberg, Joseph H. 1963. 'Some universals of grammar with particular reference to the order of meaningful elements'. In *Universals of Language*. Cambridge MA: The MIT Press, 73–113.

Greenberg, Joseph H. 1966. *The Languages of Africa*. Bloomington: Indiana University Press.

Greenberg, Joseph H. 2000. *Indo-European and its Closest Relatives: The Eurasiatic Language Family*. Vol. 1: *Grammar*. Stanford: Stanford University Press.

Greenberg, Joseph H. 2002. *Indo-European and its Closest Relatives: The Eurasiatic Language Family*. Vol. 2: *Lexicon*. Stanford: Stanford University Press.

Greenberg, Joseph H. 2005. *Genetic Linguistics: Essays on Theory and Method*. Edited by William Croft. Oxford: OUP.

Silverstein, Michael 2002. 'Joseph Harold Greenberg'. *American Anthropologist 104*, 630–635.

Wade, Nicholas 2001. 'Joseph Greenberg, 85, singular linguist, dies'. *The New York Times* May 15.

Tesnière, Lucien
(1893–1954)

French linguist, known especially for being the founder of Dependency Grammar, a theory of syntax based on dependency relations within the sentence. His most important book is *Elément de syntaxe structurale*, which was published posthumous in 1959.

Already during his school years, Tesnière proved to be extremely gifted for languages. He finished his studies in Leipzig and Vienna in 1913 and 1914. In Leipzig, he met Nikolaj Trubeckoj and joined the Prague Linguistic Circle. He was drafted into the army during the First World War, and managed to make advantage of the years spent on several fronts by learning more languages, including Hebrew, Russian, Dutch, Finnish, and Hungarian. He got his first job in Strasbourg, where he taught until 1934, and later moved to the University of Montpellier, where he taught comparative linguistics.

Tesnière's first field of research was Slavic linguistics, on which he published various works, as for example his *Petite grammaire russe* (1934). Already during his years in Strasbourg, Tesnière worked out the principles of his theory of valency, which he could not publish due to financial restrictions: thus, the theory could not be made available to a wide audience until his Montpellier years, when he published *Cours élémentaire de syntaxe structurale* (1938), followed by *Cours de syntaxe structurale* (1943) and *Esquisse d'une syntaxe structurale* (1953), published short before his death.

Tesnière called his theory 'structural syntax', thus making clear that his main interest concerned the structure of sentences and constituents. He conceived of structure as an underlying principle of constructions, rather than simply as their linear order, and wrote "Structural syntax aims to reveal the deep structural reality hidden behind apparent linear character of language, based on the spoken chain" ("La syntaxe structurale a pour objet de révéler la réalité structurale profonde qui se cache derrière l'apparence linéaire du langage sur la chaîne parlée." 1953: 4).

Tesnière abandoned the logical conception of sentence structure, based on subject and predicate, and, viewing the verb as central, provided a theory based on the notion of dependency. He is especially credited with working out the notion of valency, according to which verbs predetermine sentence structure because they have slots (valencies) that must be obligatorily filled by dependents. The word valency itself is borrowed from chemistry: Tesnière referred to the verb as to the atom of the sentence, and viewed the sentence as a molecule, constructed as the verb atom binds with other atoms. Valency is not only a property of verbs: other words as well may predetermine their surrounding structure, such as prepositions.

Even if Tesnière was the first to elaborate a complete theory of valency and dependency, the idea that specific words, notably verbs, have slots that must be filled underlies the notion of transitivity, which has a long tradition in Western grammatical description. In 1934, Bühler introduced the critical notion of *Leerstellen* 'empty slots' into German grammar, crediting medieval scholastics with the neighboring notion of *connotatio*. The term *Dependenzgrammatik* had been introduced in the German grammatical tradition in the nineteenth century, but it was rediscovered later, when Tesnière works became known in Germany.

According to Tesnière a sentence can be thought of as the staging of a small drama (*un petit drame*), in which a number of actors is involved, together with some additional entities. He called the first type of participants *actants* and the second *circumstants*. In this perspective, the verb is the central part of the sentence, in that it expresses the action (=event) which is referred to in the sentence and provides the slots (valencies) for required participants, which take the roles that the verb assigns them: thus, the verb is the organizer of the sentence. Tesnière model was influential in European structuralism, even outside linguistics: the term actant, referring to a participant of an event, then spread to semiotics, and was used notably by Algirdas Greimas in the description of actantial narrative schemes in the study of narrative texts.

Further reading

Bühler, Karl 1934. *Sprachtheorie. Die Darstellungsfunktion der Sprache*. Jena: Fischer.

Forsgren, Kjell-Aake 2006. 'Tesnière, Lucien Valerius' (1893–1954). In K. Brown (ed.), 593–594.

Greciano, Gertrud and Helmut Schumacher (eds.) 1996. *Lucien Tesnière— Syntaxe structurale et operations mentales. Akten des deutsch-französischen Kolloquiums anlässlich der 100. Wiederkehr seines Geburtstags*. Tübingen: Niemeyer.

Tesnière, Lucien 1934. *Petite grammaire russe*. Paris: Henri Didier.

Tesnière, Lucien 1953. *Esquisse d'une syntaxe structurale*. Paris: Klincksieck.

Tesnière, Lucien 1959. *Éléments de syntaxe structurale*. Paris: Klincksieck.

Wackernagel, Jacob
(1853–1938)

Swiss linguist, and a member of the second generation of the Neogrammarians. Wackernagel was born in Basle, where he studied classical philology and taught ever until retirement, except for a period in Göttingen. Among his contemporaries, he occupies a special position because of his interest for syntax, a field that had been investigated to a much lesser extent than phonology and morphology. A survey of the courses he gave in his years as professor shows that syntax was a recurring topic already in the 1880s; in 1904 Wackernagel was offering a course in historical syntax, a topic which can still sound innovative today.

As most Neogrammarians, Wackernagel too gave his name to a Law of Indo-European linguistics. In his 1892 essay 'Über ein Gesetz der indogermanischen Wortstellung' ('On a law concerning Indo-European word order', repr. in Wackernagel 1953), Wackernagel pointed out that in the ancient Indo-European languages a number of particles, conjunctions, pronouns, and verb forms took a peculiar position in the sentence, nowadays known as Wackernagel position or P2, occurring after the first accented word. All words in P2 shared a common prosodic feature, they were unaccented (or weakly accented). This tendency is most visible in Sanskrit and in Homeric Greek, but Wackernagel found its traces in other Indo-European languages as well. In particular, the occurrence of the verb in P2 was important to Wackernagel for reconstructing the pattern of the Proto-Indo-European sentence. In Vedic Sanskrit, finite verbs with preverbs are stressed in subordinate clauses, whereas in main clauses the stress shifts to the preverb. Some verbs are never stressed, most notably the verb 'be'. Among common sentence patterns in Vedic there is one in which a preverb is sentence-initial. Based on the prosodic features of the finite verbs, Wackernagel reconstructed Proto-Indo-European as having essentially the same word order as Modern High German with respect to the verb, that is, having the verb obligatorily in second position in main clauses and final position in subordinate clauses.

Wackernagel's Law has been variously evaluated in his times; especially the idea that the position of the finite verb in Proto-Indo-European was the same as in German did not meet general consent. However, the fact that various types of unaccented items were placed in P2 found a striking confirmation when Hittite was finally deciphered in 1916, for unstressed pronouns and particles follow Wackernagel's Law virtually exceptionless in this language.

Wackernagel's other major accomplishment in the field of syntax is constituted by the two volumes of lectures on syntax (*Vorlesungen über Syntax*), which appeared in 1926–1928, in which the scholar addressed several problems connected with the syntactic behavior of nouns and verbs in the Indo-European languages (mostly based on Latin, Greek, and Germanic). Wackernagel's approach, which takes each inflectional category as its starting point, is typical of historical linguistics in the late nineteenth–early twentieth century, and owes to the fact that syntax was previously conceived of as a kind of appendix to morphology. In Wackernagel's times linguists were in the process of leaving behind the confusion between syntax and morphology, but the importance of morphology for delimiting syntactic problems was still reflected, among other things, in the fact that, although he announced a further volume on sentence structure (*Satzlehre*), Wackernagel never wrote it, in spite of his own pioneering research on word order.

The newly individuated field of syntax could not yet rely on a theoretical framework. For this reason, Wackernagel's syntactic description remains pretheoretical, his insight mostly deriving from his deep knowledge of languages and texts.

It must be added that constraints on the placement of clitics apparently constituted a popular field of research toward the end of the nineteenth century, as shown by contemporary research in the field of the Romance languages by Adolf Tobler and Adolfo Mussafia, which resulted in the formulation of the so-called Tobler-Mussafia Law on the placement of clitics in the early Romance languages, even before Wackernagel's name became associated with P2 clitics.

Further reading

Collinge, N. E., *The Laws of Indo-European*. Amsterdam: Benjamins, 1985.

Eichner, Heiner and Helmut Rix (eds.) 1990. *Sprachwissenschaft und Philologie. Jacob Wackernagel und die Indogermanistik heute*. Wiesbaden: Reichert.

Mussafia, Adolfo 1886. 'Una particolarità sinttatica della lingua italiana dei primi secoli', in G. I. Ascoli et al. (eds.), *Miscellanea di filologia e linguistica in memoria di Napoleone Caix e Ugo Angelo Canello*. Firenze: LeMonnier, 255–261.

Tobler, Adolf 1912. 'Besprechung von J. Le Coultre, De l'ordre des mots dans Chrétien de Troyes', *Vermische Beiträge zur französischen Grammatik 5*, 395–414. Leipzig (originally published in 1875).

Wackernagel, Jacob 1926–1928. *Vorlesungen über Syntax.* 2 vols. Basle: Birkhäuser.

Wackernagel, Jacob 1953. *Kleine Schriften.* 2 vols. Göttingen: Vandenhoek & Ruprecht.

Section 2

Behagel, Otto
(1854–1936)

German linguist and Germanist Otto Behagel taught at the universities of Heidelberg, Basle, and Giessen. He was especially interested in Modern and Middle High German, and his work is not theoretically oriented; however, some of his intuitions on syntax capture important features of discourse structure.

Behagel formulated a number of 'laws' which regard the order of constituents, and reflect general tendencies that have a motivation connected with the distribution of information in sentences. In particular he stated that "what belongs together tends to occur together" (Behagel's first law); "less important information, i.e. already known to the hearer, tends to occur earlier in sentences than important information" (Behagel's second law); "light constituents are placed earlier in sentences than heavy constituents." The last statement is known as "Law of Growing Members," or as simply as "Behagel's Law."

Further reading

Behaghel, Otto 1909. 'Beziehungen zwischen Umfang und Reihenfolge von Satzgliedern'. *Indogermanische Forschungen 25*, 110–142.

Behaghel, O. 1932. *Deutsche Syntax. Eine geschichtliche Darstellung*, 2nd edn. 4 vols. Heidelberg, Winter.

Best, Karl-Heinz 2007. 'Otto Behaghel (1854–1936)'. *Glottometrics 14*, 80–86.

Bresnan, Joan W.
(b. 1945)

American linguist Joan Bresnan developed with Ronald Kaplan a formal theory of syntax known as Lexical-Functional Grammar. After that, using statistical measurements, she developed a new research program in which she questions static and algebraic theories of language acquisition and proposes to study language as an object inherently variable and stochastic in nature.

Joan Bresnan earned her Ph.D. in linguistics in 1972 at MIT with the dissertation *Theory of Complementation in English Syntax*. There she studied with Noam Chomsky with whom she had frequent disagreements regarding Wh-movement. This led her to formulate an alternative theory. Presently, Joan Bresnan is professor of linguistics at Stanford University, where she has been teaching since 1983. Her current topics of research include the syntax of Australian aboriginal languages and Bantu languages. She is interested in linguistic typology and is one of the developers of optimality theory.

Further reading
Bresnan, Joan 2001. *Lexical Functional Syntax*. Malden MA: Blackwell.

Bresnan, Joan and Judith Aissen 2002. 'Optimality and functionality: Objections and refutations', *Natural Language and Linguistic Theory 20*, 81–95.

Kaplan, Ronald and Joan Bresnan 1982. 'Lexical-functional grammar: A formal system for grammatical representation'. In J. Bresnan (ed.) *The Mental Representation of Grammatical Relations*. Cambridge, MA: The MIT Press, 173–281.

Croft, William
(b. 1956)

American linguist William Croft is one of today's leading typologists. He graduated in 1986, from Stanford, where he studied with Joseph Greenberg. The title of his dissertation was *Categories and relations in syntax: the clause-level organization of information*. After teaching for several years in Manchester, Croft is presently working at the University of New Mexico.

Ever since his dissertation, Croft has devoted much of his research to grammatical and syntactic constructions across languages, which he views as fundamentally conditioned by meaning. Another major focus of research has been language change, to which he has devoted his 2000 book *Explaining language change: an evolutionary approach*. In this book, Croft investigates language change in a framework inspired by evolutionary biology. Presently he is working within a framework which is a typologically oriented variant of Construction Grammar, called Radical Construction Grammar. He has a strong stance for a cognitive approach to language, and is one of the exponents of the functional-typological approach, which combines cognitivism with functionalism.

Further reading

Croft, William 1994. 'The semantics of subjecthood'. In M. Yaguello (ed.) *Subjecthood and Subjectivity*. Paris: Ophrys, 29–75.

Croft, William 2000. *Explaining Language Change: An Evolutionary Approach*. Harlow, Essex: Longman.

Croft, William 2007. 'Typology and linguistic theory in the past decade: A personal view'. *Linguistic Typology 11*, 79–91.

Delbrück, Berthold
(1842–1922)

German scholar Berthold Delbrück was one of the leading Indo-European linguists of his times. He studied at the universities of Halle (Saale) and Berlin, where he earned his Habilitation with a dissertation devoted to Sanskrit syntax in 1866, a pioneering work in comparative syntax. In 1870 he became professor of comparative and Sanskrit linguistics at the University of Jena, where he remained until he retired in 1913. He was one of the historical linguists known as Neogrammarians.

Delbrück's interest in comparative syntax brought him to join Karl Brugmann in a major project, the *Grundriß der vergleichenden Grammatik der indogermanischen Sprachen* ("Outline of the Comparative Grammar of the Indo-European languages"), in five volumes, for which Brugmann provided the volumes on phonology and morphology, and Delbrück provided the volumes on syntax. The work was published in various editions, the final one having appeared in 1916, and remains an important reference tool even today.

Delbrück's approach to syntax was comparatively new for his time, when syntax was often treated as an appendix to morphology, and mostly concerned the function of inflectional categories. Delbrück, instead, also described sentence structure and sentence types, and addressed the question of what can be defined as a sentence. In his conception, a sentence is defined as a possible utterance, that is, as a unit of discourse, rather than in logic-based terms of predication.

Further reading
Delbrück, Berthold 1888. *Altindische Syntax*. Halle: Weisenhauses.
Delbrück, Berthold 1901. *Vergleichende Syntax der indogermanischen Sprachen*. 2nd edn. 3 vols. Straßburg: Trübner.
Graffi, Giorgio 2001. *200 Years of Syntax. A Critical Survey*. Amsterdam: Benjamins.

Dixon, Robert Malcolm Ward
(b. 1939)

R. M. W. Dixon was born in England, where he earned his BA and MA at Oxford and his Ph.D. in linguistics at the University of London in 1968. His thesis, *The Dyirbal Language of North Queensland*, was the result of extensive field research carried out from 1963 in Australia. Shortly thereafter, Dixon left England and moved to Australia, where he became professor at the Australian National University, a position he held until 1999. In 2000, he moved to La Trobe University, where he is currently teaching.

After some early works in linguistic theory, Dixon's interest for field work led him to concentrate on the description of Australian languages, but it was his book on *The Jarawara Language of Southern Amazonia* that earned him the Leonard Bloomfield award from the Linguistic Society of America in 2006. His deep knowledge of numerous, genetically unrelated languages relies on control of empirical data earned in his research trips and make him one of the leading typologists.

In the field of syntax, Dixon's name is especially linked with the description of different types of alignment system and with the development of a typology of grammatical relations. His research on ergativity was first documented in 1979 by a long article in *Language*, and later by his book *Ergativity*, published in 1994, which remains the most exhaustive and insightful introduction to the field.

Further reading

Aikhenvald, Alexandra 2006. 'Dixon, Robert M. W'. In Keith Brown (ed.), 737–739.

Dixon, R. M. W. 1972. *The Dyirbal Language of North Queensland*. Cambridge: CUP.

Dixon, R. M. W. 1977. *A Grammar of Yidiny*. Cambridge: CUP.

Dixon, R. M. W. 1979. 'Ergativity'. *Language* 55, 59–138.

Dixon, R. M. W. 1994. *Ergativity*. Cambridge: CUP.

Dixon, R. M. W. 2004. *The Jarawara Language of Southern Amazonia*. Oxford: OUP.

Fillmore, Charles J.

(b. 1929)

American linguist Charles Fillmore earned his Ph.D. in linguistics from the University of Michigan in 1961. He taught at Ohio State University and Stanford before moving to Berkeley in 1971, where he taught until his retirement in 1994.

Fillmore became especially influential in the late 1960s with his theory of deep cases known as Case Grammar, and was one of the initiators of the reaction against main stream Transformational Generative Grammar, known as Generative Semantics. His Frame Grammar provided a basis for Cognitive Linguistics and later for Construction Grammar. Presently, Fillmore is collaborating to the development of the usage-based approach known as Emergent Grammar.

Further reading

Fillmore, Charles 1968. 'The case for case'. In Bach and Harms (ed.): *Universals in Linguistic Theory*. New York: Holt, Rinehart & Winston, 1–88.

Fillmore, Charles 1982. 'Frame semantics'. In Linguistic Society of Korea (ed.) *Linguistics in the Morning Calm*. Seoul: Hanshin Publishing Co., 111–137.

Givón, Talmy
(b. 1936)

Talmy Givón was born in Israel, and is one of the founders of functionalism in American linguistics. He earned his BA from the Hebrew University of Jerusalem in 1959; he then continued his studies at UCLA, where he earned his Ph.D. in linguistics in 1969. He started teaching as an assistant professor at UCLA during his graduate studies; later he moved to the University of Oregon, where he founded the Linguistic Department.

Givón is the leading exponent of contemporary American functionalism, in particular of the approach known as West Coast Functionalism, which he contributed to create. Much of Givón's research is devoted to syntax, which he views as intimately connected with semantics, and with sentence and discourse pragmatics. His major contribution to the outline of functional syntax is constituted by the two volumes *Syntax: A Functional-Typological Introduction,* (vol. I, 1984; vol. II 1990), later thoroughly revised and published as *Syntax: An Introduction* (2 vols, 2001).

Further reading
Brdar, Mario 2006. 'Givón, Talmy'. In Keith Brown (ed.), 86–87.
Givón, Talmy 1984–1990. *Syntax: A Functional-Typological Introduction* (2 vols.). Amsterdam: Benjamins (2nd, rev. edn., 2001).

Goldberg, Adele
(b. 1963)

American linguist Adele Goldberg earned her BA in mathematics and philosophy at the University of Pennsylvania, and her Ph.D. in linguistics at the University of California at Berkeley, where she studied with George Lakoff. She taught at the University of Illinois from 1997 to 2004, when she became professor of linguistics at Princeton.

Goldberg is best known for her research in the field of Construction Grammar. Her Ph.D. thesis on constructions, published in 1995, was awarded the Gustave O. Arlt Humanities Award in 1996 and has been translated into Japanese, Korean, and Chinese. She is currently the chief editor of the journal *Cognitive Linguistics*.

Further reading
Goldberg, Adele 1995. *Constructions: A Construction Grammar Approach to Argument Structure*. Chicago: University of Chicago Press.
Goldberg, Adele 2006. *Constructions at Work: The Nature of Generalization in Language*. Oxford: OUP.

Halliday, Michael Alexander Kirkwood
(b. 1925)

British linguist Michael Alexander Kirkwood Halliday studied Chinese linguistics at the University of London and at Cambridge, where he earned his Ph.D. During this period, he also lived in China for three years. In 1965 he became professor of general linguistics at University College London. In 1975 he was appointed and moved to the University of Sydney, where he taught until his retirement in 1987.

Halliday is especially known as the founder of Systemic Functional Grammar. His major interest has always been in the use of language in social contexts. In constructing his own linguistic theory, Halliday was influenced by his teacher, J. R. Firth (1890–1960), whose research mainly concerned prosodic phonology. Firth insisted on the relevance of context in his analysis of both sound and meaning; besides he held that no single system of analytical principles could adequately account for language; rather, different systems are required for different situations.

Halliday's first sketch of Systemic Grammar was published in 1961; he then refined the theory, which is fully illustrated in his 1985 book *An Introduction to Functional Grammar* (2 edn. 1994).

Further reading
Firth, John Rupert 1957. *Papers in Linguistics 1934–1951*. Oxford: OUP.

Halliday, M. A. K. 1961. 'Categories of the theory of grammar'. *Word* 17.

Halliday, M. A. K. 1973. *Explorations in the Functions of Language*. London: Edward Arnold.

Halliday, M. A. K. 1978. *Language as Social Semiotic: The Social Interpretation of Language and Meaning*. London: Edward Arnold/Baltimore: University Park Press.

Halliday, M. A. K. 1994. *An Introduction to Functional Grammar*. 2 edn. London: Edward Arnold.

Harris, Zelling
(1909–1992)

Zelling Harris was born in Ukraine; he moved to Philadelphia, Pennsylvania, with his family when he was four years old. He earned his BA (1930), MA (1932), and Ph.D. (1934) at the University of Pennsylvania, where he started teaching in 1931. He founded the first linguistics department in the United States at that university in 1946. After retiring from the University of Pennsylvania in 1979, he taught at Columbia University. In 1966, he was named Benjamin Franklin Professor of Linguistics at the University of Pennsylvania. He was a member of the American Philosophical Society and the National Academy of Sciences. He was president of the Linguistic Society of America in 1955.

Harris was interested in finding formal and mathematical properties of language, in particular characteristics that correspond to meaning and information. He used distributional views of language, as in earlier American Bloomfieldian structuralism. Moreover, inspired by algebra, he introduced the concept of transformation, which would be developed later by his former student Noam Chomsky. In 1982 he published *A Grammar of English on Mathematical Principles*, his most relevant work.

Further reading

Brabanter, Philippe de 2001. 'Zellig Harris's theory of syntax and linguistic reflexivity'. *Belgian Essays on Language and Literature L 3*, 53–66.

Harris, Zelling 1970. *Papers in Structural and Transformational Linguistics*. New York: Humanities Press.

Harris, Zelling 1982. *A Grammar of English on Mathematical Principles*. New York: Wiley.

Harris, Zelling 1988. *Language and Information*. New York: Columbia University Press.

Jackendoff, Ray S.
(b. 1945)

American linguist Ray Jackendoff made important contributions to Transformational Generative Grammar, such as the elaboration of X-bar syntax. He earned his BA in Mathematics at Swarthmore College and his Ph.D. at MIT in 1969 with the dissertation *Some Rules of Semantic Interpretation for English*. He teaches linguistics and philosophy at Tufts University since 2005, after having taught at Brandeis University for more than thirty years.

Ray Jackendoff argues against Noam Chomsky's syntactically centered view of language in which syntax is the only generative component in language. According to Jackendoff, syntax, semantics, and phonology are connected to each other via interface components as well as to other processing systems, such as the perceptual systems. In his research works he formalizes the proper interface rules of these components. In *Simpler syntax*, coauthored with Peter Culicover, both authors argue that the most explanatory syntax is the one that inputs the minimum possible structure necessary to mediate between phonology and meaning. As a consequence, their theory of language provides a far richer mapping between syntax and semantics than other frameworks.

Further reading

Jackendoff, Ray S. 1977. *X-bar Syntax: A Study of Phrase Structure*. Cambridge MA: The MIT Press.

Jackendoff, Ray S. 2002. *Foundations of Language: Brain, Meaning, Grammar, Evolution*. Oxford: OUP.

Jackendoff, Ray S. 2005. *Simpler Syntax*. Oxford: OUP.

Kayne, Richard S.
(b. 1944)

American linguist Richard S. Kayne has made prominent contributions to the study of general Transformational Generative syntax, presenting some complementary proposals to Chomsky's ideas. He has focused on English and the Romance languages syntax, mainly French.

Richard Kayne received his BA in mathematics in 1964 at Columbia College and his Ph.D. in 1969 at MIT with his dissertation *The transformational cycle in French syntax*, which later was published by MIT. He taught at the University of Paris VIII, from 1969 to 1986, at the City University of New York from 1988 to 1997 and at New York University since 1997.

Further reading

Kayne, Richard S. 1975. *French Syntax: The Transformational Cycle.* Cambridge MA: The MIT Press.

Kayne, Richard S. 1994. *Antisymmetry in Syntax.* Cambridge MA: The MIT Press.

Lakoff, George
(b. 1941)

American linguist George Lakoff is one of the most prominent exponents of Cognitive Linguistics, of which he has been one of the founders and developers. He is best known for his theory of metaphor, which he presented in several publications, among which the book *Metaphors we live by*, which he coauthored in 1980 with Mark Johnson. In 1966, he received his Ph.D. at the Indiana University. He taught at Harvard and at the University of Michigan before moving in 1972 to Berkeley, where he presently teaches cognitive linguistics.

Before his Ph.D., Lakoff was one of Noam Chomsky's students at MIT. In the early 1960s, he became critical of Chomsky's views regarding the autonomy of syntax, and started working on a semantic-based model. In a paper of 1963, which was published only several years later, he used for the first time the name of Generative Semantics. In the 1960s and 1970s, Lakoff worked at developing Generative Semantics together with Ross, McCawley, Fillmore and others.

Besides language, Lakoff has explored several other fields of human activity, including literature, philosophy, mathematics, and politics. He is the cofounder of the Rockridge Institute, which aims to promote progressive political values. His ideas about frames and political discourse are often controversial, as shown by the discussion that has arisen by his book in 2006. *Whose Freedom?: The Battle over America's Most Important Idea*, which was harshly criticized by Stephen Pinker.

Further reading
Lakoff, George 1971. 'Toward generative semantics'. In J. McCawley (ed.) *Notes from the Linguistic Underground*. New York: Academic Press, 43–61.

Lakoff, George and Mark Johnson 1980. *Metaphors We Live By*. Chicago: University of Chicago Press.

Lakoff, George and Mark Turner 1989. *More than Cool Reason: A Field Guide to Poetic Metaphor*. Chicago: University of Chicago Press.

Lakoff, George 1996. *Moral Politics*. Chicago: University of Chicago Press.

Lakoff, George and Mark Johnson 1999. *Philosophy in the Flesh*. New York: Basic Books.

Lakoff, George and Rafael Núñez 2000. *Where Mathematics comes From*. New York: Basic Books.

Lakoff, George 2006. *Whose Freedom?: The Battle over America's Most Important Idea*. New York: Farrar, Straus and Giroux.

Lamb, Sydney M.
(b. 1929)

Sydney M. Lamb, the originator of stratificational grammar, was born in Denver, Colorado in 1929. He earned his BA from Yale University in 1951 and his Ph.D. in 1958 from the University of California, Berkeley, where he taught from 1956 to 1964. After teaching at Yale University in 1964, he joined Rice University in Houston, Texas.

Lamb did research in the native languages of California, and his contributions include historical linguistics, computational linguistics, and theoretical linguistics. His most influential book is his 1966 *Outline of Stratificational Grammar* where he argues for the following levels necessary for sentence analysis: sememic level, lexemic level, morphemic level, and phonemic level, which, according to him, are hierarchically related and realized by the elements in the structural level below them. Lamb's notion of levels and relations between levels was greatly influenced by the theory of Glossematics, developed in the 1930s by Louis Hjelmslev.

In recent years, Lamb has been developing the theory further, especially by exploring its relationships to neurological structures and to thinking processes. This work is described in his books *Pathways of the Brain: The Neurocognitive Basis of Language*, published in 1999, and *Language and Reality*, published in 2004.

Further reading

Hjelmslev, Louis 1953. *Prolegomena to a Theory of Language*. Baltimore: Waverly Press, 1953 (first published 1943). 2nd revised edn. Madison: University of Wisconsin Press, 1961.

Lamb, Sydney M. 1966. *Outline of Stratificational Grammar*. Washington: Georgetown University Press.

Lamb, Sydney M. 1988. 'Autobiographical sketch'. In Konrad Koerner (ed.), *First Person Singular III*. Amsterdam: Benjamins.

Lamb, Sydney M. 1999. *Pathways of the Brain: The Neurocognitive Basis of Language*. Amsterdam: Benjamins.

Lamb, Sydney M. 2004. *Language and Reality*. London: Continuum Books.

Langacker, Ronald W.
(b. 1942)

American linguist Ronald W. Langacker is one of the leading exponents of cognitive linguistics, and the creator of Cognitive Grammar. He received his Ph.D. from the University of Illinois at Urbana-Champaign in 1966; immediately thereafter, he became professor of linguistics at the University of California at San Diego, where he taught until his retirement in 2003. He continued the American tradition of anthropological linguistics in the early years of his career with his extensive research on the Uto-Aztecan languages.

During the 1960s, Langacker worked in the paradigm of Transformational Generative Grammar, and elaborated some important notions, such as the notion of c-command, which, with later refinements, remains relevant today (see Langacker 1969). In the early 1970s, he became critical of the interpretive view of semantics assumed in Transformational Generative Grammar, and was one of the founders of Generative Semantics. His Space Grammar (Langacker 1982) provided the foundations for Cognitive Grammar and for Construction Grammar.

In the field of syntax, Langacker also gave an important contribution to research on change and diachrony with his 1977 paper on reanalysis, which "represents the first theoretical attempt to investigate the general nature, rather than a specific case, of reanalysis" (Li and Thompson 1977: xi).

Langacker published several influential books, among which the two volumes of *Foundations of Cognitive Grammar*, the most exhaustive introduction to Cognitive Grammar to date.

Further reading
Langacker, R. W. 1977. *Studies in Uto-Aztecan Grammar.* Vol. 1: *An Overview of Uto-Aztecan Grammar.* Dallas: Summer Institute of Linguistics and University of Texas at Arlington.
Langacker, Ronald W. 1982. 'Space grammar, analysability, and the English passive', *Language 58*, 22–80.
Langacker, Ronald W. 1990. *Concept, Image, and Symbol: The Cognitive Basis of Grammar.* Berlin: Mouton De Gruyter.

Lasnik, Howard
(b. 1945)

American linguist Howard Lasnik earned a BS in Mathematics and English at the Carnegie Institute of Technology in 1967, a M.A. in English at Harvard University in 1969, and a Ph.D. in Linguistics at MIT in 1972 with the dissertation *Analyses of Negation in English*. He taught at the University of Connecticut for thirty years, from 1972 to 2002, and since 2002 he has taught at the University of Maryland as Distinguished University Professor.

Lasnik is a prolific author who has played a key role in the development and the theorizing of the Transformational Generative framework, from the Extended Standard Theory, to Government and Binding Theory and the Minimalist Program. He has coauthored key articles with Noam Chomsky, such as "Filters and control" in 1977.

Further reading

Chomsky, Noam and Howard Lasnik 1977. 'Filters and control', *Linguistic Inquiry 8*, 425–504.

Chomsky, Noam and Howard Lasnik 1993. 'The theory of Principles and Parameters'. In I. J. Jacobs et al (eds.) *Syntax: An International Hanbook of Contemprory Research*. Berlin: De Gruyter, 505–569.

Lasnik, Howard 1999. *Minimalist Analysis*. Oxford: Blackwell.

Lehmann, Winfred Philip
(1916–2007)

American linguist Winfred P. Lehmann was one of the founders of historical syntax, which he investigated in typological perspective. He studied at the University of Wisconsin, where he earned his M.A. in Germanic Linguistics and his Ph.D. in 1941.

After the Second World War, he joined the Department of German at Washington University. In 1949 he moved to the University of Texas at Austin, where he created the Linguistic Department, and taught until retirement.

Among Lehmann's research fields was machine translation, but he is remembered especially for his contribution to Indo-European studies and historical linguistics. He was among the first to use Greenberg's universals (Greenberg 1963) for language reconstruction and to explain language change. His 1974 book *PIE Syntax* is a reconstruction of the syntax of Proto-Indo-European, which also explains changes in the Indo-European languages, based on the assumption that generalizations drawn from word order universals could provide a full description of syntax. This book also represents Lehmann's most consistent attempt to embrace the theory of Transformational Generative Grammar. After the publication of *PIE Syntax*, research on historical syntax almost exclusively focused on changes in word order for about a decade.

Later, in *Theoretical Bases of Indo-European Linguistics*, Lehmann provided an eclectic view of how syntactic theory can combine with historical linguistics.

Further reading
Friedrich, Paul 1975. 'Proto-Indo-European syntax. The order of meaningful elements'. Memoir 1, *Journal of Indo-European Studies*.

Lehmann, Winfred P. 1974. *Proto-Indo-European Syntax*. Austin, TX: University of Texas Press.

Lehmann, Winfred P. 1993. *Theoretical Bases of Indo-European Linguistics*. London: Routledge.

Miller, Gary D. 1975. 'Indo-European: VSO, SOV, SVO or all three?'. *Lingua 37*, 31–52.

Lightfoot, David W.
(1945)

British linguist David W. Lightfoot in one of the first linguists who used Transformational Generative syntax to explain historical processes and syntactic changes in languages in his 1979 book *Principles of diachronic syntax*. He was born in Plymouth, UK in 1945. He received his BA in classics at the University of London, King's College in 1966. He earned his MA and Ph.D. at the University of Michigan in 1970 with the dissertation *Natural Logic and the Moods of Classical Greek*.

Lightfoot is a prolific author who has widely published books and articles on historical change, syntactic theory, and language acquisition, which he views as intimately related. He has taught at McGill University, the University of Utrecht, the University of Maryland, and Georgetown University, where he has been dean of the Graduate School for Arts and Science and Assistant Director of the National Science Foundation.

Further reading

Lightfoot, David W. 1979. *Principles of Diachronic Syntax*. Cambridge: CUP.

Lightfoot, David W. 1991. *How to Set Parameters: Arguments from Language Change*. Cambridge, MA: The MIT Press.

Lightfoot, David W. 1999. *The Development of Language Aquisition, Change and Evolution*.Oxford: Blackwell Publishers.

Lightfoot, David W. 2006. *How New Languages Emerge*. Cambridge: CUP.

Mathesius, Vilém
(1882–1945)

Czech linguist and one of the founders of the Prague Circlé in 1926, together with Roman Jakobson, Nikolaj Trubeckoj and others. After studies in Slavic, Germanic, and Romance languages, he took his *habilitation* in English linguistics, and became professor of English at Carl University in Prague in 1919, where he created the English Department.

In spite of various personal problems (he became virtually blind in 1922), Mathesius was one of the most influential scholars of his time, the initiator of modern studies on the information structure of sentences and discourse. One of his sources of inspiration was a book published in 1844 by German-French philologist Henri Weil (1818–1868), which contrasted word order in various languages, pointing out that in certain languages, such as Latin and Classical Greek, communicative factors play a major role in determining word order.

In his seminal lecture read in 1911 at the Royal Bohemian Society of Sciences "On the potentiality of linguistic phenomena", Mathesius discussed the notion of stylistic registers, thus demonstrating his early interest in language usage, which remained his major field of research. In his subsequent publications, a collection of which has been published in 1961 in Czech and in 1975 in English, he introduced the terms *theme* and *rheme*, which have become part of current terminology in the analysis of discourse.

Further reading
Firbas, Jan 1968. 'On the prosodic features of the Modern English finite verb as means of Functional Sentence Perspective'. *Brno Studies in English 7*, 11–48.

Mathesius, Vilém 1975. *A Functional Analysis of Present Day English on a General Linguistic Basis*. The Hague: Mouton (English translation of *Obsahový rozbor současné angličtiny na základě obecně lingvistickém*, edited by J. Vachek, Prague).

Vachek, Josef and Libuše Dušková 1983. *Praguiana: Some Basic and Less Known Aspects of the Prague Linguistics School*. Amsterdam: Benjamins.

Weil, H. 1844. *De l'ordre des mots dans les langues anciennes comparées aux langues modernes*. Translated by C. W. Super as *The Order of Words in the Ancient Languages Compared with That of the Modern Languages*, 1978. Amsterdam: Benjamins.

McCawley, James D.
(1938–1999)

American linguist James McCawley was born in Scotland, and migrated to Chicago as a child. Extremely gifted intellectually, he entered the University of Chicago at age 16, and earned his MS in mathematics in 1958. He then got interested in linguistics and continued his study at MIT, where he studied with Noam Chomsky, and finished his Ph.D. in 1965. In 1964 he started teaching at the University of Chicago, where he remained until his death.

In the late 1960s, McCawley started disagreeing with the view of Transformational Generative Grammar regarding the autonomy of syntax. In his 1968 paper "The role of semantics in a grammar", one of the most important contributions to Generative Semantics, he expounded his view on syntax, which he considered crucially dependent on semantics and pragmatics. McCawley's skepticism about the centrality of syntax is reflected in the title of his contribution to Moravcsik and Wirth (1980), "An un-syntax", in which he claimed that "much of what has been thought of as syntax is largely a reflection of other things, such as morphology, logic, production strategies, and principles of cooperation" (1980: 168).

Further reading

McCawley, J. D. (1968). 'The role of semantics in a grammar'. In E. Bach and R. T. Harms (eds.) *Universals in Linguistic Theory*. New York: Holt, Rinehart and Winston, 124–169.

McCawley, J. D. (1980). 'An un-syntax'. In Moravcsik E. and Wirth J. (eds.), 167–194.

Harris, Randy Allen 1993. *The Linguistics Wars*. Oxford: OUP.

Lawler, John 2003. 'Memorial for John McCawley'. *Language 79*, 614–625.

Postal, Paul M.
(b. 1936)

American linguist Paul M. Postal, together with David M. Perlmutter, developed the Relational Grammar model, a formal, nontransformational grammar, which had a major, although indirect, impact on current formal syntactic theories of syntax. Paul Postal was born in Weehawken, New Jersey, received his BA in Anthropology and Philosophy at Columbia College in 1957, and his Ph.D. in Anthropology from Yale University in 1963 with the dissertation *Some syntactic rules in Mohawk*. From 1963–1965, he taught linguistics at MIT, where he started collaborating with David Parlmutter, who was finishing his Ph.D. dissertation on *Deep and Surface Structure Constraints in Syntax*.

Postal and Perlmutter became involved in the Generative Semantics movement; later they developed their own model of Relational Grammar. In the meantime, Postal had moved to the City University of New York from 1965–1967 and then to New York University from 1993 to present, while Perlmutter taught many years at the University of California in San Diego, where he is an Emeritus professor.

Further reading

Johnson, David E. and Paul M. Postal 1980. *Arc Pair Grammar*. Princeton: Princeton University Press.

Perlmutter, David 1971. *Deep and Surface Structure Constraints in Syntax*. New York: Holt, Reinhart & Winston.

Postal, Paul M. 1974. *On Raising: One Rule of English Grammar and its Theoretical Implications*. Cambridge MA: The MIT Press.

Perlmutter, David 1980. 'Relational Grammar'. In E. Moravcsik and J. Wirth (eds.), 195–229.

Postal, Paul M. and Bryan Joseph (eds.) 1990. *Studies in Relational Grammar 3*. Chicago: University of Chicago Press.

Pike, Kenneth Lee
(1912–2000)

American linguists Kenneth Lee Pike, the founder of Tagmemics, developed his career in linguistics at the Summer Institute of Linguistics (SIL) and at the University of Michigan. He was born in East Woodstock, Connecticut in 1912, and earned his BA in theology and missions at Gordon College in Boston, Massachusetts in 1933 and his Ph.D. in linguistics at the University of Michigan in 1942, where he became a distinguished faculty member from 1947 to 1977. He was made adjunct Professor at the University of Texas at Arlington in 1981. He was president of the Summer Institute of Linguistics from 1942 to 1979.

After earning his BA in theology and missions, Pike wrote many grammars using tagmemics, and translated the Bible in several aboriginal languages from Australia, Africa, Asia, and South America. His analysis of Mixtec, an Otomangean language spoken in Oaxaca, Mexico, was seminal in his approach to language. His theory of language, tagmemics, was widely used by the SIL missionaries in their descriptive work. He divided his time between the University of Michigan and the SIL, where he trained many missionaries in linguistics and in translation of the Bible.

Further reading
Pike, Kenneth L. 1967. *Language in Relation to a Unified Theory of the Structure of Human Behavior*. The Hague: Mouton.
Pike, Kenneth L. and Evelyn G. Pike 1977. *Grammatical Analysis*. Texas: Summer Institute of Linguistics and the University of Texas at Arlington.

Ross John Robert
(b. 1938)

American linguist John Robert Ross was born in Boston, Massachusetts in 1938. He studied his BA at Yale University, his MA at the University of Pennsylvania, and his Ph.D. at MIT, where, after working with Noam Chomsky, he wrote his 1967 widely influential dissertation in formal syntax, *Constraints on Variables in Syntax*.

Despite of its relevance to the field of syntax, his dissertation was published only in 1986 with the title *Infinite Syntax!*. In his dissertation John Ross proposed several terms describing syntactic phenomena that are well known and analyzed to this day, such as syntactic islands, crossover effects, extraposition, gapping and heavy NP shift, among others. He was professor at MIT from 1966 to 1985. After working outside the United States for a while, he returned to the United States to teach at the University of North Texas.

Starting from 1963, John Ross developed the theory of Generative Semantics in collaboration with George Lakoff, James McCawley, Paul Postal, and others.

Further reading
Lakoff, George and John R. Ross 1976. 'Is deep structure necessary?'. In J. D. McCawley (ed.) *Notes from the Linguistic Underground*. New York: Academic Press, 159–164.
Ross, John R. 1986. *Infinite Syntax!*. Norwood: ABLEX.

Van Valin, Robert D. Jr.
(b. 1952)

Robert Van Valin is the main proponent of Role and Reference Grammar, a theory that he developed in collaboration with other scholars, most notably William Foley. Both Van Valin and Foley earned their Ph.D. in Linguistics at the University of California, Berkeley. Together, they published *Functional Syntax and Universal Grammar* (1984), which contained an outline of the theory.

As other functionally oriented linguists, Van Valin is against Chomsky's assumption regarding the autonomy of syntax, and has criticized some of the basic notions of the Minimalist Program, arguing that "the truly universal part of universal grammar is semantically driven" and has proposed that "deviations from this semantic core are motivated at least in part by discourse-pragmatics" (Van Valin ms.).

Further reading

Foley, William A. and Robert D. Van Valin, Jr. 1984. *Functional Syntax and Universal Grammar.* Cambridge: CUP.

Van Valin Robert D. Jr. ed. 1993. *Advances in Role and Reference Grammar.* Amsterdam: Benjamins.

Key Texts

Bloomfield, Leonard 1933. *Language*. New York: Holt.

Bresnan, Joan 2001. *Lexical-Functional Syntax*. Oxford: Blackwell.

Chomsky, Noam 1957. *Syntactic Structures*. The Hague: Mouton.

Chomsky, Noam 1965. *Aspects of the Theory of Syntax*. Cambridge MA: The MIT Press.

Chomsky, Noam 1981. *Lectures on Government and Binding*. Dordrecht: Foris.

Chomsky, Noam 1986. *Knowledge of Language*. New York: Praeger.

Chomsky, Noam 1995. *The Minimalist Program*. Cambridge MA: The MIT Press.

Comrie, Bernard 1989. *Language Universals and Linguistic Typology: Syntax and Morphology*. 2nd edn. Oxford: Blackwell/Chicago: University of Chicago Press.

Croft, William 1991. *Syntactic Categories and Grammatical Relations: The Cognitive Organization of Information*. Chicago: University of Chicago Press.

Dik, Simon C. 1997a. *The Theory of Functional Grammar*. Part 1: *The Structure of the Clause*. Second, revised edition. Edited by Kees Hengeveld. Berlin/New York: Mouton de Gruyter.

Dik, Simon C. 1997b. *The Theory of Functional Grammar*. Part 2: *Complex and Derived Constructions*. Edited by Kees Hengeveld. Berlin/New York: Mouton de Gruyter.

Dowty, David 1979. *Word Meaning and Montague Grammar*. Dordrecht: Reidel.

Fillmore, Charles 1968. 'The case for case'. In E. Bach and R. Harms (eds.) *Universals in Linguistic Theory*. New York: Holt, Rinehart & Winston, 1–88.

Givón, Talmy 1984–1990. *Syntax: A Functional-Typological Introduction* (2 vols). Amsterdam: Benjamins (2nd, rev. edn., 2001).

Goldberg, Adele 1995. *Constructions: A Construction Grammar Approach to Argument Structure*. Chicago and London: Chicago University Press.

Greenberg, Joseph 1963. 'Some universals of grammar with particular reference to the order of meaningful elements'. In *Universals of Language*. Cambridge: MIT Press, 73–113.

Grimshaw, Jane 1997. 'Projection, heads and optimality'. *Linguistic Inquiry 28*, 373–422.

Haegeman, Liliane 1991. *Introduction to Government and Binding Theory*. Blackwell: Oxford.

Halliday, M. A. K. 2004. *An Introduction to Functional Grammar*, 3rd edn., Revised by Ch. Matthiesen, London: Edward Arnold.

Harris, Alice and Lyle Campbell 1995. *Historical Syntax in Cross-Linguistic Perspective*. Cambridge: CUP.

Harris, Zelling 1951. *Methods in Structural Linguistics*. Chicago: University of Chicago Press.

Hopper, Paul and Sandra Thompson 1980. 'Transitivity in grammar and discourse'. *Language 56*, 251–299.

Hopper, Paul J. 1998. 'Emergent Grammar'. In M. Tomasello (ed.) *The New Psychology of Language*. Vol. 1. Mahvah (NJ): Lawrence Erlbaum Associates, 155–175.

Hornstein, Norbert, Jairo Nunes, and Kleanthes Grohmann 2006. *Understanding Minimalism*. Cambridge: CUP.

Hudson, Richard 1984. *Word Grammar*. Oxford: Blackwell.

Johnson, David E. and Paul M. Postal 1980. *Arc Pair Grammar*. Princeton: PUP.

Kayne, Richard 1994. *Antisymmetry in Syntax*. Cambridge MA: The MIT Press.

Keenan, Edward and Bernard Comrie 1977. 'Noun phrase accessibility and universal grammar'. *Linguistic Inquiry 8*, 63–69.

Koopman Hilda and Dominique Sportiche 1991. 'The position of subjects'. *Lingua 85*, 211–258.

Langacker, Ronald W. 1977. 'Syntactic reanalysis'. In Ch. N. Li (ed.) *Mechanisms of Syntactic Change*. Austin: University of Texas Press, 57–139.

Langacker, Ronald W. 1982. 'Space Grammar, Analysability, and the English Passive'. *Language 58*, 22–80.

Langacker, Ronald W. 1987. *Foundations of Cognitive Grammar*. Vol. 1: *Theoretical Prerequisites*. Stanford: Stanford University Press.

Langacker, Ronald W. 1991. *Foundations of Cognitive Grammar*. Vol. 2: *Descriptive Application*. Stanford: Stanford University Press.

Lightfoot, David W. 1979. *Principles of Diachronic Syntax*. Cambridge: CUP.

Moravcsik, Edith 2006. *An Introduction to Syntactic Theory*. London: Continuum Books.

Pollard, Carl and Ivan A. Sag 1994. *Head-Driven Phrase Structure Grammar*. Chicago: University of Chicago Press.

Pollock, Jean Yves 1989. 'Verb movement, UG and the structure of IP'. *Linguistic Inquiry 20*, 365–424.

Reinhart, Tanya 1983. *Anaphora and Semantic Interpretation*. London: Croom Helm.

Rizzi, Luigi 1990. *Minimality*. Cambridge MA: The MIT Press.

Roberts, Ian 2007. *Diachronic Syntax*. Oxford: OUP.

Ross, John R. 1986. *Infinite Syntax!* Norwood: ABLEX.

Shopen, Timothy 1985. *Language Typology and Syntactic Description*. 3 vols. Cambridge: CUP.

Tesnière, Lucien 1959. *Éléments de syntaxe structurale*, Klincksieck: Paris.

Tomasello, Michael 1998–2002. *The New Psychology of Language*. 2 vols. Mahvah (NJ): Lawrence Erlbaum Associates.

Van Valin, Robert D. and Randy LaPolla 1997. *Syntax: Structure, Meaning and Function*. Cambridge: CUP.

Wackernagel, Jakob 1892. 'Über ein Gesetz der indogermanischen Wortstellung'. *Indogermanische Forschungen 1*, 333–436 (repr. in *Kleine Schriften*. Gottingen: Vandenhoek and Ruprecht, 1953).

Bibliography

Abney, Steven R. 1987. *The Noun Phrase in its Sentential Aspect.* Substitute thesis for dissertation. MIT, Cambridge.

Andersen, Henning (ed.) 2001. *Actualization: Linguistic Change in Progress.* Amsterdam: Benjamins.

Anderson, Stephen 2005. *Aspects of the Theory of Clitics.* Oxford: OUP.

Arrivé, Michel and Driss Ablali 2001. 'Hjelmslev et Martinet: Correspondance, traduction, problemes theoriques'. *La Linguistique 37*, 33–57.

Bartsch, Renate and Theo Vennemann 1972. *Semantic Structures: A Study in the Relation between Semantics and Syntax.* Frankfurt am Main: Athenäum.

Behaghel, Otto 1909. 'Beziehungen zwischen Umfang und Reihenfolge von Satzgliedern'. *Indogermanische Forschungen 25*, 110–142.

Bloomfield, Leonard 1933. *Language.* New York: Henry Holt and Company.

Boeckx, Cedric 2006. *Linguistic Minimalism.* Oxford: OUP.

Bresnan, Joan 1982. 'The passive in lexical theory'. In Joan W. Bresnan (ed.) *The Mental Representation of Grammatical Relations.* Cambridge MA: The MIT Press, 3–86.

Bresnan, Joan 2001. *Lexical-Functional Syntax.* Oxford: Blackwell.

Brown, Keith (ed.) 2006. *Encyclopedia of Language and Linguistics.* 2nd edn. Oxford: Elsevier.

Butler, Chris 2003. *Structure and Function: A Guide to Three Major Structural-Functional Theories.* Vol. 1: *Approaches to the Simplex Clause.* Vol. 2: *From Clause to Discourse and Beyond.* Amsterdam: John Benjamins.

Bybee, Joan 2007. *Frequency of Use and the Organization of Language.* Oxford: OUP.

Caplan, David 1981. 'Prospects for neurolinguistic theory'. *Cognition 10*, 59–64.

Chomsky, Noam 1957. *Syntactic Structures.* The Hague: Mouton.

Chomsky, Noam 1965. *Aspects of the Theory of Syntax.* Cambridge MA: The MIT Press.

Chomsky, Noam 1970. 'Remarks on nominalization'. In Roderick Jacobs and Peter Rosenbaum (eds.) *Readings in English Transformational Grammar*. Waltham, MA: Blaisdell, 184–221.

Chomsky, Noam 1973. 'Conditions on transformations'. In S. R. Anderson and P. Kiparsky (eds.) *A Festschrift for Morris Halle*. New York: Holt, Rinehart & Winston, 232–286.

Chomsky, Noam 1977. 'On *wh*-movement, In Peter. Culicover', In Th. Wasow, and A. Akmajian (eds.) *Formal Syntax*. New York: Academic Press, 71–132.

Chomsky, Noam 1980. 'On binding'. *Linguistic Inquiry 11*, 1–46.

Chomsky, Noam 1981. *Lectures on Government and Binding*. Dordrecht: Foris.

Chomsky, Noam 1982. *Some Concepts and Consequences of the Theory of Government and Binding*. Cambridge, MA: The MIT Press.

Chomsky, Noam 1986. *Knowledge of Language*. New York: Praeger.

Chomsky, Noam 1991. 'Some notes on economy of derivation and representation'. In R. Freidin (ed.) *Principles and Parameters in Comparative Grammar*. Cambridge, MA: The MIT Press: 417–454.

Chomsky, Noam 1995. *The Minimalist Program*. Cambridge, MA: MIT Press.

Chomsky, Noam 2000. 'Minimalist inquiries: The framework'. In R. Martin, D. Michaels, and J. Uriagereka (eds.) *Step by Step*. Cambridge, MA: The MIT Press, 89–155.

Chomsky, Noam 2001. 'Derivation by phase'. In M. Kenstowicz (ed.) *Ken Hale. A Life in Language*. Cambridge, MA: The MIT Press, 1–52.

Chomsky, Noam 2004. 'Beyond explanatory adequacy'. In A. Belletti (ed.) *Structures and Beyond: The Cartography of Syntactic Structure*, vol. 3. Oxford: OUP.

Chomsky, Noam 2005. 'On phases'. In C. P. Otero et al. (eds.) *Foundational Issues in Linguistic Theory*. Cambridge, MA: The MIT Press.

Chomsky Noam and Howard Lasnik 1993. 'The theory of principles and parameters'. In I. J. Jacobs et al. (eds.) *Syntax: An International Handbook of Contemporary Research*. Berlin: De Gruyter, 506–569.

Comrie, Bernard 1976. 'The syntax of causative constructions: Cross-language similarities and divergences'. In M. Shibatani (ed.) *The Grammar of Causative Constructions*. New York: Academic Press, 261–312.

Comrie, Bernard 1985. *Tense*. Cambridge: CUP.

Corbett, Greville G. 2000. *Number*. Cambridge: CUP.

Corbett, Greville G., Norman M. Fraser, and Scott McGlashan (eds.) 1993. *Talking Heads. Heads in Grammatical Theory.* Cambridge: CUP.

Croft, William 1991. *Syntactic Categories and Grammatical Relations: The Cognitive Organization of Information.* Chicago: University of Chicago Press.

Croft, William 1995. 'Autonomy and functionalist linguistics'. *Language 71*, 490–532.

Croft, William 2001. *Radical Construction Grammar.* Oxford: OUP.

Croft, William 2003. *Topology and Universals.* 2nd edn. Cambridge: CUP.

Croft, William and D. Alan Cruse 2004. *Cognitive Linguistic.* Cambridge: CUP.

Culicover, Peter and Ray Jackendoff 2005. *Simpler Synyax.* Oxford: OUP.

Dalrymple, Mary 2006. 'Lexical Functional Grammar'. Keith Brown (ed.), 82–94.

Dik, Simon C. 1978. *Functional Grammar.* Amsterdam: North Holland/ London: Academic Press.

Dik, Simon C. 1997. *The Theory of Functional Grammar.* 2 vols. 2nd edn. Edited by K. Hengeveld. Berlin: Mouton De Gruyter.

Dixon, R. M. W. 1977. *A Grammar of Yidiny.* Cambridge: CUP.

Dixon, R. M. W. 1980. *The Languages of Australia.* Cambridge: CUP.

Dixon, R. M. W. 1991. *A New Approach to English Grammar on Semantic Principles.* Oxford: Clarendon Press.

Dixon, R. M. W. 1994. *Ergativity.* Cambridge: CUP.

Droste, Flip G. and John E. Joseph (eds.) 1991. *Linguistic Theory and Grammatical Description.* Amsterdam: Benjamins.

Dryer, Matthew S. 1988. 'Object-verb order and adjective-noun order: Dispelling a myth'. *Lingua 74*, 77–109.

Edmondson, Jerold A. and Donald A. Burquest (eds.) 1992. *A Survey of Linguistic Theories.* Dallas, TX: The Summer Institute of Linguistics.

Fillmore, Charles J. 1963. 'The position of embedding transformations in a grammar'. *Word 19*, 208–231.

Fillmore, Charles J. 1968. 'The case for case'. In E. Bach and R. Harms (eds.) *Universals in Linguistic Theory.* New York: Holt, Rinehart & Winston, 1–88.

Fillmore, Charles J., Paul Kay, and Mary C. O'Connor 1988. 'Regularity and idiomaticity in grammatical constructions'. *Language 64*, 501–538.

Gabelentz, Georg von der 1891. *Die Sprachwissenschaft*. Leipzig: Tauchnitz. New edition with an essay by E. Coseriu, 1972. Tübingen: Narr.

Gazdar, Gerald, Ewan Klein, Geoffrey K. Pullum, and Ivan Sag 1985. *Generalized Phrase Structure Grammar*. Cambridge MA: Harvard UP.

Givón, Talmy 1971. 'Historical syntax and synchronic morphology: An archaeologist's field trip'. *Chicago Linguistic Society 7*, 394–415.

Goldberg, Adele 1995. *Constructions: A Construction Grammar Approach to Argument Structure*. Chicago: University of Chicago Press.

Graffi, Giorgio 2001. *200 Years of Syntax. A Critical Survey*. Amsterdam: Benjamins.

Greenberg, Joseph 1963. 'Some universals of grammar with particular reference to the order of meaningful elements', in *Universals of Language*. Cambridge MA: The MIT Press, 73–113.

Grimshaw, Jane 1997. 'Projection, heads and optimality'. *Linguistic Inquiry 28*, 373–422.

Haegeman, Liliane 1991. *Introduction to Government and Binding Theory*. Oxford: Blackwell.

Hale, Kenneth L. 1973. 'Person marking in Walbiri'. In Stephen R. Anderson & Paul Kiparsky (eds.) *A Festschrift for Morris Halle*. New York: Holt, Rinehart & Winston, 308–344.

Halliday, M. A. K. 2004. *An Introduction to Functional Grammar*, 3rd edn., Revised by Ch. Matthiesen, London: Edward Arnold.

Halliday, M. A. K. 2006. 'Systemic Theory'. In Keith Brown (ed.), 443–448.

Harris, Alice and Lyle Campbell 1995. *Historical Syntax in Cross-Linguistic Perspective*. Cambridge: CUP.

Harris, Randy 1993. *The Linguistics Wars*. Oxford: OUP.

Harris, Zelling 1946. 'From morpheme to utterance', *Language 22*, 161–183.

Harris, Zelling 1951. *Methods in Structural Linguistics*. Chicago: University of Chicago Press.

Harris, Zelling 1957. 'Co-occurrence and transformations in linguistic structure'. *Language 33*, 283–340.

Hauser, Marc, Noam Chomsky, and Tecumseh Fitch 2002. 'The evolution of the language faculty: Clarifications and implications'. *Science 298*, 1569–1579.

Hawkins, John A. 1983. *Word Order Universals*. New York: Academic Press.

Heine, Bernd 1993. *Auxiliaries: Cognitive Forces and Grammaticalization*. Chicago: University of Chicago Press.

Hengeveld, Kees and J. Lachlan Mackenzie 2005. 'Functional Discourse Grammar'. In Keith Brown (ed.) 668–676.

Hopper, Paul 1987. 'Emergent Grammar'. *Proceedings of the 13th Annual Meeting of the Berkeley Linguistics Society 13*, 139–157.

Hopper, Paul J. 1998. 'Emergent Grammar', In M. Tomasello (ed.) *The New Psychology of Language*. Vol. 1. Mahvah (NJ): Lawrence Erlbaum Associates, 155–175.

Hopper, Paul and Sandra Thompson 1980. 'Transitivity in grammar and discourse'. *Language 56*, 251–299.

Hopper, Paul and Sandra Thompson 1984. 'The discourse basis for lexical categories in universal grammar'. *Language 60*, 703–753.

Hopper, Paul and Elizabeth Closs Traugott 1993. *Grammaticalization*. Cambridge: CUP.

Hornstein, Norbert, Jairo Nunes and Kleanthes K. Grohmann 2005. *Understanding Minimalism*. Cambridge: CUP.

Hudson, Richard 1980a. 'Constituency and dependency'. *Linguistics 18*, 179–198.

Hudson, Richard 1980b. 'A second attack on constituency'. *Linguistics 18*, 489–504.

Hudson, Richard 1984. *Word Grammar*. Oxford: Blackwell.

Hudson, Richard 1987. 'Zwicky on heads'. *Journal of Linguistics 23*, 109–132.

Jespersens, Otto 1933. *Essentials of English Grammar*. London: Allen & Unwin.

Johnson, David E. and Paul M. Postal 1980. *Arc Pair Grammar*. Princeton: PUP.

Jones, Linda K. 1980. 'A Synopsis of Tagmemics'. In Moravcsik, E. and J. Wirth (eds.) 1980, 77–95.

Kayne, Richard 1994. *Antisymmetry in Syntax*. Cambridge MA: The MIT Press.

Keenan, Edward 1976. 'Towards a universal definition of "subject"'. C. N. Li (ed.) *Subject and Topic*. New York: Academic Press, 303–333.

Kim, Jong-Bok 2000. *The Grammar of Negation: A Constraint-Based Approach*. Stanford: CSLI Publications.

Klavans, Judith L. 1985. 'The independence of syntax and phonology in cliticization'. *Language 61*, 95–120.

Klima, Edward 1964. 'Negation in English'. In Jerry A. Fodor and Jerrold J. Katz (eds.) *The Structure of Language*. New York: Prentice Hall, 46–323.

Kuryłowicz, Jerzy 1949. 'Le problème du classement des cas'. *Biuletyn Polskiego Towarzystwa Językoznawczego 9*, 20–43.

Lakoff, George 1987. *Women, Fire, and Dangerous Things: What Categories Reveal about the Mind*. Chicago: University of Chicago Press.

Lamb, Sydney 1966. *Outline of Stratificational Grammar*. Washington, DC: Georgetown University Press.

Lambrecht, Knud 1994. *Information Structure and Sentence Form: Topic, Focus, and the Mental Representation of Discourse Referents*. Cambridge: CUP.

Landau, Illan 2001. *Elements of Control: Structure and Meaning in Infinitival Constructions*. Dordrecht: Foris.

Langacker, Ronald W. 1969. 'On Pronominalization and the Chain of Command'. In D. A. Reibel and S. A. Schane (eds.) *Modern Studies in English: Readings in Transformational Grammar*. Englewood Cliffs, N. J.: Prentice-Hall, 160–186.

Langacker, Ronald W. 1977. 'Syntactic reanalysis'. In Ch. N. Li (ed.) *Mechanisms of Syntactic Change*. Austin: University of Texas Press, 57–139.

Langacker, Ronald W. 1982. 'Space grammar, analysability, and the English passive'. *Language 58*, 22–80.

Langacker, Ronald W. 1987. *Foundations of Cognitive Grammar: Theoretical Prerequisites*. Stanford : Stanford University Press.

Lehmann, Christian 1983. 'Rektion und syntaktische Relationen'. *Folia Linguistica 17*, 339–378.

Lehmann, Christian 1985. 'On grammatical relationality'. *Folia Linguistica 19*, 67–109.

Lehmann, Christian 1988. 'Towards a typology of clause linkage'. In J. Haiman and S. A. Thompson (eds.) *Clause Combining in Grammar and Discourse*, 181–225.

Lepschy, Giulio 1982. *A Survey of Structural Linguistics*. London: André Deutsch.

Levine, Robert D. and Detmar Meurers 2006. 'Head-Driven Phrase Structure Grammar: Linguistic Approach, Formal Foundations, and Computational Realization'. Keith Brown (ed.), 237–252.

Li, Charles N. and Sandra A. Thompson 1976. 'Subject and topic: A new typology of language'. In C. N. Li, (ed.), *Subject and Topic*. New York: Academic Press, 457–489.

Li, Charles 1977. Introduction to Ch. Li (ed.) *Mechanisms of Syntactic Change*. Austin: University of Texas Press, xi–xix.

Luraghi, Silvia 1990. *Old Hittite Sentence Structure*. London/New York: Routledge.

Lyons, John 1977. *Semantics*. Vol. 2. Cambridge: CUP.

Matthews, Peter H. 1993. *Grammatical Theory in the United States from Bloomfield to Chomsky*. Cambridge: CUP.

Matthiessen, C. M. I. M. and M. A. K. Halliday, forthcoming. 'Systemic Functional Grammar'. In Fred C. C. Peng and J. Ney (eds.) *Current Approaches to Syntax*, Amsterdam: Benjamins/London: Whurr.

Meillet, Antoine 1912. 'L'évolution des formes grammaticales'. *Scientia* 12/26, 6. Repr. in A. Meillet, *Linguistique historique et linguistique générale* 1 Paris: Champion, 1921, 130–148.

Moravcsik, Edith 1995. 'Government'. In *Syntax. Ein internationales Handbuch*. Berlin: Mouton De Gruyter, 705–721.

Moravcsik, Edith and Jessica Wirth (eds.) 1980. *Current Approaches to Syntax*. New York: Academic Press.

Newmeyer, Frederick 1986. *Linguistic Theory in America*. Orlando: Academic Press.

Ngonyani, Deo and Peter Githinji 2006. 'The asymmetric nature of Bantu applicative constructions'. *Lingua 116*, 31–63.

Otten, Heinrich 1981. *Die Apologie Hattusilis III. Das Bild der Überlieferung*, Wiesbaden: Harrassowitz.

Partee, Barbara H. and Herman L. W. Hendriks 1997. 'Montague grammar'. In J. van Benthem and A. ter Meulen (eds.) *Handbook of Logic and Language*. Amsterdam: Elsevier/Cambridge, MA: The MIT Press, 5–91.

Pollard, Carl and Ivan A. Sag 1987. *Information-Based Syntax and Semantics*. Vol. 1. *Fundamentals*. Stanford: CSLI Publications.

Pollard, Carl and Ivan A. Sag 1994. *Head-Driven Phrase Structure Grammar*. Chicago: University of Chicago Press.

Pollock, Jean Yves 1989. 'Verb movement, UG and the structure of IP'. *Linguistic Inquiry 20*, 365–424.

Pustejovsky, James 1995. *The Generative Lexicon*. Cambridge MA: The MIT Press.

Radford, Andrew 1988. *Transformational Grammar: A First Course*. Cambridge: CUP.

Reinhart, Tanya 1983. *Anaphora and Semantic Interpretation*. London: Croom Helm.

Rose, John 1967. *Constraints on Variable in Syntax*. Ph.D. Diss.: MIT.

Ross, John R. 1986. *Infinite Syntax!* Norwood: ABLEX.

Sadock, Jerrold M. 1991. *Autolexical Syntax: A Theory of Parallel Grammatical Representations*. Chicago: University of Chicago Press.

Sag, Ivan A., Thomas Wasow, and Emily Bender 2003. *Syntactic Theory: A Formal Introduction*. 2nd edn. Chicago: University of Chicago Press.

Sapir, Edward 1911. 'The problem of noun incorporation in American languages'. *American Anthropologist 13*, 250–282.

Sapir, Edward 1921. *Language*. New York: Harcourt, Brace & Co.

Schiller, Eric, Elisa Steinberg, and Barbara Need (eds.) 1996. *Autolexical Theory: Ideas and Methods*. Berlin: Mouton De Gruyter.

Schwischay, Bernd ms. 'Introduction à la syntaxe structurale de L. Tesnière'. http://www.home.uni-osnabrueck.de/bschwisc/archives/tesniere.pdf

Spreng, Bettina forthcoming. 'Events in Inuktitut: Voice alternations and viewpoint aspect'. *Proceedings of the 41st Annual Meeting of the Chicago Linguistic Society*. Chicago: University of Chicago Press.

Sulkala, Helena and Merja Karjalainen 1992. *Finnish*. Routledge, London.

Takahashi, Kiyoko and Rumiko Shinzato 2003. 'On Thai copulas, *khUU1* and *pen1*: A cognitive approach'. *Proceedings of the 2nd Seoul International Conference on Discourse and Cognitive Linguistics: Discourse and Cognitive Perspectives on Human Language*, 131–145.

Tesnière, Lucien 1953. *Esquisse d'une syntaxe structurale*, Paris: Klincksieck.

Tesnière, Lucien 1959. *Éléments de syntaxe structurale*. Paris: Klincksieck.

Thompson, Sandra A. 1978. 'Modern English from a typological point of view: Some implications of the function of word order'. *Linguistische Berichte 54*, 19–35.

Thompson, Sandra A. 1988. 'A discourse approach to the cross-linguistic category "adjective"'. In John Hawkins (ed.) *Explanations for Language Universals*. Oxford: Blackwell, 167–185.

Timberlake, Alan 1977. 'Reanalysis and actualization in syntactic change'. In Ch. N. Li (ed.) *Mechanisms of Syntactic Change*. Austin: University of Texas Press, 141–177.

Tomasello, Michael 2002. 'Introduction'. In M. Tomasello (ed.) *The New Psychology of Language*. Vol. 2. Mahvah (NJ): Lawrence Erlbaum Associates.

Traugott, Elizabeth 1988. 'Pragmatic strengthening and grammaticalization'. *Proceedings of the 14th Annual Meeting of the Berkeley Linguistic Society,* 406–416.

VanValin, Robert D. Jr. 1990. 'Semantic parameters of split intransitivity'. *Language 66,* 221–260.

VanValin, Robert D. Jr. 2006. 'Role and reference grammar'. In Keith Brown (ed.), 641–650.

Van Valin, Robert D. Jr. 2002. ms. 'Minimalism and explanation'. J. Moore and M. Polinsky (eds.), *Explanations in Linguistics*, Stanford: CSLI, 281–297. http://wings.buffalo.edu/soc-sci/linguistics/research/rrg/vanvalin_papers/ Min-Expl.pdf

Van Valin, Robert D. and Randy LaPolla 1997. *Syntax: Structure, Meaning and Function*. Cambridge: CUP.

Vendler, Zeno 1957. 'Verbs and Times'. *Philosophical Review 56,* 143–160.

Wackernagel, Jacob 1953. *Kleine Schriften*. 2 vols. Göttingen: Vandenhoek & Ruprecht.

Wanner, Dieter 1987. *The Development of Romance Clitic Pronouns*. Berlin: Mouton De Gruyter.

Weil, H. 1844. *De l'ordre des mots dans les langues anciennes comparées aux langues modernes*. Translated by C. W. Super as *The Order of Words in the Ancient Languages Compared with That of the Modern Languages*, 1978. Amsterdam: Benjamins.

Wells, Rulon 1947. 'Immediate constituents'. *Language 23,* 81–117.

Yuasa, Etsuyo and Jerrold Sadock 2002. 'Pseudo-subordination: A mismatch between syntax and semantics'. *Journal of Linguistics 38,* 87–111.

Zwicky, Arnold M. 1977. *On Clitics*. Bloomington, IN: Indiana University Linguistics Club.

Zwicky, Arnold M. 1985. 'Heads'. *Journal of Linguistics 21,* 1–30.